MW00580534

An Introduction
to Judaic Thought
and Rabbinic Literature

Martin Sicker

Westport, Connecticut
London

Library of Congress Cataloging-in-Publication Data

Sicker, Martin.
  An introduction to Judaic thought and rabbinic literature / Martin Sicker.
      p. cm.
  Includes bibliographical references and index.
  ISBN 0–275–99465–1 (alk. paper)
  1. Judaism—Sacred books. 2. Rabbinical literature. I. Title.
  BM496.6.S53 2007
  296.1—dc22   2006038819

British Library Cataloguing in Publication Data is available.

Copyright © 2007 by Martin Sicker

All rights reserved. No portion of this book may be
reproduced, by any process or technique, without the
express written consent of the publisher.

Library of Congress Catalog Card Number: 2006038819

ISBN-10: 0-275-99465-1
ISBN-13: 978-0-275-99465-5

First published in 2007

Praeger Publishers, 88 Post Road West, Westport, CT 06881
An imprint of Greenwood Publishing Group, Inc.
www.praeger.com

Printed in the United States of America

The paper used in this book complies with the
Permanent Paper Standard issued by the National
Information Standards Organization (Z39.48-1984).

10   9   8   7   6   5   4   3   2   1

R0412274928

CHICAGO PUBLIC LIBRARY
SOCIAL SCIENCES AND HISTORY
400 S. STATE ST   60605

Contents

Introduction

As the title of this book indicates, it is concerned with Judaic thought and rabbinic literature, two categories that require some explication. First, the title is intended to draw a distinction between Judaic and Jewish thought; that is, whereas all of Judaic thought is Jewish, not all of Jewish thought is Judaic. As the term is used in this book, Judaic thought refers to the ideas underpinning the normative rabbinic Judaism that has dominated and shaped Jewish life, in one way or another, for more than two millennia. There is, of course, a great deal of Jewish thought, that is, the ideas articulated by Jews, that transcends the bounds of normative Judaism, although it may be asserted that even in such non-Judaic thought one frequently may discern strands of traditional Judaic ideas. However, the focus of the subject matter of this book precludes consideration of such materials in its pages.

It is perhaps a truism that all literature, including nonfiction, is in a sense autobiographical. What is included or omitted in a work such as this, and the approach taken to the collection and analysis of data and information that are presented in it, are necessarily reflections of the author's point of view. I therefore feel obligated to inform the reader of some pertinent information that will clarify the perspective brought to this book. My primary concern here is with *traditional* Judaic thought, that is, the body of sometimes highly diverse ideas that may be found in the corpus of rabbinic literature from remote antiquity to modern times.

The definition of what constitutes rabbinic literature is not as straightforward as might be imagined at first consideration. Whether it includes everything written by persons acknowledged by the title of "rabbi" or whether it is more or less inclusive in scope is a matter of perspective. For one thing the meaning of the term "rabbi" has varied over time. The term itself did not come into use until the first century, when it referred to a scholar accorded the honor of membership in the supreme religious council, the Sanhedrin, or senate. There were of course many scholars of great merit who never made it on to the council, whose membership was limited to seventy, but this in no way was a reflection on their abilities or qualifications. It should be noted that prior to the first century, the authoritative leaders of the community served without carrying such a title.

When, due to historical factors that brought about the collapse of autonomous Jewish institutions by the end of the fifth century, the formal process of ordination by which one became a "rabbi" was brought to an end, the title subsequently was accorded to individuals as an honorific, regardless of whether they had the scholarly qualifications demanded in earlier times. We thus find that a wide variety of persons in medieval times were accorded the honor by later generations even though they were not recognized scholars of the traditional teachings of Judaism. With the cessation of traditional ordination, scholars were granted what is known in Latin as *facultas docendi* or the authority to teach and, in many instances, persons so authorized by their teachers were known as "rabbis," especially in Europe, whereas in the Near East they were more often honored with the title of *hakham* or "sage." It is noteworthy that the ancient scholars recorded in the Talmud and Midrash—works to be discussed later—were described collectively as the *hakhamim* or "sages." In modern times, the title of "rabbi" is awarded to graduates of rabbinical seminaries representing the Orthodox, Reform, Conservative, and Reconstructionist movements in modern Judaism, although there are some significant differences in the curricula followed in the various schools and the qualifications necessary for ordination. The point being made here is simply that Judaic thought and rabbinic literature are not clerical preserves and are open to anyone interested and capable of exploring their depths and participating in their further elaboration.

For purposes of this book, rabbinic literature is taken to include those works that deal with elaborating the normative legal and ethical precepts found in the biblical texts and oral traditions that fall within the scope of what is known as Rabbinic Judaism. What is not given consideration in this book are the works that fall into literary genres that have little direct connection with normative Judaism, such as philosophy and mysticism. Although many of such works are very significant in their own right and, therefore, may merit consideration as important works of Jewish and in many cases Judaic thought, they nonetheless do not fit comfortably within the category of rabbinic literature.

Because all of rabbinic literature is ultimately based on the *TaNaKH* or the Hebrew Bible, the first chapter of this book is devoted to a discussion of that ancient collection. Its primary concern is with setting the stage for understanding how the written biblical texts are perceived in Judaic thought. In the process, it will also point out what distinguishes the *TaNaKH* from the Christian Old Testament, the very name of which indicates a belief of its supersession by a New Testament, a notion that Judaism categorically rejects. What is not discussed in the chapter on the *TaNaKH* is the content of the individual works, about which there is already a virtual mountain of widely available descriptive materials. The focus, instead, is placed on aspects of the work that have particular relevance for Judaic thought and rabbinic literature.

The second chapter deals with the patterns of interpretation of normative biblical precepts that prevailed for some seven centuries between the era of Ezra the Scribe in the fifth century BCE and the end of the second century CE. This chapter will discuss and provide examples of the different approaches to biblical exegesis that enabled the early sages and rabbis to apply biblical precepts to the real world of man and society, and the collections of literature that recorded those intellectual activities for future reference. In the course of the discussion, attention will be given to the rules of interpretation, the hermeneutic, that were employed by the rabbis in their examination of the biblical texts to determine how general statements were to be transformed into specific rules to be observed in practice.

The third chapter is devoted to exploring the reasons why there was a trend toward codification of applied law and practice and the eventual composition of the *Mishnah*, a legal compendium that served as the basis for the continuing evolution of Jewish law to the present day. Because, like all other compendia, decisions had to be made about what to include—the editorial policy that reflected such decisions will be discussed along with what happened to the materials that were excluded. The organization and content of the work will be discussed along with illustrative examples of the thought processes at work. Examples also will be given of how and why the omitted materials dealt with the issues differently than those included in the new basic document.

The fourth chapter explores how subsequent generations subjected the *Mishnah* to the same type of critical analysis that earlier rabbis applied to exegesis of the biblical texts, ultimately producing vast collections of such materials recorded in two distinct versions of what is known as the Talmud. The principal similarities and differences between the Babylonian Talmud and the Jerusalem Talmud will be discussed, and some examples of rabbinic reasoning and method will be presented.

The fifth chapter directs the reader's attention to the vast store of nonlegal material to be found in the Talmuds as well as in numerous separate collections. These teachings and speculations cover a wide range of topics and provide a window into the diverse philosophical, theological, and ethical perspectives that characterize rabbinic thought. These materials are for the most part concerned with understanding the subtexts that underlay the simple meaning of the biblical writings and thus involve frequently surprising exegeses that have served as the subjects of innumerable sermons throughout the centuries. The major collections of these materials, generally categorized as Midrash, are discussed and illustrated by examples drawn from them.

The sixth chapter returns to the normative concerns of the literature and discusses the processes of codification of rabbinic law from the medieval period to the present. In addition to the codes, consideration is also given to the enumeration of the traditional 613 precepts of Judaism, which has engendered a literary genre of its own, both in descriptive and poetical–liturgical forms. The chapter also discusses the responsa literature, that is, the rabbinic responses to questions raised about issues of personal, communal, and ritual significance, which have arisen through the centuries, including emergent issues that were not covered in the authoritative codes, and some examples of this literature are provided for illustrative purposes.

The seventh chapter is devoted to interpretations of the biblical texts, especially of the Torah or Pentateuch. This genre differs significantly from the efforts of the ancient rabbis with regard to both the legal and narrative portions of the biblical writings. Rabbinic biblical commentators are primarily concerned with explaining what the biblical texts are actually saying or implying, for the most part without reference to the implications for normative practice. Indeed, in some instances rabbinic biblical interpretations may be at variance with accepted traditions and practices. What is especially interesting about this category of the literature is that, like the authors of the ideas and comments collected in the Midrash, the commentators are completely free to read the biblical texts from their own perspectives, and thus often find their views disputed by later commentators, a process that will be illustrated by a number of examples.

The commentaries discussed in this chapter represent but a small sample of the voluminous work produced over the centuries in this genre. The commentators chosen are those who are most often cited by other commentators, as well as some, whose works, for varying reasons, have been included in the collection known as *Mikraot Gedolot* ("Great Scriptures") or the Rabbinic Bible, which consists of the biblical text almost literally surrounded by these commentaries, giving students the opportunity to read a verse and then consider often varying interpretations of it. Of course, the Rabbinic Bible is only accessible to those with knowledge of Hebrew, although English translations of some of the commentaries included therein are slowly becoming available in separate editions. For purposes of comparison, the commentary or excerpt from a commentary by each of the authors cited on a single verse of text will illustrate their relatively freewheeling approach to interpretation.

The eighth and final chapter is devoted to a brief consideration of the state of Judaic thought and rabbinic literature at the outset of the twenty-first century, which is clearly more variegated than at any time in the long history of Judaism. Primary consideration will be given to how the thought and literature of earlier eras and generations are reflected in the manner in which rabbinic thinkers and writers associated with the various contemporary movements—or trends as some prefer to call them—in Judaism deal with the issues first raised in the biblical teachings, and struggled with over the course of some two millennia by the authors and contributors to the vast library of Judaic thought discussed in the preceding chapters.

What will quickly become evident to those previously unfamiliar with rabbinic literature is the fact that virtually none of it, with the exception of a relative handful of recent popular works of dubious significance, is designed or intended for casual perusal. Rabbinic writing is often painfully concise, with a style and idiom of its own, and requires substantial intellectual investment on the part of the reader to make it comprehensible. In other words, rabbinic literature is not designed for reading but for study, and has proved highly rewarding for those who have successfully struggled with it over the centuries. It is my hope that this brief introduction to the subject may help the reader gain some insight into the nature of a highly complex literature that has grown from the teachings of Moses, more than three thousand years ago, to the vast libraries of rabbinic thought and interpretation that exist today.

Chapter 1

The *TaNaKH* or Hebrew Bible

The *TaNaKH* or Hebrew Bible, often referred to by Christian designation as the Old Testament, is in essence an anthology of ancient literary works composed in Hebrew (the books of Daniel and Ezra in a combination of Hebrew and Aramaic) over a period of a millennium that includes a variety of prophetic, historical, and other kinds of writing. How and by whom this anthology was brought into being are only two of the numerous questions regarding the work that immediately come to mind. Was it simply a collection of all the ancient materials of interest that were available to the compilers, or were there criteria that were applied by some ancient religious authorities in determining what was to be included in it? And, if the latter were the case, who established those criteria and decided which writings satisfied them and therefore would be included in the biblical collection? Moreover, does the incorporation of a work in the biblical corpus confer any special sanctity on it? These are but a few of the questions that this chapter will discuss and seek to answer, acknowledging at the outset that the documentary evidence in support of such answers is rather skimpy at best and in many instances simply nonexistent.

It is clear that the books that comprise the library known as the *TaNaKH* or Hebrew Bible as we have it do not constitute the entire corpus of literary works produced in ancient Israel. In fact, a number of other works not included in Scripture are actually cited or referred to in it. Thus, in the biblical narrative of the journeys undertaken by the Israelites in the wilderness of Sinai, a poetic passage is cited there that is a direct quotation from *the book of the Wars of the Lord* (Numbers 21:14). Similarly, in the biblical recounting of Joshua's famous prayer for divine intervention to delay the onset of darkness until the decisive battle with the Amorites was concluded, it states: *And the sun stood still, and the moon stayed, until the nation had avenged themselves of their enemy,* and then adds, *Is this not written in the book of Jashar* (Joshua 10:13). There is a second lengthy biblical passage that quotes the famous lamentation of David over the deaths of Saul and Jonathan (2 Samuel 1:18–27) from *the book of Jashar.* There are also numerous biblical references to *the book of the chronicles of the kings of Israel* (1 Kings 14:19; 15:31; 16:5, 14, 20, 27; 22:39), and to *the book of the chronicles of the kings of Judah* (1 Kings 15:7, 23; 22:46). In addition, there is a biblical statement that the acts of David *are written in the words of Samuel the seer, and in the words of Nathan the prophet, and in the words of Gad the seer* (1 Chronicles 29:29), indicating another three literary works that are no longer extant. Similarly, with regard to the acts of Solomon, the biblical text states, *are they not written in the words of Nathan the prophet, and in the prophecy of Ahijah the Shilonite, and in the visions of Jedo the seer* (2 Chronicles 9:29), adding another two items to the list of lost works. Finally, there is a biblical notation that Solomon *spoke three thousand proverbs; and his songs were a thousand and five* (1 Kings 5:12), suggesting that the works containing these compositions are also among the lost.

A number of reasons for the disappearance of these and presumably many other ancient works have been suggested. First and probably foremost, literacy was not very widespread in the ancient world, which meant in effect that the basic economics of publishing for a limited market tended to constrain the number of works that could be reproduced. A related factor was the state of publishing technology in antiquity, reflected in the difficulty of accurately hand-copying manuscripts, which made reproduction of books extremely time consuming and therefore costly. Moreover, in some cases the materials on which ancient writings were inscribed were perishable and therefore tended to further limit the survivability of works that were not constantly reproduced; only selected works would have been copied on long-lasting but expensive parchment. It may also be assumed that a good number of works were simply lost as a consequence of the almost continual warfare that afflicted ancient Israel. Another contributing circumstance was the fact that significant changes took place in the orthography or shape of the letters of Hebrew script during the two century-long Persian period of hegemony over the Land of Israel. As recorded in the post-biblical anthological work known as the Talmud (to be discussed later), in reference to the literary legacy attributed to Moses: "Originally the Torah was given to Israel in Hebrew [that is, Paleo-Hebrew] characters and in the sacred [Hebrew] language; later, in the times of Ezra, the Torah was given in *Ashurith* [Proto-Hebrew] script and

Aramaic language. [Finally], they selected for Israel the *Ashurith* script and Hebrew language."[1] Just as was the case in the change of modern German script from Gothic to Latin letters, the change in Hebrew script probably drove many works available only in the older script out of reproduction and circulation, as scribes struggled to adapt their skills to the new script. Finally, the process of finalizing the contents of Scripture, presumably in accordance with some defined selection criteria of which we have no certain knowledge, effectively consigned many but not all of the excluded writings to oblivion. A number of such writings, many of which were originally composed in Hebrew or Aramaic and subsequently translated into other languages, were preserved and ultimately incorporated into the extra-biblical collections known as the Apocrypha and Pseudepigrapha.

In Jewish tradition, the books of the Hebrew Bible are grouped in three categories of works, *Torah* (Pentateuch), *Neviyyim* (Prophets), and *Ketuvim* (Writings or Hagiographa), which in the aggregate are widely known by the acronym *TaNaKH*. The works included in the three categories are discussed in general terms in the following paragraphs. For detailed descriptions of the actual contents of each of these works, the reader may consult any of the numerous introductory works on the Bible, a great number of which are in print and readily available.

Torah (PENTATEUCH)

The first five books, traditionally attributed to Moses, that are included in the biblical library are generally known as the Torah. It is a curious fact, however, that for much of Jewish history the collection of books that fall within the category of Torah did not have a firmly established collective name. That is, there has been no single designation commonly used by Jews at all times and places for the principal component of the Hebrew Scriptures.

Some of the early names applied to the collection of books that comprise the Torah are *Sefer Torat Moshe* or *Book of the Torah of Moses* (Joshua 8:31; 2 Kings 14:6; Nehemiah 8:1); *Sefer Moshe* or *Book of Moses* (2 Chronicles 25:4; Ezra 6:18; Nehemiah 13:1); *Sefer haTorah* or *Book of the Torah* (Joshua 8:24; 2 Kings 22:8; Nehemiah 8:3); and *Sefer Torat Adonai* or *Book of the Torah of God* (2 Chronicles 17:9, Nehemiah 9:3). In the later rabbinic literature, the collection is referred to as *Hamishah Sifre Torah* or "The Five Books of the Torah,"[2] or, the more popular, *Hamishah Homshei Torah* or "The Five Fifth-Parts of the Torah."[3] The latter names reflect and derive from the practice, since about the fifth century BCE, of transcribing copies of the five component parts of the Torah for private use and study on five separate scrolls for convenience of handling—which gave rise to the use of the Greek term Pentateuch, that is, "the five-volume book," subsequently known in Hebrew as the *Humash*, to describe the five books attributed to Moses.

The English names commonly assigned to the five books of the Torah, as well as those similarly employed in the Romance languages, derive from the Latin, which in turn derive from the names employed by the Greek-speaking Jews who translated into Greek the Hebrew designations commonly applied to the works in ancient Judea. According to a tradition preserved in the rabbinic literature, these names were *Sefer Beriat haOlam* (Book of the Creation of the World) or Genesis; *Sefer Yetziat Mitzraim* (Book of the Exodus from Egypt) or Exodus; *Torat Kohanim* (Book of the Priestly Code) or Leviticus; *Homesh haPekudim* (Book of the Numbered) or Numbers; and *Mishneh Torah* (The Repetition of the Torah) or Deuteronomy.

It should be noted that the name Leviticus, which seems to refer to the Levites rather than to the priests, probably derives from the Torah's repeated references to the priests as *hakohanim haleviyim* or Levitical priests (Deuteronomy 17:9, 18; 18:1), presumably to draw a clear distinction between the institutionalized priesthood, all of whom are direct descendants of Aaron the Levite, and the first-born sons of the other tribes and clans who previously performed priestly functions. The name *Mishneh Torah*, which was assigned to the fifth book, is actually derived from a verse in the book where the term refers to "a copy of the Torah" (Deuteronomy 17:18), which is not an accurate translation of Deuteronomy, the latter literally meaning "second law." Nonetheless, both names are apropos because the book is essentially a recapitulation of the teachings of the first four books, and is thus in a sense a second rendition of the Torah.

An alternate approach taken in antiquity was to name a book either by its opening word or words, or by its first significant word. According to this scheme, the first book of the Torah, Genesis, is known in Hebrew as *Bereshit* or "In the beginning," the first word of the book. It is of interest to note that, in the opinion of some of the rabbis of the Talmud, and reiterated in a tenth-century composition by Aaron ben Moses Ben-Asher, a noted expert on the Hebrew text, the presumably lost *book of Jashar*, which means the book of the "upright," is actually just another name for the book of Genesis, which deals with the lives of the "upright," the patriarchs of Israel.[4]

The second book, Exodus, is known as *Shemot* or the "names," derived from the first verse of the book, *Now these are the names of the sons of Israel*. It is noteworthy that it is also known in the Talmud as *Homesh Sheni* or the Second Fifth [of the Torah].[5] The third book, Leviticus, is known as *Vayikra* or "And He called," the first word of the book. The fourth book, Numbers, is known as *Bamidbar* or "In the wilderness," from the first verse of the book, *And the Lord spoke unto Moses in the wilderness of Sinai*. The fifth book, Deuteronomy, is known as *Devarim* or "words," from the first verse of the book, *These are the words which Moses spoke*. This method of naming the books of the Torah ultimately prevailed among Jews and is today the preeminent manner in which the books of the Torah are identified in Jewish literature, although one will still find occasional references in the Hebrew rabbinic literature to the earlier names *Torat Kohanim* and *Mishneh Torah*, instead of *Vayikra* and *Devarim*, for Leviticus and Deuteronomy.

NEVIYYIM (PROPHETS)

The books that fall within this category have long been placed in the arbitrary subcategories of *Neviyyim Rishonim* or "Former Prophets" and *Neviyyim Aharonim* or "Latter Prophets." The significance of this classification is not entirely clear; it seems likely that the division into two categories was employed simply as a means to reduce the physical size of the scrolls containing all of these works by copying them on two separate scrolls, according to their classification. In any case, "Former Prophets" includes the books of Joshua, Judges, Samuel, and Kings. The "Latter Prophets" includes the books of the so-called literary prophets (a designation not used in Hebrew), which refers to the works bearing the names of specific prophets that, in whole or in part, were preserved. It should be borne in mind, however, as pointed out above, that some additional prophetic works that might have been included were lost. The "literary prophets" include Isaiah, Jeremiah, Ezekiel, and the so-called twelve "Minor Prophets" (a designation not used in Hebrew), Hosea, Joel, Amos, Obadiah, Jonah, Micah, Nahum, Habbakuk, Zephaniah, Haggai, Zechariah, and Malachi.

It should be noted, however, that the designations of "former" or early prophets and "latter" prophets were not used in this literary sense in antiquity, where only Haggai, Zechariah, and Malachi were considered "latter prophets" because they prophesied entirely in the period following the destruction of the Temple of Jerusalem in 586 BCE. Thus, in response to the question of who constituted the "former prophets," one ancient sage answered, "They are David, Samuel, and Solomon." In response to the same question, another sage noted that the prophets Haggai, Zechariah, and Malachi were excluded from that category and are therefore considered "latter prophets."[6] The characterization of some of the prophets as "minor" is entirely unrelated to their comparative stature or the substance of their writings; the designation simply relates to the size of their books, the works of the minor prophets being of a size that permitted all twelve of them to be copied on a single relatively small scroll or as is common practice today, to be printed in a single slim volume as the *Trei-Assar* (Twelve) or *The Twelve Prophets*.

The books of the "Former Prophets," Joshua, Judges, Samuel, and Kings, are often characterized as historical books because they continue the narrative of the history of Israel from the Exodus and its aftermath, where the Torah ends, to the destruction of the kingdoms of Israel and Judah. However, they clearly are not histories in the modern sense of the term and are therefore considered prophetic books in Jewish tradition because they are written from a prophetic perspective. For the prophetic historiographers, it was how the divine challenge and human response were played out on the stage of history that was of primary concern, and their descriptions of that repeated drama inevitably produced a very different sort of historical writing than the typically self-glorifying chronicles of other ancient peoples. Actual events, accurately recorded, were of considerably lesser interest to them than the motivations behind and the consequences that flowed from the responses of the Israelites to the historical challenges with which they were presented.

KETUVIM (WRITINGS)

The works that fall into this general category, sometimes characterized as Hagiographa, include *Psalms, Proverbs, Job, The Five Megillot* or *Scrolls* (which include *Song of Songs, Ruth, Lamentations, Ecclesiastes*, and *Esther*), *Daniel, Ezra, Nehemiah*, and *Chronicles*. Although *Psalms* and *Proverbs* may have been written during the same period as some of the prophetic works, it is assumed that they were not included in the prophetic collections either because their inspiration was perceived to be human rather than divine, or because they were not seen as fully compatible with the ideological perspective that permeates the books of the prophets. It is suggested that some of the books, such as *Ezra, Daniel*, and *Chronicles*, that did fit the prophetic mold were probably put in final form after the prophetic canon had already been established and were therefore excluded from it. It is not clear when the designation of *Ketuvim* or Writings became the accepted name of the collection of these diverse works, which were frequently referred to in antiquity simply as "other writings."

CANONIZATION OF SCRIPTURE

The term canon, in the sense of an authoritative body of works, as applied to the *TaNaKH*, refers to the closed nature of the biblical corpus.

The term was first used in this sense by the Church Fathers in the fourth century. There is no specific Hebrew equivalent of the term, although as a practical matter, for Judaism the *TaNaKH* is the canon. Works not included, such as the books categorized as Apocrypha and Pseudepigrapha, are designated as *sifrei hitzonim* or external books, that is, those books that are outside the canon. A canonical book in Judaism is a book that is accepted as authoritative for religious doctrine and practice, and is a book to be studied and expounded both publicly and in private. The original concept of the biblical canon as revealed religion was distinctively Jewish, making the Bible the animating force of Jewish life. It was also a revolutionary step in the history of religion, and was later adopted by both Christianity and Islam.

It seems clear that the different components of the Hebrew Scriptures were canonized or given their final composition during different historical periods. Thus, there is reason to believe that the Torah most probably was canonized about 622 BCE, following the religious reformation that took place during the reign of King Josiah. Tradition has it that the books of the prophets entered the canon sometime during the period of Persian hegemony immediately prior to the Macedonian conquest of Judea, which took place in the latter third of the fourth century BCE. There is no record of any controversy at the time surrounding the choice of which prophetic works to include. It does appear, however, that the inclusion of the book of Ezekiel in the canon was a matter of some controversy many years later because his vision of the temple of the future and its priestly laws was deemed by some religious authorities to contradict the provisions set forth in the Torah.[7] For example, Ezekiel asserted: *The priests shall not eat of any thing that dieth of itself, or is torn, whether it be fowl or beast* (Ezekiel 44:31). This was considered problematic because the Torah had already stipulated that eating anything that died of itself or was torn by a beast is forbidden to every Israelite (Exodus 22:30; Leviticus 3:24). Ezekiel's statement, by stipulating that *the priests* were not to eat of such animals, could be construed as saying that it was permissible for others to do so, therefore presenting an apparent contradiction that raised the question of whether the book should be removed from common use despite its canonicity. Advocates for retaining the work evidently were successful and the challenge to it was dropped.

It appears that the earliest the books of Writings could have been incorporated in the biblical canon is about the middle of the second century BCE. This estimate is based on the fact that the Song of Songs contains some Greek words, as does the book of Daniel, which suggests that Hellenistic influences had already reached the point where its language crept into writings that would achieve canonical status. However, the controversies over canonization recorded in the Talmud clearly suggest a much later date for finalization of the canon, as we know it. It is clear that Rabbi Akiba, who thrived in the period following the destruction of the Second Hebrew Commonwealth in 70 CE, definitively excluded the works found in the Apocrypha and Pseudepigrapha from incorporation into the Hebrew canon.

NUMBER AND ORDER OF BOOKS IN THE *TANAKH,*

In Jewish tradition, the *TaNaKH* consists of twenty-four books: the five books of the Torah; Joshua; Judges; Samuel; Kings; Isaiah; Jeremiah; Ezekiel; The Twelve Prophets; Psalms; Proverbs; Job; Song of Songs; Ruth; Lamentations; Ecclesiastes; Esther; Daniel; Ezra-Nehemiah; and Chronicles. At least one biblical scholar has suggested that setting the number of books in the Hebrew canon at twenty-four is an artificial construct that curiously parallels the number of letters in the Greek alphabet, which accounts for the two most esteemed books in the Hellenistic world, Homer's *Iliad* and *Odyssey*, each having twenty-four books.[8] The obvious implication of this is that the Jewish religious authorities might have deemed it appropriate to attempt to counteract Hellenistic influences in every conceivable way, including the number of books in the biblical canon. It is noteworthy in this regard that the ancient Jewish historian Josephus, who lived in the first century, considered the *TaNaKH* to consist of only 22 books, corresponding to the number of letters in the Hebrew alphabet. He reached this number by attaching the book of Ruth to Judges and Lamentations to Jeremiah.[9]

Given the Hellenistic influences that became increasingly prominent following the Macedonian conquest of the region in the late fourth century BCE, it should come as no surprise that the earliest translations of the biblical writings were into Greek, a process that began about the middle of the third century BCE in Alexandria, Egypt. Although it is unlikely that the original Greek Septuagint deviated much from the Hebrew original in structure, this is not the case with the versions of the Septuagint that are presently available. As a result, Greek bibles, beginning with later augmented editions of the Septuagint, and their Latin derivatives, such as the Vulgate, tend to deviate from the Hebrew versions in two significant respects: the inclusion of works excluded from the Hebrew canon and the arrangement of the books included. The Hellenistic canon eliminates *Ketuvim* or Hagiographa as a division and distributes the works contained therein among a four-part canon, consisting of Torah (Pentateuch), history, poetic and didactic books, and prophetic works.

Typically, the contents of non-Hebrew bibles list 39 books, exclusive of Apocrypha. This number is arrived at by dividing the books of

Samuel, Kings, and Chronicles in two, separating Ezra-Nehemiah into two books, and by counting the writings of each of the twelve Minor Prophets as separate books, even though they traditionally were written on a single scroll. In fact, the present subdivisions of the Minor Prophets were not known in Hebrew editions of the Bible prior to the Bomberg edition of 1521. The widely accepted reason the books of Samuel, Kings, and Chronicles were divided in two in the Greek translation was because each work in Greek made use of approximately fifty percent more words than the Hebrew original. Thus, each of the three books contain about 25,000 words in Hebrew, where as the Greek translation contains 37,000–38,000 words. For the sake of convenience in handling, each of these large works was divided in two and copied on separate scrolls.

The actual sequential order of the books varies in different non-Hebrew biblical collections. It is a curious fact, however, that although the order of the books in the Hebrew bibles has generally been consistent, to the best of our knowledge, for more than a millennium, as evidenced by early medieval codices, that order is remarkably inconsistent with that specified by the ancient sages and reflected in the major law codes of Judaism and in a number of German and French manuscripts. Thus, although all existing printed Hebrew editions of the books of the Prophets follow the Spanish and oriental manuscripts and list their order as Joshua, Judges, Samuel, Kings, Isaiah, Jeremiah, Ezekiel, and the Twelve Prophets, we are told: "Our Rabbis taught: The order of the Prophets is, Joshua, Judges, Samuel, Kings, Jeremiah, Ezekiel, Isaiah, and the Twelve Prophets."[10] It is not clear why the ancient sages changed the chronological order of the three major literary prophets from Isaiah, Jeremiah, and Ezekiel to that of Jeremiah, Ezekiel, and Isaiah. Ironically, modern biblical scholarship, which maintains that the latter part of the book of Isaiah is actually a separate work by a later prophet of the same name, identified as Deutero-Isaiah or Second Isaiah, should have little problem with the change. However, there can be little if any doubt that the ancient sages considered the entire work attributed to Isaiah to be the product of a common author. Later sages attempted to supply the following rationale for placing the book of Isaiah, who preceded both Jeremiah and Ezekiel, after their works: "Because the Book of Kings ends with a record of destruction and Jeremiah speaks throughout of destruction and Ezekiel commences with destruction and ends with consolation and Isaiah is full of consolation; therefore we put destruction next to destruction and consolation next to consolation."[11] Although plausible, this rationale is by no means compelling since only the latter part of Isaiah dwells on consolation and passages of consolation are to be found in Jeremiah as well. The fact that the Hebrew editions simply ignore the ancient rabbinic stipulation of the order of the prophetic books is visible testimony of the failure of the sages to justify the anachronistic placement of the book of Isaiah in the order of the canon. Adding to the irony is the fact that the code of Jewish law composed by Joseph Caro in the sixteenth century, and still considered authoritative by traditionalists today, restates the order stipulated by the sages, at a time when Hebrew bibles were being printed using the original chronological order of the prophets, and widely disseminated.[12]

Compounding the problem, a similar discrepancy obtains with regard to the order of the books listed in the *Ketuvim*, the collection of the remaining biblical writings. The ancient sages ordained: "The order of the Hagiographa is Ruth, the Book of Psalms, Job, Proverbs, Ecclesiastes, Song of Songs, Lamentations, Daniel and the Scroll of Esther, Ezra and Chronicles."[13] However, by contrast with the books of *Neviyyim*, the order of the *Ketuvim* found in manuscript bibles varies widely. It is only since 1488, when the first printed Soncino edition of the entire Hebrew Bible appeared, that the order of the Hagiographa found in Hebrew editions of the Bible has been consistent in a manner that deviates sharply from that stipulated by the ancient sages. The commonly established order of the books in *Ketuvim* in all printed editions is Psalms, Proverbs, Job, Song of Songs, Ruth, Lamentations, Ecclesiastes, Esther, Daniel, Ezra-Nehemiah, and Chronicles. Once again, it remains a mystery why the order of the books does not conform to the ancient specification.

CANONICAL SANCTITY

Although, as indicated above, there is no Hebrew equivalent for the term "canon," there was a rabbinic criterion by which the effective canonical status of a book could be determined. That criterion was whether or not direct contact with a book *mettame et hayadaim* or "renders the hands unclean," a criterion that appears to have been applied to works deemed as divinely revealed or inspired. According to the *halakhah*, rabbinic law and normative practice, anyone whose hands came into direct contact with any book considered to have canonical status contracted ritual impurity in the second degree, requiring a prescribed ritual washing of the hands, a process of ritual purification normally required of one who contracted ritual impurity in the second degree in order to preclude its transference to and contamination of other objects. The following citation from the *Mishnah*, the basic rabbinic compendium of Jewish law to be discussed later, specifies this criterion and also gives a good indication of some of the debates that took place over the canonization process.

All the Holy Scriptures render the hands unclean. The Song of Songs
and Ecclesiastes render the hands unclean. R. Judah says: The Song of
Songs renders the hands unclean, but about Ecclesiastes there is dissension. R. Jose says: Ecclesiastes does not render the hands unclean, and
about the Song of Songs there is dissension . . . R. Simeon b. Azzai said: I
have heard a tradition from the seventy-two elders on the day when they
made R. Eleazar b. Azariah head of the college [of Sages], that the Song of
Songs and Ecclesiastes both render the hands unclean. R. Akiba said: God
forbid!—no man in Israel ever disputed about the Song of Songs [that he
should say] that it does not render the hands unclean, for all the ages are
not worth the day on which the Song of Songs was given to Israel; for all
the Writings are holy, but the Song of Songs is the Holy of Holies. And if
aught was in dispute the dispute was about Ecclesiastes alone. R. Johanan
b. Joshua, the son of R. Akiba's father-in-law, said: According to the words
of Ben Azzai so did they dispute and so did they decide.[14]

The conflict recorded in this passage concerned the canonicity of the
Song of Songs and Ecclesiastes, the former because of its erotic imag-
ery and the latter because of its apparent cynicism. The advocates of
considering both works as properly included in the biblical canon
ultimately carried the day primarily, it would seem, because the eroti-
cism of the Song of Songs was interpreted as a mystical allusion to the
symbiotic relationship between God and Israel, and because despite
its evident cynicism the book of Ecclesiastes ends on a positive note
calling on all to put aside their notions about the world and rely on
divine guidance.

There are at least three theories regarding the purpose of this seemingly arcane rule about rendering the hands ritually impure that are
of interest because they deal with the question of the sanctity of the
biblical texts and their care. One theory suggests that the rule is related
to the fundamental concept of making a clear distinction and separation between the holy and the profane, a concept emphasized by the
Pharisees and their rabbinic successors that suffuses much of Jewish
religious law and tradition. According to this theory, they washed their
hands after handling a sacred book, not because the holy book somehow contaminated them, something that does not seem reasonable,
but rather to emphasize the transition from the holy to the profane.
The washing highlighted that the hands that were now to be engaged
in some profane activity were no longer in the same state of ritual
purity as they were when they previously held a sacred book. In effect,
the washing disrupted the contiguity of contact between the holy and
the profane, keeping them in separate conceptual spheres. The obvious
problem with this theory is that there is no comparable stipulation that
one must first wash one's hands before going from the profane to the
sacred, at least not with regard to touching a book of the *TaNaKH*.

A second and more plausible theory proposes that the rule was intended as a prophylactic measure to assure that the sacred scrolls were treated with appropriate deference and care. It is suggested that the rule, which originated in the period when the Temple in Jerusalem existed, was directed against the common practice of the priests who used to keep their biblical scrolls and *terumah*, the agricultural tithe, in close proximity. The food attracted mice, which then harmed the scrolls. Accordingly, it was argued, the rule regarding rendering the hands unclean was intended to protect the scrolls from being treated in this manner.[15] The logic behind the rule was that it would soon become apparent to the priests that it was in their interest to keep the biblical scrolls and food stores in separate places to avoid repeatedly having to go to wash their hands every time they touched a scroll and then wished to partake of the *terumah*, the consumption of which necessitated that they be in a state of ritual purity. The need to repeatedly wash their hands could be especially onerous, given the state of indoor plumbing in antiquity.

The third theory, which is related to some extent to the one just discussed, proposes that the rule originally applied only to the Torah scroll that was maintained in the court of the Temple of Jerusalem. The idea was that by decreeing that touching the scroll defiled the hands, requiring the prescribed purification procedure, it would dissuade people from mishandling the scroll. Later on, however, the rule was applied to all Torah scrolls as a consequence of a broader factional dispute between the parties of the Pharisees, who, in broad terms, represented the interests of the popular masses, and the Sadducees, who represented the interests of the aristocracy and the priesthood. The dispute between them arose in the second century BCE and grew into a struggle for societal dominance that lasted until the destruction of the Temple of Jerusalem and with it the Second Commonwealth in 70 CE. A great point of contention between the Pharisees and Sadducees was the authority of the unwritten or Oral Torah, to be discussed later, which the Pharisees maintained had originated at the same time as the Written Torah, a concept the Sadducees rejected. Accordingly, it is argued, when the Pharisees were in a position to impose their will on the religious establishment they sought to deemphasize the popular reading of the Torah scrolls by the priests, thereby giving greater status to the Oral Torah. The rule about rendering the hands unclean made it difficult if not impossible for the priests to read from the Torah scrolls and to eat of the *terumah*, which we may assume was their practice during long study sessions.

By implication, then, since all the works included in the Hebrew Scriptures render the hands unclean, that is, are considered canonical, all other works regardless of merit are of necessity noncanonical. And to make this point even clearer, it was specified that "the Gospels and the books of heretics do not render the hands unclean, and the books of Ben Sira and all the books written thenceforward do not render the hands unclean."[16] It is noteworthy that the exclusion from canonicity applied not only to Jewish works that the ancient sages disapproved of, such as the Gospels and heretical writings, but also to apocryphal works such as Ben Sira or Ecclesiasticus, Jubilees, and Maccabees, writings that the sages and later rabbis referred to or cited approvingly.

Although sanctity is attributed to all the works included in the biblical canon, tradition has ascribed a relative order of degree of sanctity to the included works, which is manifested in the manner in which they are to be handled. The Torah, as the primary source of all Judaic thought and practice, is held to possess a higher sanctity than the remaining books of the *TaNaKH* that are considered as predicated on and therefore subsidiary to it. Accordingly, a *Humash*, which includes all five books of the Torah, may be laid on top of the individual books of the Torah, and individual books of the Torah may be laid on top of books of the Prophets and the Writings. However, it is impermissible to place either a book of the Prophets or of the Writings on top of a book of the Torah, just as one may not place an individual book of the Torah on top of a complete *Humash* or Pentateuch.[17]

INTERNAL ARRANGEMENT OF THE TEXTS

Anyone who looks in a Torah scroll will notice, aside from the special orthography that is employed, that although the text is identical with that found in printed editions, the way it is presented differs radically. In the Torah scroll there are no chapter subdivisions, no punctuation marks, and no musical notations or accents, all of which are to be found in the printed editions. The reasons for these anomalies are grounded in the history of the biblical texts and the transition from hand-written scrolls to printed books.

Ancient books were originally written as scrolls, as indicated above, and a perusal of the Torah scroll as well as a scroll of the Book of Esther, the only books of the Bible that are still produced in scroll form for synagogue use, will reveal that the scrolls do in fact have subdivisions in the form of paragraphs, but not sections or chapters. The paragraphs, which enclose complete thoughts and expressions, are indicated either by the absence of any additional writing on the line following the final word of the paragraph, as is the case with a modern English paragraph, or by a space the width of nine letters separating the last word of a paragraph and the first word of a succeeding paragraph that begins on the same line. These and a host of additional rules were established by tradition in antiquity as a means of preserving the integrity of the biblical texts as handed down from generation to generation and from copyist to copyist. By the eighth century, the laws and customs that related to the preparation, inscription, and the shape and adornment of the letters in the Torah scroll were compiled in a tractate, *Soferim* (Scribes), as well as in the subsequent legal compilations of rabbinic authorities. Those scholars who were deeply engaged in these and other traditions relating to the preservation of the integrity of the written texts were known as Masoretes, that is, masters of the scribal traditions or "Masorah."[18]

Another issue that engaged the Masoretes was the oral traditions that accompanied the written text since antiquity. Because the Hebrew alphabet consists entirely of consonants, traditions evolved as to how unwritten vowels were to be applied to make the written text comprehensible in terms of tense and gender, effectively creating a formal grammar that reflected common traditional usage. By formalizing the readings of the biblical texts, the Masoretes were able to ensure consistency and textual integrity in the transmission of the texts of the *TaNaKH* over future generations. The significance of what they did may be appreciated if one recognizes that the change of an unwritten vowel in a biblical word can radically alter the meaning of the text in which it appears. Nonetheless, tradition precluded the instructional notes of the Masoretes from being included directly in the Torah scrolls used for public reading in the synagogue. However, there was no such restriction on their use in scrolls of individual biblical works and, over time, in codices as well, a codex being in effect a primitive book consisting of sheets of parchment or paper laid on top of each other and bound between two pieces of wood, which eventually became books as we know them today. Accordingly, to be assured that one is reading the Torah scroll correctly, one need only refer to a standard Hebrew copy of the *Humash* or any of its individual books to see the text accompanied by diacritical and accent marks, as well as punctuation, that are absent in the scroll. All printed editions of the *TaNaKH* or Hebrew Bible embody what has become known as the Masoretic text, a standard that has prevailed for a millennium in both earlier scribal and later printed form.

One additional significant difference between the printed Hebrew *Humash* and the Torah scroll is the subdivision of the printed texts into both labeled *parshiot* (portions) and numbered *perakim* (chapters), which reflect two very different organizational principles. With regard to the former, the custom of the Babylonian (Mesopotamian) Jewish communities was to read the entire Torah publicly in the synagogue annually. For this purpose, and in recognition of some of the peculiarities of the lunar calendar, the Torah was subdivided into 54 *parshiot* or portions, each of which was given a distinct name, usually a key word in the opening sentence of the portion. Thus, the first *parshah* or portion of the book of Genesis or *Bereshit* is also named *Bereshit*, because it begins with the text, *In the beginning* (Gen. 1:1). The second *parshah* is named *Noah*, because it begins with the text, *These are the generations of Noah* (Gen. 6:9). The third *parshah* is named *Lekh Lekha*, because it begins with the text, *Now the Lord said unto Abram: Get thee [lekh lekha]* (Gen. 12:1). The same pattern follows throughout all 54 *parshiot* or portions that make up the Torah. It is noteworthy that in the tradition followed in the land of Israel, the public Torah reading was completed over a three-year cycle causing the text to be subdivided into 154, or 167 according to a variant tradition, portions called *sedarim*. Nonetheless, the printed editions of the Torah all follow the Babylonian tradition.

It will be noted that the *parshiot* or portions described above do not follow the chapter arrangements found in the printed biblical texts, the second *parsha* of Genesis beginning with the ninth verse of chapter six and the third *parsha* beginning with chapter 12. The numerical *perakim* or chapters derive entirely from Christian sources, beginning with their subdivision of the Greek Septuagint, followed by the Latin Vulgate, editions according to such a scheme, which varied from edition to edition until the thirteenth century when they were standardized by the Archbishop of Canterbury, Stephen Langton (d. 1228), into the form now universally accepted. This numerical scheme was subsequently adopted in editions of the Hebrew Bible to facilitate participation in the religious disputes into which the representatives of the Jewish communities of Europe were drawn repeatedly. The first Hebrew biblical manuscript organized according to this numerical scheme dates to approximately 1330, and it became fairly standard afterward.

The organization of the texts by chapters clearly is useful for easily finding a particular text in editions with different page numberings, which presumably is the reason why the method was adopted by early clerics. However, it should be noted that there are instances where the subdivision by numbered chapters is not as innocuous as it may appear at first glance, and clearly reflects theological positions or sectarian interests inconsistent with or inimical to traditional Judaic perspectives. An example of this may be seen at the conclusion of the initial account of the seven days of creation, which in the numbered chapter subdivision separates the seventh day from the first six days by a chapter break. In the Hebrew Bible, the story of creation is told in the first seven paragraphs of the book of Genesis, each paragraph dealing with the events of a single day, after which tradition calls for a break in the public reading. However, according to the superimposed numbered chapter arrangement, the first chapter of Genesis concludes with the creation on the sixth day, and the paragraph that relates what took place on the seventh day is relegated to the following chapter. This arrangement, which makes no sense from a Judaic standpoint, surely was not accidental. However, if considered within the context of the medieval Christian polemic against Judaism and its practices, one may infer the reasoning behind it. There can be no question that attempts were made to deemphasize the Jewish view of the Sabbath as the culmination of creation, which considers the Sabbath itself to be a divine creation, as the text says: "And on the seventh day God finished His work which He had made; and He rested on the seventh day" (Gen. 2:2). Short of tampering with the text itself, severing the story of the creation of the seventh day as a day of rest from the preceding narrative by a chapter break presumably made it easier to justify the transfer of the Sabbath of the seventh day from Saturday, as established in Judaism, to Sunday, as reflected in those European calendars that begin the week with Monday.

Another example of the use of chapter divisions to meddle with the text may be seen in the penultimate verse of the second chapter of Genesis: "Therefore shall a man leave his father and his mother, and shall cleave unto his wife and they shall be one flesh" (Gen. 2:24). Anxious to introduce a chapter break at this point, which culminates the story of the creation of woman, the next episode being that of the moral fall of man in the garden of Eden, but uncomfortable with ending the preceding chapter with the verse cited and thus highlighting the point it makes, an additional verse was added to the chapter. The problem was that Gen. 2:24 seemed to challenge the monastic ideal of celibacy by strongly advocating marital union. Accordingly, the next verse, "And they were both naked, the man and his wife, and were not ashamed" (Gen. 2:25), was added to end the chapter on the note of shamelessness rather than on the desirability of marriage. From a Jewish theological perspective, placing a chapter break at this point is of no particular significance, because in the Torah scroll all the text from Gen. 2:4 through 3:15 is contained within a single long paragraph. It is troublesome, however, from a Hebrew literary perspective because it interrupts what is evidently a biblical play on words involving the nuanced use of the word *arum* in both 2:25 and 3:1. Read together, the text states: "And they were both naked (*arum*), the man and his wife, and were not ashamed. Now the serpent was more subtle (*arum*) than any beast of the field which the Lord God had made." In other words, the serpent that played such a pernicious role in the story was, in all outward appearances, as innocent as Adam and Eve were before eating of the tree of the knowledge of good and evil. Accordingly, Jewish commentators see in this usage of a word that carries the meaning of both guileless and mischievous the implicit suggestion that, as one scholar put it, "seeming simplicity is often the most dangerous weapon of cunning,"[19] which is one of the lessons to be learned from the episode. The position of the chapter break severs the linkage between the two Hebrew verses, a linkage that is almost self-evident in the Hebrew but that is, as a practical matter, completely lost in translation.

THE HEBREW BIBLE IN ENGLISH TRANSLATION

Translating Hebrew into a noncognate language such as English is both difficult and problematic, the subtleties of the one being obscured and sometimes distorted by the subtleties of the other. Moreover, because idiomatic expressions and usages cannot be translated literally and retain their meaning, and because differences in grammar may preclude literal translation, English translations, as well as those in other languages, of the Hebrew Scriptures are unavoidably also interpretations, the accuracy of which may be subject to dispute, especially when they affect fundamental concepts. This is not to suggest that the meaning of the biblical texts is absolutely clear to those who have a good knowledge of Hebrew. The fact is that there is a vast library of Hebrew commentaries on the Hebrew Scriptures that often reflect a wide variety of interpretations of a single text. The problem, however, is significantly compounded by translations of the text, which in effect, give a specific interpretive meaning to a text in the process of rendering it in English. In other words, one cannot be sure that the translation truly reflects the intent of the original, because the translation itself may necessarily negate alternative understandings of the text. The benefit of reading the text in the original language is that the various interpretations of it are extraneous to the text and can be examined and evaluated objectively, something that is made more difficult when the text itself represents an interpretive bias of which the reader may be unaware.

A classic example of this problem may be seen in the ways that the first verse of the Bible has been translated into English and other languages. A brief comparison of the translations provided in the 1917 and 1962 Jewish Publication Society editions will reflect very different understandings of what the text is telling us. In the earlier edition, which is based for the most part on the King James Version and reflects a more literal translation, the opening verse reads: *In the beginning God created the heaven and the earth.* In the later revised edition, however, the verse is rendered: *When God began to create heaven and earth.* What is at issue here is the translation of the Hebrew word *be'reshit*, rendered in the earlier edition as, *in the beginning*, and in the later edition as *when . . . began*. The appropriate understanding of this first word of Genesis has been the subject of a controversy that first flared among Jewish medieval biblical scholars, and continues until this day among modern commentators.

In the earliest known translation of Scripture, the Greek *Septuagint* (third century BCE), *bereshit* is rendered as *en archi* or "in the beginning." Similarly, the Latin *Vulgate* renders the word as *in principio*, with the same meaning of "in the beginning," as do the eight major English translations from the Tyndale (1530) to the Revised Standard Version (1960). It thus seems fair to say that there was a general consensus regarding the meaning of the word in antiquity, although there is some difference between how the word is rendered in the Aramaic translations and paraphrases produced between the second and eighth centuries. However, it was in the medieval period that the meaning of the term became not only a matter of grammatical disagreement among Jewish scholars, but also one with major theological implications, which I have discussed at length in *The Biblical Creation Narrative: A Study in Interpretation*, and will not delve into here.

AUTHORSHIP OF THE BOOKS OF THE BIBLE

Unquestionably, it would be of inestimable value to know the identity of the author or authors of the various biblical books. Identifying the authors surely would enable us to better understand why the works are presented in their current form, and might provide the answers to many questions about the apparent anomalies to be found in the texts. But, the ability to do this convincingly has thus far proven to be beyond the competence of modern biblical scholarship and this will most likely continue to remain the case for the foreseeable future. One cannot even state with confidence that the books specifically attributed to the prophets and other named persons are the actual literary products of those persons. And, if this is the case with the books of the Prophets and the Hagiographa, it is certainly the case with regard to the books of the Torah, the latter serving as the critical foundation for virtually all of subsequent Judaic thought.

Accordingly, if one accepts the assertion that Moses authored the Torah in response to the direct divine revelation received by him, as seems to be the explicit assertion of the biblical text, the work may be understood as truly representing a divine prescription for a future civilization in the purest possible sense. After all, if we conceive of God as omnicompetent, as tradition maintains, then the divinely ordained prescriptions revealed through Moses must represent ultimate and perfect reason. Presumably, the deity could have chosen another scheme for the ideal society. The fact that no other is revealed suggests that this is the one that God in His infinite wisdom deemed most appropriate for humankind, at least in its general fundamental principles, and as particularly applicable to the exemplary civilization and society intended to be created by the children of Israel.

Alternatively, one may prefer to believe that the prescriptions of the Pentateuch are the personal work of Moses, conceived by him in accordance with his own insights, or perhaps formulated under divine inspiration. In this case, the Torah may be understood as setting forth a Mosaic political philosophy and theory of governance, thinly veiled as political theology. Similarly, one may prefer to accept a theory of non-Mosaic authorship, or authorship by a variety of hands over an extended period of time, in accordance with the documentary hypotheses of modern higher biblical criticism.

Regardless of the validity of any of these theories of authorship, the basic premise that underlies the work remains unaffected. The Pentateuch as we have it, and as it has been known for some two and a half millennia, still represents the social and political philosophy of its authors or editors couched in theological terms. The critical distinction between the traditional view that the Torah reflects divine revelation and the two alternative views suggested above concerns the matter of author infallibility alone. It does not affect the reality that the Torah, irrespective of alternate theories of authorship, has served as the basis of Judaism and Jewish history for at least two and a half millennia. As already suggested, the actual authorship of the books of the biblical canon is not and probably never will be known for certain, at least not in a sense that would satisfy reasonable scientific criteria. It is of interest for present purposes, however, to consider briefly how the problem of authorship has been addressed in the literature of Judaism, the view of the sages reflected in the following passage.

Who composed the Scriptures?—Moses composed his own book and the portion of Balaam and Job. Joshua composed the book that bears his name and [the last] eight verses of the Pentateuch. Samuel composed the book that bears his name and the Book of Judges and Ruth. David composed the Book of Psalms, including in it the work of the elders, namely Adam, Melchizedek, Abraham, Moses, Heman, Yeduthun, Asaph, and the three sons of Korah. Jeremiah composed the book that bears his name, the Book of Kings, and Lamentations. Hezekiah and his colleagues composed Isaiah, Proverbs, the Song of Songs and Ecclesiastes. The Men of the Great Assembly composed Ezekiel, the Twelve Minor Prophets, Daniel and the Scroll of Esther. Ezra composed the book that bears his name and the genealogies of the Book of Chronicles up to his own time . . . Who then finished it [the Book of Chronicles]?—Nehemiah the son of Hachaliah.[20]

The classical Jewish view on the question of the authorship of the books of the Torah is, of course, that Moses composed it in accordance with the divine revelation granted to him to convey to the children of Israel. However, even the ancient sages conceded that there were some passages that could not have reasonably been penned by Moses, most notably the final eight verses of Deuteronomy that deal with his death and burial. Accordingly, the composition of these was attributed to Moses' successor Joshua.

The statement that Moses composed the parables of Balaam that are found in Numbers 23–24 seems strange, given that they are included in a book, the composition of which has already been ascribed to Moses, a problem with which commentators have struggled over the centuries. There are at least two possible explanations of the statement. First, we may infer that the sages are implicitly asserting that Moses had written those passages separately and later incorporated them into the biblical text. This was the position of the thirteenth–fourteenth-century scholar Yom Tov ben Abraham Ishbili of Seville (known as Ritba), who asserted that Moses had written a separate work on Balaam that was subsequently lost except, presumably, for the passages incorporated into the biblical text. A second explanation, championed by the sixteenth-century commentator Judah Loew ben Bezalel of Prague (known as Maharal), is that the purpose of the statement is to make clear that, contrary to the unrecorded opinion of some that those passages, which concerned a non-Israelite prophet, were a later interpolation from an alien source, they were in fact written by Moses.[21]

Another biblical text that evidently troubled later commentators is the instruction given to the people by Moses to set up large plastered stones and to "write upon them all the words of this law" (Deut. 27:3), a charge that was dutifully carried out by Joshua, who wrote "upon the stones a copy of the law of Moses" (Josh. 8:32). Tradition has it that the number of stones was twelve, each of which represented a tribe of the people of Israel. The problem is that it was difficult to conceive how the entire Torah could be written on even twelve very large stones. This problem was addressed succinctly by the tenth-century Mesopotamian commentator Saadia Gaon, who interpreted Moses' instruction as requiring that it was the "principles of this law" that were to be copied, and by implication not the entire Torah.[22] Saadia's interpretation was subsequently adopted by the twelfth-century Spanish commentator Abraham ibn Ezra, with the comment that what Saadia meant by "principles of this law" was the enumeration of the traditional 613 precepts of the Torah, which the latter had listed in brief composition in the poetical form of *Azharot*, which will be discussed later.[23] Moreover, the Hebrew for the phrase "a copy of the law of Moses," employed above in the citation from the book of Joshua, is *mishneh Torah*, which as noted earlier has traditionally been a name assigned to the book of Deuteronomy and not the entire Pentateuch. The significance of all this is that when it is asserted by the ancient sages, based on the biblical text itself, that Moses wrote the entire Torah, the actual reference may be to the laws and precepts of the Torah and not necessarily to its narrative portions as well. Ibn Ezra's critical comments on this and a number of other biblical passages evidently inspired the seventeenth-century philosopher Baruch (Benedict de) Spinoza, who cites Ibn Ezra extensively, to author a major critique regarding the authorship of the entire biblical corpus.[24] Spinoza's critique effectively launched the mode of analysis known as Higher Criticism that continues to dominate the contemporary world of nontraditional biblical scholarship.

Notwithstanding the contentious issues of authorship, the twenty-four books of the Hebrew Scriptures constitute the bedrock of Judaism and Judaic thought as it has evolved and developed for more than two millennia. The subsequent development of the literature of Judaism in all its variegated forms took place in the light of Scripture and the traditions derived from it. This vast body of literature has from earliest times reflected two relatively distinct orientations corresponding to those found in Scripture itself, one that focuses on precept and normative guidance for the society and civilization that it prescribes, and the other on the narrative of the trials and tribulations of the children of Israel and their patriarchs and rulers over the course of the people's early history.

With regard to the former orientation, there emerged a vast literature devoted to the translation of biblical precept and guidance into the rules, regulations, and behavioral norms for a living society that essentially described and prescribed the path it should follow. These normative stipulations are encompassed under the general rubric of *halakhah* or the "way", which may be defined broadly as applied biblical law. With regard to the latter orientation, an equally vast if not greater body of literature emerged that dealt not only with the narrative content of Scripture but also with a wide range of topics that fall outside the prescriptive realm of *halakhah*. This literature encompasses both political and cultural history and all that pertains thereto, as well as theological, theosophical, and philosophical speculation, and a variety of other topics, all of which come under the general rubric of *aggadah* or "narrative." These relatively distinct bodies of rabbinic literature are nonetheless often complementary, and familiarity with both is essential to a proper comprehension of Judaic thought, as it has evolved from antiquity to the present. The history and various aspects of both types of rabbinic literature are discussed at some length in the chapters that follow.

Chapter 2

Midrash Halakhah

Putting aside the intriguing questions concerning biblical authorship, for which no compelling answers have been or are likely to be found, it is important to bear in mind that the *Hebrew* Scriptures remain the foundation stone of the entire edifice of Judaism and its literature as they have evolved over a period of more than three millennia. The question that will be of primary concern in this and the remaining chapters of this book, is how the substantive teachings of Scripture, their content and intent, were transmitted and construed over time in the life and thought of the faith community of Israel. It is important to understand at this point that when we speak of the "substantive teachings of Scripture," from a Judaic perspective this refers exclusively to the Torah, the five books of Moses, and not to the other parts of the *TaNaKh*. According to well-established tradition, precept and law in Judaism may be derived only from the Torah, and not from any of the other biblical writings, although the latter are of critical importance to the philosophy and ethics of Judaism. The problem inherent in accurately conveying the intent of the provisions of the Torah may be seen reflected in its own rather sketchy description of the process through which biblical precept and law were to be presented to the people of Israel.

> *And Moses wrote this law [Torah], and delivered it unto the priests the sons of Levi . . . and unto all the elders of Israel. And Moses commanded them, saying: At the end of every seven years . . . in the feast of tabernacles, when all Israel is come to appear before the Lord thy God in the place which He shall choose, thou shalt read this law [Torah] before all Israel in their*

hearing ... that they may hear, and that they may learn, and fear the Lord your God, and observe to do all the words of this law [Torah] (Deut. 31:9–12).

The critical question, of course, is whether the *words of this law* are sufficiently clear and explicit to facilitate ready translation into observance and practice, without further explanation and elaboration. Even a cursory examination of the biblical texts will reveal that this is hardly the case. For example, the people are instructed to observe the Sabbath, but what that means in practice is by no means self-evident. The biblical text does not specify how one is to go about observing the day, a day of rest, what one should or should not do during that time period, that is, how "rest" is to be defined, or even when the day of rest is to begin and end. Similar issues with regard to virtually all the biblical stipulations demanded that those who conveyed the law to the public, the Levites and the elders, also explain what was intended and how to act in conformity with them. This in turn raised the obvious problem of how to assure that the various persons entrusted with public instruction all said the same things to their audiences, without which there could be no commonality of practice in their various communities. This raised the corollary concern that all written texts lend themselves to various interpretations that may prove mutually inconsistent. Accordingly, it became critically important to ascertain the true intent of the author if the texts were to be correctly understood. In other words, from the very outset it was essential that Moses, as lawgiver, also had to serve as master teacher of the Levites and the elders to assure a common comprehension of what the transmitted texts intended and required.

The self-evident implication of this circumstance gave rise to the idea that there had to be oral interpretations and traditions that accompanied the original written texts, which would enable those who received them to deal with all the questions and issues implicit in the necessarily delimited written word. Accordingly, the ancient sages suggested that this idea was stated implicitly in the written text, *These are the statutes [hukim] and ordinances [mishpatim] and laws [torot], which the Lord made between Him and the children of Israel in mount Sinai by the hand of Moses* (Lev. 26:46). They understood the meaning of these three categories of teachings to be as follows: "The *statutes [hukim]* are what may be expounded [*midrashot*] from the text, the *ordinances [mishpatim]* are the laws [*dinim*]. *Torot* [plural of Torah] teaches that two Torahs were given to Israel, one in writing and one orally ... teaching that the Torah, its rules, and its grammar, and its explanation were given through Moses at Sinai."[1]

It should be noted that the idea of a dual Torah had been strongly contested by some groups within the broad Judaic fold in antiquity, again in the early medieval period, and again by some in modern times. Nonetheless, it has remained the keystone of rabbinic thought for more than two millennia. Indeed, some advocates of the idea have pointed out that it is quite clear that the biblical text itself indicates that there were oral laws and traditions incorporated in the Torah as normative precepts that dated from the time of the Patriarchs, which long anteceded the promulgation of the written texts. These included, for example, requirements such as circumcision, which the narrative of the book of Genesis records as being first divinely imposed on Abraham centuries earlier, and traditions such as tithing, a practice which the patriarch appears to have observed on his own initiative (Gen. 14:20) and which was followed by his grandson Jacob (Gen. 18:22). Accordingly, it might be asserted that not only was there an Oral Torah that was presented by Moses together with the Written Torah, but that in fact some of it was already normative practice before being stipulated in the Written Torah.

An obvious and important question is why the oral interpretations of and traditions regarding the biblical texts, given their evident importance, were not written down to assure their preservation and integrity.[2] The probable reasons for this are two-fold. First, it would clearly have been undesirable to have two alternate sets of Scriptures. Second, and perhaps an even more important consideration, there is finality to a written text that does not pertain to that which is oral. Oral traditions and teachings are permeable and can be added to or modified over time, and thus allow for growth and development in accordance with the needs of time and place. Judaism thus places extraordinary value on its oral traditions and teachings and has only put them into writing when historical circumstances threatened their very preservation. However, this statement should not be understood as asserting that these traditions and teachings were never actually written down but rather that they were never published until it was deemed essential to do so. There can be no doubt that many teachers throughout the ages recorded notes of discussions with their own teachers, colleagues, and students as aids to memory. Accordingly, the process of publishing the various works of the oral literature necessarily involved the acquisition and compilation of such notes from a variety of authors living in different times and places, in addition to oral materials literally passed down by word of mouth for generations. It was the evident availability of such source documents and reliable oral transmissions that enabled the final editors of the works that put them on permanent record for the future to set forth vibrant discussions of a point of law or tradition, the participants in which may have never actually known each other and in some instances may not even have lived in contemporary time frames.

Although one cannot assert with any certainty when the existence
of a body of oral tradition that amplified and explained the Mosaic
texts was first established, it seems clear that such oral traditions were
already well known in scholarly circles by the third century BCE. In
what may be the oldest fragment in the entire corpus of post-biblical
literature, a "chain of tradition" that purported to account for the historical transmission of oral traditions originating with Moses was set
forth as a parallel to the biblical statement regarding the transmission
of the written text: "Moses received Torah from Sinai and transmitted
it to Joshua, Joshua to the elders, the elders to the prophets, and the
prophets transmitted it to the Men of the Great Assembly."[3] This "chain
of tradition" varies from that in the biblical text in two significant ways.
The transmission of the Written Torah is from Moses to the priests and
from them to the elders, whereas the transmission of the Oral Torah
is described as having been from Moses to Joshua, and from Joshua
to the elders, and from them to the prophets. In the latter process the
priesthood is not presumed to play any distinctive role as guardians of
the traditions, perhaps a reflection of adverse historical circumstances
at the outset of the Second Temple period. Another consideration is the
fact that whereas the biblical texts speak of "*the* Torah," presumably
referring specifically to the Mosaic writings, the post-biblical text is
assumed to be speaking of "Torah" in the broader sense of teachings,
both past and future, referring to or derived from "the Torah," but not
specifically articulated therein.

The Great Assembly, the final link in the chain of transmission of the
oral tradition, is presumed to have been a national communal body,
the very existence of which as an ongoing institution remains the subject of a scholarly controversy that is of only peripheral interest here.
Modern historical scholarship reflects at least four different theories
regarding the Great Assembly. At one end of the spectrum, it has been
argued that it was nothing more than an ad hoc congress of notables
that was convened only rarely in ancient Israel to deal with the collective needs of the people during times of major communal crises. At
the other end of the range of opinion, there is the view that accords it
status as a longstanding institution that came into being in the time of
Nehemiah (fifth century BCE), during the period of Persian suzerainty
over the land of Israel and the reconstitution of the Judean community there. It is presumed to have continued to function for about two
centuries as conservator of the Mosaic tradition and ad hoc communal
legislative body until the threshold of the Hasmonean era that began
in the early second century BCE.[4] In any case, following the decline
and eventual dissolution of the Great Assembly as a central communal
institution, the mantle of leadership in preserving the integrity of the
oral traditions fell to the ancient sages or rabbis who constituted yet

another link in the "chain of tradition," whose recorded teachings constitute a massive literature covering a wide range of topics, all related in one way or another to the Mosaic legacy.

Just what was it that was actually transmitted as oral traditions that were presumed to have originated simultaneously with or in some instances before the written biblical text of the Torah? Primarily, it was the ways in which the specific biblical precepts were to be observed or carried out in practice, detailed information and guidance that the Written Torah did not provide. It is this transformation of biblical precept into rules and regulations that can be applied to the various facets of communal, family, and religious life that is encompassed by the term *halakhah*, mentioned earlier. However, it is important to understand that *halakhah* goes beyond law, as that term is usually defined. In addition to prescribing what may or may not be done, *halakhah* also seeks to inculcate what ought or ought not to be done beyond that which is required by law. In other words, *halakhah*, deriving from the root *halakh*, meaning to go or walk, refers to the way things are to be done or ought to be done in the ideal society envisioned by the Torah.

To provide the necessary authority for the regulatory stipulations they promulgated, the ancient rabbis asserted that the practices required by oral tradition but not specified in the biblical texts essentially had the same force of law as the latter. Secondarily, but nonetheless of great consequence for the future development of Judaism, the oral tradition encouraged and provided techniques for critical study of the biblical texts, which allowed the astute scholar to uncover layers of subtexts that gave fresh meaning to a number of texts that were considered troublesome and stipulations that were deemed impracticable for various reasons. The following example will illustrate this point.

The biblical text states unequivocally: *An Ammonite or a Moabite shall not enter into the assembly of the Lord* (Deut. 23:4). The later sages saw this exclusionary rule as highly problematic because it seemed to directly impugn the legitimacy of David, who was a descendant of Ruth, a Moabite woman who had elected to cast her lot with Israel, to be the king of Israel and Judah and progenitor of the coming Messiah. The rabbinic literature thus records a tradition relating to the events surrounding the favor shown by King Saul to David and the effort by one of the king's non-Israelite counselors to discredit the rising star in the king's court. "Doeg the Edomite then said to him [Saul], 'Instead of enquiring whether he is fit to be king or not, enquire rather whether he is permitted to enter the assembly or not!' 'What is the reason?' 'Because he is descended from Ruth the Moabitess.'" As such, he would be biblically disqualified from entering the assembly, let alone ascending the throne of Israel. The problem, we are told, was resolved by a critical reading of the biblical text. "We learned: *An Ammonite*, but not an Ammonitess; *A Moabite,* but not a *Moabitess.*"[5] That is, because the biblical injunction specifies an Ammonite and a Moabite, the gender of the terms being clearly masculine, it was reasoned that the restriction was not intended to apply to feminine members of the named peoples. Thus, without changing a word of the biblical text, its own choice of words was read in a manner that delimited the scope of the injunction. This interpretation of the Written Torah became part of the Oral Torah that was handed down through the generations.

Another example of this sort of critical examination of the biblical texts may be seen in the situation where two biblical precepts seem to address the same issue but appear to conflict with each other. The biblical text stipulates: *The wages of a hired servant shall not abide with thee all night until the morning* (Lev. 19:13). The simple sense of this is that the worker has to be paid the same night following completion of his work. However, there is another biblical stipulation that seems to contradict the former: *In the same day thou shalt give him his hire, neither shall then sun go down upon it* (Deut. 24:15), indicating he has to be paid during the day. The guiding principle for resolving this apparent conflict was that where two biblical texts appeared to deal with the same issue, it must be assumed that the second text intends to say or stipulate something not included in the first. In the case at hand, the sages resolved the difficulty by arguing that the first verse applied to a day worker who received his payment at night, and the second verse applied to a night worker who received his pay during the day following his work. In both cases the imperative is to compensate the worker within a short period of time after the conclusion of his work day, whether it end in the evening as in the first case or in the morning as in the second. Once again, new meaning is given to the biblical texts without tampering with them.

This general approach to reading the biblical texts critically and deriving implicit information from them heightened understanding of their meaning and intent and provided guidance with regard to how the precepts should be carried out. The interpretive process through which this took place has been dubbed *midrash halakhah,* or legal exegesis. Although we have no certain knowledge when this analytic process first began, Scripture itself provides textual evidence that such critical reading of the Torah was already practiced in the first half of the fifth century BCE by Ezra the Scribe, who *had set his heart to seek [i.e., interpret] the law of the Lord, and to teach in Israel statutes and ordinances* (Ezra 7:10). Thus, at the solemn assembly at which Ezra presented the Torah to the people, he and his associates *caused the people to understand the Law . . . And they read in the book, the Law of God, distinctly; and they gave the sense, and caused them to understand the reading* (Neh. 8:7–8).

It was through application of the critical techniques of *midrash halakhah* that post-exilic Judaism first began to take on the shape, the contours of which are still clearly visible to this day. This is not to suggest, however, that the path from divinely ordained biblical precept to human reformulation as *halakhah* was smooth. It clearly was not. As in all intellectual enterprises, differences of scholarly opinion arose, some of which were simply irreconcilable. Such a dispute arose among the sages of the late first century and early second century CE, the subject matter of which is only of secondary importance for present purposes. What is particularly notable is the manner in which the dispute was resolved. Although the story of the dispute is presented in a clearly legendary form, it nonetheless remains a remarkable expression of Judaic tradition, which accords extraordinary importance to independent human reasoning as a critical element in interpreting and carrying out the divine precepts set forth in the Torah.

In the case under consideration, the sage R. Eliezer ben Hyrcanus stood in opposition to his colleagues, insisting that he was correct in his understanding of the proper application of the law and that they, the majority, were wrong.

> On that day R. Eliezer brought forth every imaginable argument, but they did not accept them. Said he to them: "If the *halakhah* agrees with me, let this carob-tree prove it," whereupon the carob-tree was torn a hundred cubits out of its place . . . "No proof can be brought from a carob-tree," they retorted. Again he said to them: "If the *halakhah* agrees with me, let the stream of water prove it," whereupon the stream of water flowed backwards. "No proof can be brought from a stream of water," they responded. Again he urged: "If the *halakhah* agrees with me, let the walls of the schoolhouse prove it," whereupon the walls inclined to fall. But R. Joshua rebuked them, saying: "When scholars are engaged in a *halakhic* dispute, why are you interfering?" As a result, they did not collapse out of respect for R. Joshua, nor did they resume their upright position out of respect for R. Eliezer, and they are still standing in an inclined position. Again he said to them: "If the *halakhah* agrees with me, let it be proved from heaven," whereupon a Heavenly Voice cried out: "Why do you dispute with R. Eliezer, seeing that in all matters the *halakhah* agrees with him." But R. Joshua arose and exclaimed: *It is not in heaven* [Deut. 30:12]. What did he mean by this? R. Jeremiah said: [He meant] that the Torah had already been given at Mount Sinai, and we pay no attention to a Heavenly Voice, because You long ago wrote in the Torah at Mount Sinai, *After the majority must one incline* [Ex. 33:2].[6]

This passage is truly remarkable in more than one respect. For one thing, it clearly indicates that the application of *midrash halakhah* may yield diametrically opposite results when employed by different critical scholars, making it essential, as a practical matter, that there be a means of resolving the dispute in the public interest, so that the society might remain cohesive in its religious practices, even though it may prove to be impossible to achieve intellectual consensus on the matter. The solution affirmed here is that in a case where the applicable *halakhah* is in dispute, for all practical purposes it must be settled in accordance with view of the majority, that is, presumably, a majority of those generally deemed competent to render halakhic decisions. Another crucial aspect of this passage is its rather explicit assertion that the revelation of the Torah at Sinai was duly recorded in a written text, which is fixed for all eternity, and that once it and the oral traditions accompanying it were given to Israel, the divine role with regard to it is concluded. Men will determine what the *halakhah* is in any given instance, without interference from above. How was this latter and arguably arrogant assertion viewed on high? The story continues with a supposed meeting of one of the sages with the ancient prophet Elijah, who was asked: "What did the Holy One, blessed be He, do at that hour? He laughed [with joy] and replied, saying: 'My sons have defeated Me, My sons have defeated Me.'"[7] That is, God had set the ground rules and His children now insisted that He stick by them, even though He preferred R. Eliezer's understanding of the intent and application of the *halakhah* over that of the other sages who constituted the majority of those entrusted with instructing the community in its regard.

The text-critical methodology of *midrash halakhah* was the predominant approach to the determination of the intent and meaning, and application in practice, of the biblical precepts from early post-exilic times until the completion of the *Mishnah*, to be discussed in the next chapter, a span of more than seven centuries, and continued to be applied by individual scholars for some time thereafter. During that long period, the methodology of *midrash halakhah* became progressively more systematized, especially through the efforts of the early sage Hillel, who thrived in the period spanning the latter years of the first century BCE and the early years of the first century CE. He adopted and promulgated seven rules of hermeneutics, the analytic methods that greatly facilitated legal exegesis and soon became a subject of study and application in the seminaries and study groups that emerged to fill the need for trained exegetes and decisors of *halakhah*, that is, persons with the acknowledged competence to render halakhic decisions, known in Hebrew as *poskim*.

The methods of *midrash halakhah* reached their point of highest development and perfection in the academies of R. Akiba and R. Ishmael respectively, two of the most prominent scholars of the early second century CE. There was a good deal of interaction between these schools, some of the same scholars attending each at different times, which led to an ongoing cross-pollination of ideas. A stylistic nuance emerged in the literature produced by schools that enabled one to determine to which school a scholar was primarily attached. Thus in the school of primary attachment, the scholar was known by his name alone, whereas in the school of secondary attachment his name was augmented by a patronymic. Accordingly, in the school of R. Akiba one prominent scholar was referred to as R. Simeon, and in the school of R. Ishmael he was known as R. Simeon ben Yohai.

The methodological differences between R. Akiba and R. Ishmael, at least eight of which have been identified, sometimes resulted in very different halakhic conclusions, and resulted in disagreements among their disciples and proponents that were ultimately resolved in favor of one or the other by later decisors.[8] However, it should be understood that these disagreements were part of a legitimate intellectual debate among scholars who were also colleagues, but who approached the challenges of legal exegesis from somewhat different perspectives. Both made use of the methodology applied by the venerated Hillel, although to very different degrees. It was R. Ishmael who expanded on the pioneering work of Hillel by increasing the number of hermeneutic rules for the interpretation of Scripture to thirteen, thereby adding to the intellectual tools available with which to probe the biblical texts for answers to questions that were not raised in earlier times. It is noteworthy that the thirteen rules of R. Ishmael are listed at the very beginning of the *Sifra*, a work attributed to the school of R. Akiba, attesting to the respect accorded by the different schools to each other. These hermeneutic rules, which are recited daily as part of the traditional Morning Prayer service, an indication of the importance attributed to them in Jewish tradition, are as follows:

1. Argument from a minor premise to a major premise, and vice versa. Logic dictates that if a less serious case involves a requirement for stringency, the same stringency would certainly apply to a more serious case.

2. Comparison of similar expressions: In cases limited by tradition, two independent laws or cases are presumed to shed light upon each other.

3. A general principle derived from one or two verses may be applied to all cases that logically appear to be similar.

4. When a generality is followed by a specification, the law is applied only to that which is specified.

5. If the specification is mentioned first and then followed by a generalization, instances or circumstances other than the ones specified are also to be considered as included within the scope of the general rule.

6. When a specification is preceded and followed by a generalization, then the general rule applies to everything that has the same essential characteristics as the specification.

7. A general statement that requires specification. This hermeneutic rule applies in a situation in which rules (4) and (5) do not apply because it is self-evident that a stated generalization requires a specification to clarify its meaning, and the converse.

8. Anything included in a generalization that is singled out to teach something, that teaching is presumed to apply to everything encompassed by the generalization.

9. Anything included in a generalization that is singled out to discuss a provision analogous to the general category, is presumed be more lenient rather than more stringent.

10. Anything included in a generalization that is singled out to discuss a provision not analogous to the general category, may be both more lenient and more stringent, depending on the particulars.

11. Anything included in a generalization that is singled out for treatment as a new case, cannot be returned to the generalization for treatment unless Scripture does so explicitly.

12. The meaning of a stipulation may be derived from its context, or from the following biblical text.

13. Two passages that appear to be contradictory may be reconciled by a third passage.

These hermeneutic rules for legal exegesis, the elaboration and illustration of which will not be undertaken here, except for the few instances of their application discussed below, proved to be powerful tools in the hands of competent analysts of the biblical texts trained in the school of R. Ishmael.

R. Akiba, by contrast with his colleague R. Ishmael, started from the theological premise that stipulated divine perfection, which implied that the Torah, the divine revelation, was necessarily also perfect. Accordingly, he placed great emphasis on deriving meaning from seeming imperfections in the biblical texts such as defective spelling of words where letters were omitted or duplication of statements. Indeed, he was famous for his ability to derive unanticipated meaning from the use of conjunctions and qualifiers like "but" and "only." By questioning every nuance in the biblical text, conceptual as well as literary, he was able to reach interpretations that were unconstrained by the more defined rules of R. Ishmael.

The differing methodological approaches of the two sages are reflected in the works of *midrash halakhah* that were eventually produced by their schools, orally at the time to be sure, but eventually to be put in the written form of four major works of *midrash halakhah* that have come down to us, two attributed to each of the schools. It is highly likely that there were additional works produced in these academies, oral or actually written, that were lost as a result of the persistent political and social chaos in the land of Israel in the early centuries of the common era, fragments of which were preserved by later scholars and incorporated into the Talmud. Some such fragments also have been collected from a variety of sources and published separately as well.

The principal surviving works of *midrash halakhah* attributed to the school of R. Ishmael are the *Mekhilta*, and exegetical commentary on the biblical book of Exodus, and the *Sifre* on the book of Numbers. The two principal collections attributed to the school of R. Akiba are the *Sifra* on the book of Leviticus, also known as *Torat Kohanim*, and the *Sifre* on the book of Deuteronomy. However, it would be misleading to suggest that these works deal exclusively with *midrash halakhah*, because there are substantial amounts of non-halakhic material to be found in them as well. For example, the narrative portion of the book of Exodus is significantly larger than its legal content, and even though the *Mekhilta* is traditionally considered a work of *midrash halakhah*, halakhic analysis actually takes up only about two-fifths of the book, the rest dealing with the meaning and implications of the narrative portions of the biblical texts. It also should be borne in mind that the teachings and discussions collected in these works were transmitted orally over long periods of time and, as with much of this kind of material, were conveyed in very concise terms, sometimes with one or two words representing whole complex arguments that were readily understood by those intimately familiar with both the subject matter and what might be called rabbinic shorthand. As a result, even though a substantial amount of this literature is available in translation, the translations, primarily but not exclusively of those parts of it dealing with legal issues, are not always easily comprehensible to those unfamiliar with the subject matter and the abbreviated style of rabbinic writing. Accordingly, in the legal selections from these works presented below, I do not simply cite verbatim extracts, which may not be especially edifying, preferring to give the reader some insights into what the sometimes painfully brief statements are really talking about and the thought processes they reflect.

THE MEKHILTA

The *Mekhilta* (from the Aramaic *mekhilata*, meaning "a collection"), like the other works of *midrash halakhah* discussed in this chapter, records the opinions of those sages, known as *tannaim*, who thrived prior to the beginning of the third century CE. Although the contents of the *Mekhilta* clearly were familiar to the later sages known as *amoraim*, who thrived from the third to the sixth century, it was not known to them by that name and it is therefore assumed that the work received its present designation no earlier than the latter part of the latter period. The work, which according to some modern scholars was most likely compiled and edited in the form that has come down to us not earlier than the fourth century, does not deal with the entire book of Exodus, nor, as already indicated, exclusively with its legal topics. The collection covers discussions of Exodus 12:1–23:19, 31:12–17, and 35:1–3, and is made up of nine tractates, *Pisha* (Ex. 12:1–13:16), *Beshallah* (Ex. 13:17–22, 14:1–31), *Shirata* (Ex. 15:1–21), *Vayassa* (Ex. 15:22–17:7), *Amalek* (17:8–18:27), *Bahodesh* (Ex. 19:1–20:23), *Nezikin* (Ex. 21:1–22:23), *Kaspa* (Ex. 22:24–23:19), and *Shabbata* (Ex. 31:12–17, 35:1–3), which are subdivided into eighty-two sections. The following example of *midrash halakhah* drawn from the *Mekhilta* will illustrate one of the exegetical methods employed by the school of R. Ishmael.

It may be observed that the sixth, seventh, eighth, and ninth of the Ten Commandments are contained in a single biblical verse: *Thou shalt not murder. Thou shalt not commit adultery. Thou shalt not steal. Thou shalt not bear false witness against thy neighbor* (Ex. 20:13). Although unstated in the biblical text, this strongly suggests that there is an intimate connection between these precepts. It will be noted that the first three of these precepts deal with wrongs committed against another person by actually carrying out a deed, whereas the last concerns a wrong committed by an act of speech, which differentiates it from the three preceding injunctions. With regard to the first three concerning murder, adultery, and stealing, the sages observed that murder and adultery are quite specific—murder relates to the capital crime of willfully causing the death of another human being; adultery relates to the crime of violating a married woman, something for which biblical law ordains capital punishment. However, the injunction against stealing is nonspecific and could refer either to the criminally wrongful misappropriation of property or of the kidnapping of people. The question before the sages was, to which of these does the eighth commandment relate, the theft of property or the theft of people? Why this was a matter of interest will be made clear as we consider how the question is dealt with in the *Mekhilta*.

The sages of the school of R. Ishmael begin their discourse on the subject by rhetorically asking why the injunction against stealing appears in the biblical verse along with murder and adultery. The response they offer is that it is placed there because there is another verse that states: *And he that stealeth a man and selleth him, or if he be found in his hand, he shall surely be put to death* (Ex. 21:16). Their argument is that the latter verse stipulates the capital penalty for the crime of kidnapping, but biblical law also requires that there be a specific warning against committing such a crime before one can become subject to capital punishment. Accordingly, they asserted, the injunction against stealing contained in the eighth commandment is intended to constitute the required specific warning against kidnapping. But, it was objected, how do we know that it is a warning against kidnapping and not a warning against stealing property? Their rejoinder is that the warning against stealing property is given elsewhere in Scripture, specifically in the injunction: *Ye shall not steal* (Lev. 19:11). But, it was objected further, perhaps the eighth commandment is the injunction against stealing property, and *Ye shall not steal* the injunction against kidnapping. The response of the sages is that one must apply reason to the problem and understand the text in consonance with the thirteen hermeneutic rules in accordance with which the Torah is to be interpreted. In this instance it is the twelfth rule in the system of R. Ishmael, which corresponds to the seventh rule in the system of Hillel that applies. That rule stipulates that a law is interpreted by its general context. What is the general context of the injunctions against murder, adultery, and theft? It is clearly that of crimes punishable by death, and the eighth commandment must therefore similarly relate to a crime of theft that is punishable by death, and that can only be the capital crime of kidnapping. Moreover, they argued, presumably in anticipation of the challenge as to how the general context is established: "There are three laws mentioned in this section. Two of them are explicit and one not explicit. Let us learn about the non-explicit from the explicit ones. Just as the explicit ones are laws for the violation of which one incurs the penalty of death at the hands of the court, so also the non-explicit one must be a law for the violation of which one incurs the penalty of death at the hands of a court." Accordingly, the eighth commandment is understood as a prohibition against kidnapping and the instruction *Ye shall not steal* as the general prohibition against the theft of property.[9]

What is the significance of all this? First, it maintains the integrity of the tradition by demonstrating that each of the two biblical verses prohibiting stealing has a distinct purpose and is not merely a pointless restatement of the other. Secondly, as seen from a legal perspective, it makes the case that no category of theft other than kidnapping merits the penalty of capital punishment, a principle alien to many cultures and societies throughout history to the present day.

Another example from the *Mekhilta* illustrates how the methodology of the school of R. Ishmael was applied to the interpretation of the biblical version of the *lex talionis*, the ancient law of retaliation, measure for measure. Scripture stipulates that if an altercation takes place and an innocent bystander is struck, *if any harm follow, then thou shalt give life for life, eye for eye, tooth for tooth, hand for hand, foot for foot, burning for burning, wound for wound, stripe for stripe* (Ex. 21: 22–25). The question the sages debated was whether these stipulations should be understood literally or figuratively. Their conclusion was that, since there was no intention to commit homicide, *life for life*, was to be understood as intending monetary compensation, as determined by a court. Several reasons were given for this conclusion. R. Judah haNasi, patriarch of the Jewish community of Israel toward the end of the second century, derived it by analogy from the precept requiring that in the case of an ox that was known to have gored in the past, and the owner of the animal did not take care that it be adequately restrained, and it killed a person, *the ox shall be stoned, and its owner shall also be put to death. If there be laid on him a ransom, then he shall give for the redemption of his life whatsoever is laid upon him* (Ex. 21:29–30). R. Judah reasoned that since one verse states, *give life for life*, and the other *give for the redemption of his life*, the use of "give" in both makes them analogous and since in the latter case it clearly refers to monetary compensation, we may assume that it also has the same meaning in the former.

Using the same two biblical texts, R. Isaac arrived at the same conclusion through the use of the first of the 13 hermeneutic rules, dealing with inference from leniency to stringency and the converse. It should be borne in mind that in the case of the owner of the goring ox that kills, the biblical law specifies that *its owner shall also be put to death*, whereas in the case on the unintentional killing of a bystander, it states, *thou shalt give life for life*, but does not specifically impose a death sentence. R. Isaac argued as follows: "If even in a case where the penalty of death is imposed only a monetary compensation is exacted, it is but logical that in this case, where no death penalty is imposed, surely no more than a monetary compensation should be exacted."[10]

Pursuing the converse logic of the argument a step farther, if in the case of an unintentional killing monetary compensation is the appropriate penalty in practice, this is surely the case with regard to lesser injuries. Accordingly, the stipulation of an *eye for an eye* would clearly mean monetary compensation, the expression itself taking on the character of a figure of speech meaning equivalent compensation. Elsewhere in the rabbinic literature, the case is made that the principle of monetary compensation applies even in the case of the intentional maiming of another person. For example, it is argued that the idea of an *eye for an eye* could not be taken literally because it would be impossible to carry out in the case of a person's eye being harmed irreparably by a blind person, or someone's leg being broken by a person who is already crippled. Since the retaliation in kind could not be carried out, in the absence of substituting monetary compensation in its place, the perpetrator would have to be set free without penalty. Moreover, to make the penalty monetary compensation only in the case of maiming carried out by an already handicapped person would create the untenable situation of one law for the handicapped and another for everyone else, something that violates the biblical stipulation: *Ye shall have one manner of law* (Lev. 24:22).[11]

Against this background, R. Eliezer takes yet another approach to reconciling the several biblical texts dealing with the issue, employing the sixth hermeneutic rule, which is, when a general statement is followed by a specification that is followed by another general statement—you may infer only whatever is similar to the specification. To illustrate this, he turns to the cognate passages in the book of Leviticus that deal with the law of retaliation. The first general statement is, *And if a man maim his neighbor; as he hath done, so shall it be done to him* (Lev. 24:19), the implication being that the law of retaliation in kind applies. This statement is followed by the specifications: *breach for breach, eye for eye, tooth for tooth* (Lev. 24:20), which the sages already determined means monetary compensation and seems to contradict the previous statement. However, in the same verse, following the specifications, it states further: *as he hath maimed a man, so shall it be rendered unto him*, another general statement. This sets the stage for R. Eliezer to introduce the methodological argument:

> This is a general statement followed by a specific statement and by another general statement, all of which must be interpreted as including only things similar to those mentioned in the specific statement. Now, in this case the specific statement specifies that for injuries resulting in a permanent defect and affecting chief organs and visible, though inflicted intentionally, one is subject only to the payment of indemnity. Hence, for any injuries resulting in a permanent defect and affecting chief organs and visible, though inflicted intentionally, one is subject only to payment of indemnity.[12]

In effect, a critical reading of the biblical verses yields a result that negates their superficial meaning, affirming that the law of retaliation never was intended to be taken literally, except with regard to murder, which is considered a special case.

SIFRE ON NUMBERS

The second major work of the school of R. Ishmael is the *Sifre* on the book of Numbers. The name *Sifre* is Aramaic for "books," the reference being to "books of the academy," which, with regard to the school of

R. Ishmael, presumably originally referred to both this book and that which later became known as the *Mekhilta*. Because of the similarity in title, the *Sifre* on Numbers and the *Sifre* on Deuteronomy are often lumped together as though they were two parts of a single work, notwithstanding that they were the products of two very different schools. Modern scholarship suggests that neither of the works designated as *Sifre* was compiled or edited in the form handed down before the end of the fourth century. The *Sifre* on Numbers contains 161 sections, each designated as a numbered *piska*, that provide exegetical analyses of chapters 5–12, 15, 18–19, 25:1–13, 26:52–31:24, and 35:9–34 of the book of Numbers. As with the *Mekhilta*, much of the material presented does not deal with halakhic matters, although the same exegetical hermeneutics are applied.

A clear example of *midrash halakhah* drawn from the *Sifre* on Numbers may be seen at work with regard to matter of inheritance. The biblical rule states: *If a man die, and have no son, then ye shall cause his inheritance to pass unto his daughter. And if he have no daughter, then ye shall give his inheritance unto his father's brethren. And if his father have no brethren, then ye shall give his inheritance unto his kinsman that is next to him of his family, and he shall possess it* (Num. 27:8–11). In considering this passage, the sages were troubled by the anomalies they found in it. It states that if there is no son, the inheritance is *to pass* to his daughter, but if he has no daughter, they shall *give* his inheritance to the deceased's uncles. Three problems seem to leap off the page. First, the deceased's father is omitted as a possible heir. Second, the deceased's brothers, if there be any, are not listed as possible heirs whereas his uncles are. Third, the change in wording from *pass* with regard to a daughter to *give* with regard to all other potential heirs. The biblical text thus virtually cries out for explication and exegesis.

Applying the first of the 13 hermeneutic rules, the sages reasoned that the biblical text must have meant to include the deceased's father as an heir, since the father's brothers are eligible only because of the father, so that if they are eligible he must of necessity also be eligible. Moreover, logic would dictate that the deceased's father should have priority over them in the order of succession. How, then, can one account for the omission in the biblical text? It was reasoned that inclusion of the deceased's father is obviously implicit in the biblical text and therefore did not require specification.

At this point, the sages' discourse presupposes awareness of the context in which the biblical precept is announced. Scripture relates the story of the five daughters of Zelophehad, who died without any sons to inherit and continue the family line. Given that under the traditional laws of the ancient world, daughters could not inherit, they appealed to Moses not to let the absence of a male heir cause the line of their father, a loyal follower, to come to an end with his death. After divine consultation and approval, the biblical edict allowing daughters to inherit property was issued (Num. 27:1–7). Presumably, in accordance with ancient practice, if the new rule were not issued, the inheritance in landed property would have reverted to the head of the family, the dead man's father, if alive, for his disposition.

Bearing this in mind, the sages argued that this was the reason the biblical text said that his inheritance should *pass unto his daughter* and not that it should be *given* to her. That is, although traditional law required that the property revert to the deceased's father, the new rule required that he *pass* it on to his granddaughter. However, in the absence of a granddaughter, the deceased's property would be *given* to the next in line in the order of inheritance, which would be the deceased's father, and if the latter were no longer alive it would be given to the latter's brothers, and so on in the prescribed order of inheritance. As R. Ishmael, son of R. Jose, explained: "It states: *ye shall cause his inheritance to pass unto his daughter*; [this means] where there is a daughter, the inheritance is passed from the father [of the deceased], but it is not *passed* where there are only brothers [of the deceased]."[13] That is, by implication, the father of the deceased is free to *give* the reverted property now in his possession to one or more of the deceased's brothers, but that property does not *pass* to them according to the biblical laws of inheritance. It should be noted, parenthetically, that the order of inheritance found in later recapitulations of the oral law, having undergone repeated analyses of the kind discussed above, differs in a number of respects from that set forth explicitly in the biblical text.

As already indicated, the works of *midrash halakhah* produced by the school of R. Ishmael are not exclusively legal in content, as in the examples given above, but also deal with other issues related to a critical reading of the biblical texts and applying hermeneutic rules in the reconciliation of seemingly contradictory texts. An example of this may be seen where the issue before the sages was the seeming inconsistency between two biblical narrative texts. It is stated in the opening verse of the book of Leviticus, *And the Lord called unto Moses, and spoke unto him out of the tent of meeting* (Lev. 1:1), which may be read as meaning, literally, *out of the tent of meeting*. However, there is also a verse in the book of Exodus which, referring to the tent of meeting, states: *And there I will meet with thee, and I will speak with thee from above the ark-cover, from between the two cherubim which are upon the ark of the testimony* (Ex. 25:22). The clear implication of the latter text is that the communication with Moses will take place within the tent of meeting and not from outside the tent of meeting, which creates a seemingly irreconcilable conflict between the two passages. To deal with this conflict, the sages applied the last of the 13 hermeneutic rules, which is that two contradictory passages, each of which is correct in its own context, may be reconciled by the introduction of a third, and that third passage in this case is to be found in the book of Numbers. *And when Moses went into the tent of meeting that He might speak with him, then he heard the Voice speaking to him from above the ark-cover that was upon the ark of the testimony, from between the two cherubim; and He spoke unto him* (Num. 7:89). The sages argued: "What this text says is that Moses entered and stood in the tent of meeting and the divine voice descended from the heaven of heavens to between the two cherubim, and he would hear the voice speaking to him from within."[14] Accordingly, both earlier texts were correct—the divine voice spoke from above, outside the tent of meeting, but Moses only heard it inside, coming from between the cherubim.

Turning to the school of R. Akiba, we encounter a rather different approach to exegesis of the biblical texts than that of the school of R. Ishmael, and this is clearly reflected in the works produced by his school, known as the *Sifra* on Leviticus and the *Sifre* on Deuteronomy. The term *Sifra*, is Aramaic for "book," and is the singular form of *Sifre*, or "books." It has been suggested that both were originally called *Sifre* and that the application of the singular name *Sifra* to the work on Leviticus was intended to distinguish it from the other work on Deuteronomy, produced in the same school. The work is also widely known as *Torat Kohanim*, the law of the priests, because so much of Leviticus is concerned with the Tabernacle and its rituals in which the priests and Levites played the major role. The work provides critical readings of most of Leviticus, and is almost entirely devoted to legal matters, the narrative portion of the biblical book being rather small. It is noteworthy that the *Sifra* is the only one of the four major works of *midrash halakhah* that still does not have a published critical edition; nor is there a standard subdivision of the work. As a result, some editions contain a subdivision in accordance with the biblical *parsha* as defined for synagogue readings of Scripture, while others follow alternate schemes. All further subdivide the work into *perek*, *parshata*, and *piska*, which are interspersed in the work in a fashion that sometimes makes it very difficult to locate a particular text. As M.D. Heer, author of the brief article on the *Sifra* in the *Encyclopaedia Judaica* put it, "The division of the sections into chapters are also full of errors and in the printed editions the references to the chapters are given inaccurately." Nonetheless, the *Sifra* is an important and oft-cited classic of rabbinic literature.

THE *SIFRA* OR *TORAT KOHANIM*

The first example of the approach of the school of R. Akiba to *midrash halakhah* is drawn from the *Sifra* and deals with a biblical injunction that has both halakhic and ethical implications. Scripture admonishes: *Thou shalt not curse the deaf, nor put a stumbling block before the blind* (Lev. 19:14). The sense of justice that pervades Scripture here gives categorical expression to the idea that one should not take advantage of the disadvantaged, either by word or deed. With regard to the second clause about placing *a stumbling block before the blind*, the sages understood this in more than a physical sense, which would be self-evident to all but the morally obtuse. Accordingly, they treated the statement both literally and figuratively, broadening the injunction to include psychological stumbling blocks as well as tangible ones. For example, they specifically included giving inappropriate advice to a person that evidently trusts your opinion to the extent that he or she requests it of you, the trust itself considered serving as the stumbling block that can cause a disastrous fall.

However, in considering the first clause, *Thou shalt not curse the deaf*, the sages evidently were moved to ask why the injunction was limited only to the deaf and not applied to everyone, something that they deemed most appropriate. To deal with this issue they adduced another related biblical injunction, *Thou shalt not . . . curse a ruler of thy people* (Ex. 22:27). Considering both texts in tandem, they saw them not as two unrelated provisions, each of which bore independent validity, but rather as end points of the spectrum of those to whom the injunction *Thou shalt not curse* applied, the physically disadvantaged at one end and the most highly advantaged at the other. But, they asked further, why specify the deaf rather than the physically disadvantaged generally? Their answer was that the deaf were singled out to extend the application of the injunction to the dead as well as the living. That is, the dead are analogized, for this purpose, to the deaf in that neither can hear. Therefore, just as it is impermissible to curse the deaf, who cannot hear your words and react to them, so is it impermissible to curse the dead, who are similarly unable to hear and react.[15] The latter point, of course, further emphasizes the impermissibility of taking advantage of the disadvantaged.

Another example from the *Sifra* illustrates how the sages employed biblical statements as prooftexts for arguments regarding issues only tangentially related to the subject of the biblical text. The biblical text states: *And if thy brother be waxen poor, and his means fail with thee; then thou shalt uphold him . . . Take thou no interest of him or increase; but fear thy God; that thy brother may live with thee* (Lev. 25:35–36). It is the very last clause of this citation, *that thy brother may live with thee*, that serves as the linchpin of an argument between R. Akiba and a sage named Ben (Son of) Bathyra, each deriving a dramatically different implication from it. At issue between them is the question of the relative priorities of altruism and self-interest in extreme circumstances. The *Sifra* postulates, in this regard, a hypothetical situation in which two companions are traveling on a journey far from civilization. They begin to run out of water, and one of them still has a flask of water with only enough to keep one of them alive until he can reach safety. If one drinks, the other will perish. If both drink, both will perish. The question is, how should the person who has the water act with regard to his companion who has none?

Ben Bathyra concluded from his exegesis of the biblical phrase, *that thy brother may live with thee*, "that they should both drink and perish," the rationale being, as elaborated in a retelling of the story in the Talmud, "rather than that one should behold his companion's death."[16] He thus clearly adopted an extreme altruistic position. Since an objective analysis of the situation indicates that only one need die, not both, it would appear that he considers the biblical teaching as placing greater ultimate value on altruistic sentiment than it does on the preservation of human life for its own sake. That is, his reading of the biblical text, *may live with thee*, leads him to the conclusion that the phrase *with thee* implies that both parties are equal before God and should therefore either live together or die together, because the life of the one who has the water in his possession is not of greater value than that of his companion.

R. Akiba, by contrast, drew a very different conclusion from his exegesis of the biblical phrase, namely that the one who had the flask of water should drink and live, even though his companion would perish before his eyes. "R. Akiba said to him: *that thy brother may live with thee*: thy life takes precedence over his life."[17] That is, R. Akiba understood the biblical phrase "*with* thee" to mean "along with thee" and not "instead of thee." In the case under discussion, where it is possible to save only one of the two lives involved, R. Akiba would consider it a biblical obligation to do so, especially since not doing so would not in any way contribute to saving the life of other person. Since the one who has the water is in a position to preserve his own life, which is his primary obligation to the life he has been granted, his life should take precedence over that of his companion.

SIFRE ON DEUTERONOMY

The other major work produced by the school of R. Akiba is the *Sifre* on Deuteronomy, which contains 357 sections, each designated as a numbered *piska*, that provide exegetical analyses of Deuteronomy 1:1–30, 3:21–4:1, 6:4–9, 11:10–26, 15, 31:14 and 32:1ff (a great many but not all of the verses to the end of the book). Here again critical readings of the narrative portions of the biblical text are about equal in volume to the legal exegeses found in the work.

Turning topically from ethical precept to criminal law, the following example drawn from the *Sifre* on Deuteronomy will illustrate how the school of R. Akiba applied legal exegesis to the biblical teaching dealing with the crime of kidnapping and its punishment. Scripture states: *If a man be found stealing any of his brethren of the children of Israel, and he deal with him as a slave, and sell him; then that thief shall die; so shalt thou put away the evil from the midst of thee* (Deut. 24:7). Considering this stipulation as a general precept within the context of the range of related biblical precepts, the sages evidently felt compelled to raise a number of questions about it to help further define its intent and scope, and proceeded to parse the verse critically. First, they implicitly asked what was meant by *If a man be found*. Since the conclusion of the precept is that the kidnapper shall die, they presumed that the opening clause did not override the established requirements for a forewarning by witnesses that the contemplated crime was a capital offense, and not that any kidnapper who happened to be discovered was subject to capital punishment. Second, they considered the implication of the specification *If a man be found*, and argued that this precluded its applicability to someone who was by definition not a man, such as would be the case with a minor who perpetrated a kidnapping. Moreover, they read the phrase, *stealing any of his brethren of the children of Israel*, as limiting the capital punishment aspect of the rule as applying to members of his community, but not to outsiders. This should not be taken as suggesting that the sages approved of the kidnapping of strangers and selling them into slavery, which was surely not the case. Since slavery was pervasive in the world of antiquity, the biblical injunction was presumably understood as intended to restrict that practice in the community of Israel, and much biblical legislation that makes slave ownership onerous is testimony to this. The issue here is not slavery as such but communal integrity and the severity of the penalty for violating it in the described manner.

The phrase, *of his brethren of the children of Israel*, evoked the question of the redundancy of the phrase. Since the biblical injunction was addressed to the children of Israel, it would seem that *of his brethren* makes it clear that the text is referring to the children of Israel. Why then add *of the children of Israel* to the statement? The sages evidently were divided over the question. One position, taken by R. Johanan ben Barokah, was that the phrase, *of the children of Israel*, was added purposively, "Thus including him who steals his own son and sells him, who is equally liable." The majority of the sages, however, did not attribute any special legal significance to the inclusion of the seemingly redundant phrase and asserted: "He who steals his own son and sells him is not liable," that is, not liable to capital punishment, perhaps reflecting the ancient view of the scope of patriarchal authority.

Another question that troubled the sages was the point at which liability for a capital crime begins. They took the position that the kidnapper becomes liable and eligible for the death penalty at the point when the person kidnapped is taken into his possession. R. Judah, however, took a dissenting position, arguing that capital liability began only when "he takes him into his possession and uses him, as it is said *And he deal with him as a slave, and sell him*," taking *and sell him* as a critical factor in assigning capital liability. This implicitly suggested that if he kidnapped someone and did not sell him, but kept him as a slave, he would not be liable for capital punishment, an argument that the majority rejected. Parsing the text further, the sages also inferred a significant nuance from the phrase, *then that thief shall die*. That is, when all the conditions for capital liability are met, "*that (thief)*—but not one who steals someone who is a slave or is a half-slave and half-free." That is, kidnapping someone who is already in a state of full or semi-slavery should not be treated as a capital crime, which is applicable only to one who kidnaps and sells someone who was free to begin with.

Finally, there remains the question of the ultimate purpose of the biblical pronouncement, which is stated as, *so shalt thou put away the evil from the midst of thee*. The seemingly evident meaning of this is that setting forth the capital liability attached to the crime, and carrying out the required punishment, will contribute to expurgating evil from the community of Israel. In other words, the biblical statement could be understood as considering the threat of capital punishment for such a crime as a deterrent, and thus as a means of reducing the amount of evil acts perpetrated. The sages, however, chose to interpret the biblical text rather differently, taking it as meaning that it was intended as a means to "remove the evildoers from Israel."[18] There would seem to be a significant difference between a stipulation intended to *put away the evil from the midst of thee*, and one to put away "the evildoers," and one can only speculate on what caused the sages to elect to interpret the text in this manner.

Another example of legal exegesis using the critical method of reading the biblical texts perfected in the school of R. Akiba concerns the biblical insistence that, *The fathers shall not be put to death for the children, neither shall the children be put to death for the fathers; every man shall be put to death for his own sin* (Deut. 24:16). At first glance, this text looks very much like a syllogism, one that might be found in a basic textbook on logic: fathers are not to be put to death for the transgressions of their children; children are not to be put to death for the transgressions of their fathers; therefore, fathers and children are to be put to death for their own transgressions. Of course, one might question why anyone would think that fathers might be held criminally liable for the crimes of their children, and the converse, so that a biblical injunction was required to negate and reject such a notion. This question evidently did not trouble the sages, who were undoubtedly well aware that such practices were not unheard of in the ancient world, in biblical times and after, and was not raised by them. What did trouble them was the obvious redundancy in the biblical text.

The school of R. Akiba categorically rejected the notion that the biblical text might employ redundancies or any other literary device for the purpose of emphasis or clarity. Any such usage would taint the perfection of the divine word. Accordingly, any logically unnecessary word or even letter, let alone an entire phrase, had to be explained as adding something significant that was not self-evident. Approaching the text under discussion from that perspective, the sages started with the clause, *The fathers shall not be put to death for the children,* and asked: "What is it that Scripture wishes to teach us here? That fathers are not to be executed because of (the deeds of) their children? Does it not say *every man shall be put to death for his own sin?*" Given the latter statement, it is obvious that the former is superfluous, unless it is intended to teach something else. What might that be? In what alternate way might the statement be understood, consistent with the Hebrew wording, *al banim,* clearly meaning "because of the children," so as to remove its evident redundancy? The sages inferred: "Scripture means rather to tell us that fathers shall not be executed on the testimony of their children, nor children on the testimony of their own fathers." Read in this way, the redundancy not only vanishes but a new and important principle of law is introduced, the implications of which have reverberated through the centuries up to the present day. Not only is the biblical verse understood to say that the testimony of neither parents nor children can be used against each other for purposes of prosecution of a capital offense, by extension it may also be understood implying that, because such testimony is invalid, neither parents nor children may be compelled to testify against each other, at least not in a capital case.

The sages went even farther in parsing the biblical text, implicitly arguing that since fathers cannot be convicted of a capital crime on the testimony of their children, the converse may be deduced from that assertion, making the statement *neither shall the children be put to death for the fathers* unnecessary for such purpose. What, they implicitly asked, does this seemingly superfluous clause mean to convey? Their answer was as follows: "When it goes on to say, *neither (shall) the children (be put to death for the fathers),* it means to include relatives, to wit, one's brother, father's brother, mother's brother, sister's husband, father's sister's husband, mother's sister's husband, mother's husband, father-in-law, and brother-in-law."[19] In other words, the term *banim* or children is construed as referring to all the male members of the family within one degree of separation, bearing in mind that women were biblically precluded from serving as witnesses. Is such a construal legitimate? While this may be debatable, it should be borne in mind that the term *banim* has also been used in the phrase "children of Israel," referring to the entire people. Accordingly, in this case, the sages elected to limit the scope of inclusion in the term to male members of the immediate family and those directly related through marriage, all of whose testimony is to be considered invalid in a capital case.

In sum then, the legal exegesis, the *midrash halakhah*, of the biblical verse asserts that, neither parents nor children can be executed for crimes committed by the other; neither parents nor children can be convicted of a capital crime on the testimony of the other; and, for the purposes of testimony in a capital case, "children" are construed as including the entire immediate family and in-laws.

As suggested earlier, these texts are not intended or designed for casual reading but require serious study, significant intellectual rewards awaiting those who make the effort.

Chapter 3

The *Mishnah*

As important as the study and application of *midrash halakhah* was to shaping Jewish life in the post-exilic period, the method nonetheless suffered from certain deficiencies. For one thing, because it dealt directly with the biblical text, which touches on the same or similar issues in diverse places, it became repetitive and cumbersome as a body of oral teachings. For example, the precept regarding observance of the Sabbath appears in no less than ten places strewn throughout all five books of the Torah. Also, because in the recapitulation of the Mosaic laws in Deuteronomy some precepts are expressed in different ways than they are in the other books, the works of *midrash halakhah* will reflect variant exegeses. Moreover, as indicated in the preceding chapter, the works of *midrash halakhah* contain large amounts of non-halakhic material, of interest but not of primary relevance for those wishing to focus their efforts on learning and comprehending *halakhah*. All of this placed an increasingly heavy burden on students, who had to absorb an ever-growing body of unorganized knowledge.

Another and perhaps more serious problem was the fact that *midrash halakhah*, by its very nature as exegesis of the biblical texts, was unable to deal effectively with those precepts, rules, and traditions not specifically mentioned in the Torah, but held to have originated either simultaneously with the written text or even earlier from the time of the ancient patriarchs of the people. Moreover, the innumerable changes that took place in the life of the people, over the more than a millennium since tradition maintained the Law of Moses was given to them, necessitated the enactment of a variety of affirmative as well as restrictive rules for the society that either had no direct source in the Torah, or a tangential connection at best. As a result of this, and because the Torah was considered the only authoritative source of precept and law, the practice arose of taking biblical statements out of context for use as prooftexts for otherwise contentious propositions, a not altogether satisfactory basis for establishing their authority.

A third factor that may have engendered the need for a written and systematized halakhic corpus not directly tied to biblical sources was the consideration that the whole process of *midrash halakhah* had become enmeshed in the lingering struggle between the Pharisees, who were the principal practitioners of wide-ranging biblical exegesis, and the Sadducees and their later followers, who tended to be strict constructionists of the biblical texts. As reported by the historian Josephus, writing in the first century: "The Pharisees have delivered to the people a great many observances by succession from their fathers, which are not written in the law of Moses; and for that reason it is that the Sadducees reject them, and say that we are to esteem those observances to be obligatory which are in the written word, but are not to observe what are derived from the tradition of our forefathers; and concerning these things it is that great disputes and differences have arisen among them."[1] There was a justifiable concern among the Pharisees that challenges from the Sadducees and those who came under their influence to the rules derived from Scripture by exegesis might have a negative effect on their students, who would constitute the next generation of sages and communal leaders.

Finally, some modern nontraditional commentators have suggested that an additional factor that may have contributed to the decision of R. Judah haNasi, who became official patriarch of the Jewish community in the Land of Israel around 165 CE, to proceed with the publication of a more systematic treatment of traditional *halakhah* was the almost simultaneous formation of the New Testament canon by the Christians, which may have been perceived as an effort to place the received traditions of that community in a formal structure.[2]

Because of these and perhaps other problematic considerations as well, it ultimately became apparent that the growing body of oral teachings needed to be systematized for purposes of study and preservation for future generations. However, this necessitated a departure from the tradition of direct reliance on the biblical texts as the sole authoritative source of *halakhah* in order to accommodate the numerous commonly accepted teachings and traditions that did not have their origins in the written texts.

To date, historical scholarship has not yet succeeded in establishing when the idea of grouping the various teachings derived through the processes of *midrash halakhah* according to their subject matter, instead of the traditional approach of simply following the order in which the relevant matter appeared in the biblical texts, and including teachings and traditions that did not derive from the Torah, first originated. What is known is that the first three recorded halakhic rulings issued independently of a scriptural basis are attributed to Jose ben Joezer (d. c. 165 BCE), who asserted that it was permitted to eat a certain type of locust, that the liquid that flowed in the Temple slaughterhouse was not susceptible to being ritually unclean, and that one who touches a corpse becomes personally ritually unclean,[3] understood as implying that his uncleanness does not contaminate anything else that he touches. This development suggests very strongly that at the same time that *midrash halakhah* continued to be the preeminent approach to dealing with the exigencies of daily life in a post-biblical world, the need for an alternate approach to preserving those teachings, as well as teachings outside its scope, was already acknowledged and such a new approach began to take shape. This alternate approach became known as *mishnah*, repetition or recapitulation of the *halakhah*, an emerging body of topically arranged oral teachings that would not be put in final written form until the end of the second century CE. Accordingly, by the time, about the beginning of the second century, that R. Akiba and R. Ishmael were formulating and perfecting their methodological approaches to *midrash halakhah*, teaching according to the organizational method of *mishnah* was increasing and becoming more systematized at a significant pace, promising to overshadow but by no means eliminate *midrash halakhah* by the beginning of the following century.

It may seem ironic that the earliest systemization of the *halakhah* in mishnaic form is attributed to R. Akiba, who was also a preeminent practitioner of *midrash halakhah*. It was the latter's disciple R. Meir who was the critical link between the work of R. Akiba and the ultimate compilation of the *Mishnah* under the aegis of R. Judah haNasi, who was himself a student of R. Judah ben Ilai, a younger colleague of R. Akiba, whose teachings are quoted in the *Mishnah* more often than any other scholar. According to one ancient source, R. Judah haNasi made use of some thirteen different collections of *halakhah* prepared by earlier sages in composing his version of the *Mishnah*. By tradition, all the anonymous rulings recorded in the *Mishnah* are attributed to R. Meir, and the presumption is that they are based on the teachings of R. Akiba. It should also be noted that the *Mishnah* of R. Judah haNasi was not the only attempt to formulate similar collections of *halakhah*. This clearly was done by other sages of the period, and there is textual evidence that other existing collections of *halakhah* in different subject areas were incorporated in the *Mishnah*. Those that were not so incorporated continued to circulate for a time but were eventually superseded by the *Mishnah*, and subsequently disappeared. Thus, well into the third century, many years after the final redaction and publication of the *Mishnah* of R. Judah haNasi, the amoraic sages (those who thrived and taught following the publication of the *Mishnah*, and were its expositors) referred to it as *Mishnatenu* (our *Mishnah*) to distinguish it from the others that presumably were still in circulation at the time.

The problem confronting R. Judah haNasi, and what probably impelled him to undertake the compilation and publication of the *Mishnah*, was the chaotic and tenuous state of Jewish existence in the period following the especially harsh persecution of his people that took place in the Land of Israel during the reign of the Roman emperor Hadrian. As patriarch of what remained of the community, he was determined to assure its continuity and that of its distinctive culture, and it was clear that in order to do this it was essential to bring greater coherence to Jewish communal and religious life. Moreover, as a result of the destructiveness that characterized the wars with Rome, many people had fled the country seeking refuge in Parthian Mesopotamia, where there were already well-established and flourishing Jewish communities. The latter were becoming the major centers of the Jewish Diaspora and the lack of proximity to the schools of the sages in the Land of Israel made it essential that they have an authoritative collection of *halakhah* to guide them and thus assure that their communal life and religious practices would not deviate significantly from that of their brethren in the Land of Israel. For these reasons, R. Judah haNasi, as patriarch, undertook the task, assisted by others, of bringing together the mass of halakhic material accumulated over many generations that had become unwieldy because of controversies between rival authorities and contradictory traditions. It was reassembled as a coherent whole, arranged systematically, its argumentation abbreviated, its discussions summarized, and superfluous material eliminated.

The *Mishnah* also undertook to resolve prevailing halakhic disputes among the sages by rendering authoritative decisions, when this was deemed necessary, added appropriate supporting argument. It was not, however, intended to be a code of law, something that would not appear until much later in the medieval period; it was simply to be an authoritative compendium of the Oral Torah as it was taught in the schools of the period. That it was not intended to be a code of law becomes evident when one considers the fact that contradictory opinions are routinely cited in the *Mishnah*, even though the redactor's preferences are presumed to be reflected in the anonymous or other opinions cited first, which are then followed by citations of dissenting views. It is also of interest to note that for the last thousand years there has been a prolonged controversy among medieval commentators and continued among modern scholars over whether the *Mishnah* of R. Judah haNasi was actually put into writing at his direction, or whether it was promulgated and transmitted as an oral work that was first put into writing as late as some three centuries later.[4]

It should come as no surprise that numerous infusions of *midrash halakhah* are to be found in the *Mishnah*, which also incorporates earlier methods of assisting memory by grouping unrelated *halakhot* simply on the basis of their originating from the same authority, having some numerical feature in common, or employing similar formulations or key phrases. As a result, some *halakhot* are to be found in tractates wherein they are completely out of place from a topical standpoint. Thus, although the *Mishnah* is a vast improvement over the works of *midrash halakhah* in important respects, it is by no means free of flaws of its own. Moreover, notwithstanding the idea that one of the key features of the *Mishnah* was to be its seeming nonreliance on biblical texts, the *Mishnah* in fact will be seen to abound in such references, especially when dealing with topics and issues addressed in the works of *midrash halakhah*.

A clear example of the relationship between the works of *midrash halakhah* and the *Mishnah* may be seen in how the latter incorporates the passage from the *Sifre* on Deuteronomy from the school of R. Akiba that deals with the biblical precept: *If a man be found stealing any of his brethren of the children of Israel, and he deal with him as a slave, and sell him; then that thief shall die; so shalt thou put away the evil from the midst of thee* (Deut. 24:7), discussed at length in the preceding chapter. The relevant passage in the *Sifre* reads as follows:

> *If a man be found*—before witnesses—*man*—excluding a minor—*stealing any of his brethren*—and not of others—*of the children of Israel*: Thus including him who steals his own son and sells him, who is equally liable. So taught R. Johanan ben Barokah, while the Sages say: He who steals his own son and sells him is not liable. *And he deal with him as a slave*: This shows that he is not liable until he takes him into his possession. R. Judah, however, says: Until he takes him into his possession and uses him, as it is said, *And he deal with him as a slave, and sell him. Then that thief shall die*—by the method of execution intended whenever unspecified death penalty is mentioned in the Torah, namely strangulation—*that (thief)*—but not one who steals someone who is a slave or is half-slave and half-free—*and thou shalt put away the evil from the midst of thee*—remove the evildoers from Israel.[5]

The *Mishnah* treats the same subject in the context of which criminals are to be subject to the penalty of death by strangulation, and specifies, among others, one who kidnaps a member of the community. With regard to the perpetrator of such a crime, the *Mishnah* states:

> He is not liable unless he brings him into his own domain. R. Judah says: Unless he brings him into his own domain and makes use of him, for it

is written, *and he deal with him as a slave, and sell him*. If a man stole his own son, R. Johanan ben Baroka declares him liable, but the Sages declare him not liable. If he stole one that was half-slave and half-free, R. Judah declares him liable, but the Sages declare him not liable.[6]

The differences between the two renditions are notable in a number of ways. First, the *Mishnah* is much more concise. Second, many, but not all of the exegetical nuances derived from the text in the *Sifre* are omitted in the *Mishnah*, presumably not because they are irrelevant but rather because they are considered self-evident to those who follow the teachings of the school of R. Akiba. Third, the *Mishnah* omits the moral point emphasized in the very last segment of the discussion in the *Sifre*, namely the purpose behind the penalty. Why this was done is open to speculation. It may be because placing the rationale for a rule within the rule may serve to undermine it. Thus while the rationale for the rule, according to the *Sifre*, is that imposition of the severe penalty will help "remove the evildoers from Israel," there is always the possibility that it may fail in that regard, thus providing an opening to call the validity of the rule into question, something the *Mishnah* does not wish to provide.

The *Mishnah* is organized in six topical orders or *sedarim*, the complete work commonly referred to as *Shisha Sidrei Mishnah*, or by the acronym *ShaS*. The standard subdivision of the six orders of the *Mishnah* is into 63 *massakhtot* or tractates, the latter term actually signifying a web of woven fabric (*tractatus*), and this subdivision has remained constant from antiquity to this day, although one early source puts the number at 60, which may be reached by combining several closely related tractates. The tractates are subdivided into *perakim* or chapters, the aggregate number of which for the entire *Mishnah* is 523. The sequence of the orders in the *Mishnah* seems arbitrary, although some sages sought to establish the sequence on the basis of dubious correlations of the key topics of the orders with the sequence of terms in one or another biblical verse. Within each order, the sequence of the tractates has only been standard since the work was printed, the first complete printed edition being that produced in Naples in 1492.

The orders of the *Mishnah* are (1) *Zeraim* (Seeds), which contains 11 tractates with 74 chapters dealing with agricultural produce and the portions of the harvest that are to be allocated to the priests, Levites, and the poor; (2) *Mo'ed* (Festivals), which contains 12 tractates with 88 chapters dealing with the established holy days, feasts and fasts, and related matters; (3) *Nashim* (Women), which contains 7 tractates with 71 chapters dealing with family law, marriage, divorce, vows and oaths, and inheritance; (4) *Nezikin* (Damages), which contains 10 tractates with 73 chapters dealing with civil law, torts, damages, criminal law, penalties, punishments, and government; (5) *Kodashim* (Holy Things), which contains 11 tractates with 91 chapters dealing with laws pertaining to the Temple and the sacrificial rites; and (6) *Toharot* (Purities), which contains 12 tractates with 126 chapters dealing with the rules regarding ritual purity and impurity, their sources and the processes of purification. Some examples of *halakhah* contained in the tractates of the six orders of the *Mishnah* follow.

SEDER ZERAIM

The second tractate of *Seder Zeraim*, the first order of the *Mishnah*, is named *Peah*, meaning "corner" and refers to the corner of a field. It is devoted to the laws concerning some of the biblically mandated provisions for the poor and the stranger, the latter not being a landholder and therefore presumed to be without sufficient resources to be self-sustaining. The Torah stipulates: *And when ye reap the harvest of your land, thou shalt not wholly reap the corner of thy field, neither shalt thou gather the gleaning of thy harvest . . . thou shalt leave them for the poor and for the stranger* (Lev. 19:9–10). Although the Torah states quite explicitly that one is not to harvest his entire crop, but is to leave a portion of it for the poor and stranger, the biblical stipulation does not specify how large the *corner of the field* or *peah* that is to remain unharvested for that purpose should be. It is at this point that the oral tradition comes into play. Presumably reflecting a longstanding tradition in such regard, the *Mishnah* states categorically: "*Peah* should be not less than one-sixtieth [of the harvest]. And although they [the ancient sages] have said that no measure is prescribed for *Peah*, it should be [calculated] in accordance with the size of the field, the number of the poor, and the level of poverty."[7] The *Mishnah* then proceeds to detail more than twenty-five specific provisions regarding *Peah* that have no source whatever in Scripture, but that must either have been hallowed by tradition or conceived in response to specific issues that were raised and decided by the sages in response to the needs of their time.

For example, it would appear that one of the issues that was raised at some point was whether the law of *Peah* also applied to land that did not produce crops but hosted an orchard. In response to this, the *Mishnah* states: "A general rule was stated with regard to *Peah*: whatsoever is used for food, and is overseen and grows from the soil, and is gathered together and is brought in for storage is liable under the law of *Peah*. Both grain and pulse are included in this rule."[8] This would seem to include trees. However, it appears that there must also have been some question about whether the fruit of some trees was considered food, and the *Mishnah* undertook to clarify what came under the rule.

"Among trees, sumach, carob, walnut trees, almond trees, vines, pome-granate trees, olive trees, and palm trees are subject to the law of *Peah*."[9] By contrast with the general rules discussed earlier, this one turned out to be problematic, exemplifying the problem of transforming oral law into written law without losing the flexibility of the former. While it seems reasonable that the fruit of these trees were the ones primarily used for food at the time the rule was established, a large variety of other fruit trees that came into common use later would have been precluded from liability under the rule. Later rabbis therefore found it necessary to assert that the list in the *Mishnah*, despite its clear word-ing, was not intended to be exhaustive but merely illustrative of what was intended.

SEDER MO'ED

The tractate *Shabbat* (Sabbath) is the first and largest compilation in *Mo'ed* (Festivals), the second order of the *Mishnah*, which deals with the wide variety of obligatory practices related to the observance of established holy days, feasts, fasts, and matters related to such obser-vance. Although the Torah clearly mandates observance of these spe-cial times and occasions, no information is provided as to the required content of such observances. Thus, with regard to the Sabbath, the pri-mary concern of the mishnaic tractate under consideration, the fourth of the Ten Commandments, states: *Remember the Sabbath day, to keep it holy. Six days shalt thou labor, and do all thy work; but the seventh day is a Sabbath unto the Lord thy God, in it thou shalt not do any manner of work, thou, nor thy son, nor thy daughter, nor thy man-servant, nor thy maid-servant, nor thy cattle, nor thy stranger that is within thy gates* (Ex. 20:8–10). If one turns to the *midrash halakhah* for an explication of the injunction, *Six days shalt thou labor, and do all thy work*, what will be found is the following: "But is it possible for a human being to do all his work in six days? It simply means: Rest on the Sabbath as if all your work were done. Another interpretation: Rest even from the thought of labor."[10] Again, in connection with another biblical passage that stipulates, *Verily, ye shall keep My Sabbaths* (Ex. 31:13), the sages asked: "Why is this said? Because it says: *Thou shalt not do any manner of work* [Ex. 20:10], from which I know only about activities that can be regarded as labor. But how about activities that can be regarded as merely detracting from the restfulness of the Sabbath? Scripture says here: *Verily, ye shall keep My Sabbaths*, thus prohibiting even such activities as only detract from the restfulness of the day."[11]

What is conspicuously absent from these discussions is any defini-tion of what constitutes work. The methods of *midrash halakhah* are of no avail here because there are few biblical texts that even implicitly suggest what might be considered work. This limitation, however, did not affect the very same sages from relying on the oral tradition to supply that which the written Torah did not specify. Thus, the *Mishnah* declares:

> There are thirty-nine principal categories of work: (1)sowing; (2) ploughing; (3) reaping; (4) binding sheaves; (5) threshing; (6) winnowing; (7)sorting crops; (8) grinding; (9) sifting; (10) kneading; (11) baking; (12) shearing wool; (13) washing, (14) beating, or (15) dyeing it; (16) spinning; (17) weaving; (18) making two loops; (19) weaving two threads; (20) separating two threads; (21) tying [a knot]; (22) loosening [a knot]; (23) sewing two stitches; (24) tearing in order to sew two stitches; (25) trapping a deer, (26) slaughtering it, (27) flaying it, (28) salting it, (29) curing its hide, (30) scraping it, (31) cutting it up; (32) writing two letters; (33) erasing two letters in order to write two letters; (34) building, (35) tearing down; (36) putting out a fire; (37) lighting a fire; (38) striking with a hammer; (39) transporting an object from one domain to another.[12]

This list could only have emerged from some ancient legislators who felt the need to give effect to the biblical demand for observance of the Sabbath by desisting from work, and, in the absence of specific biblical guidance, surveyed the world around them to determine what kind of common activities might reasonably be construed as work. However, in contrast to the previous example drawn from the *Mishnah* dealing with the laws of *Peah*, where specification of the trees affected appeared definitive and therefore problematic to later scholars, in this instance the redactor was careful to state at the outset that the list being set forth contained thirty-nine "principal categories" of work. That is, the list was by no means to be construed as exclusive or exhaustive. This was particularly important for those ancient communities outside the Land of Israel that were more commercially and less agriculturally oriented. Thus although a city-dweller might not sew, plough, or reap a crop, there were activities he might undertake that were analogous and that therefore would come under the same prohibition.

SEDER NASHIM

As suggested above, on occasion *halakhot* are recorded in the *Mishnah* in tractates primarily devoted to unrelated topics because of a tangential connection. An interesting example of this is found in *Sotah* (The Suspected Adulteress), the fifth tractate in the third order, *Nashim*, devoted to issues concerning women. It is here that one finds a presentation of the rules relating to the mobilization of manpower for war.

In this case, there are some rather specific biblical stipulations in such regard.

> *And the officers shall speak to the people, saying: "What man is there that hath built a new house, and hath not dedicated it? Let him go and return unto his house, lest he die in the battle and another man dedicate it. And what man is there that hath planted a vineyard, and hath not used the fruit thereof? Let him go and return to his house, lest he die in the battle, and another man use the fruit thereof. And what man is there that hath betrothed a wife, and hath not taken her? Let him go and return unto his house, lest he die in battle, and another man take her." And the officers shall speak further unto the people, and they shall say: "What man is there that is fearful and faint-hearted? Let him go and return unto his house, lest his brethren's heart melt as his heart"* (Deut. 20:5–8).

In considering these biblical stipulations, the sages saw a need to clarify their intent and scope of application, an analysis that was already undertaken through *midrash halakhah* as subsequently recorded in the *Sifre*,[13] and incorporated and expanded upon in the *Mishnah*. At first glance, the biblical intent seems obvious. Placing great value on family life, it provides for deferment from active military duty for those who are just setting out to build a home, plant a new vineyard, or consummate a marriage. Moreover, it also proposes to defer service for those whose fear and faint-heartedness are palpable on the basis of the demoralizing effect it might have on other combatants.

However, the sages asked, when the biblical text speaks of one who has built a new house, does it mean that it applies only to one who literally builds a new house or, as they surmised, does application of the biblical rule extend to one who buys a new house or is given one as a gift, and does it mean only a house in which one lives? They concluded: "It is all one whether he builds a house for straw [silo], a house for cattle [barn], a house for wood [woodshed], or a house for wares [warehouse]; it is all one whether he builds or buys or inherits or whether it is given to him as a gift." Moreover, they asked, when the biblical text speaks of planting a vineyard, does it mean a vineyard exclusively? The sages concluded: "It is all one whether he plants a vineyard or plants five fruit trees, even if they are of five kinds. It is all one whether he plants vines or sinks them in the ground or grafts them; it is all one whether he buys a vineyard or inherits it or whether it is given him as a gift." Similarly, with regard to the third biblical stipulation regarding an unconsummated marriage, they concluded: "It is all one whether he betroths a virgin or a widow."[14] With regard to the *fearful and faint-hearted*, R. Akiba took the phrase literally as referring to one who "cannot endure the armies joined in battle or bear to see a drawn sword. R. Jose the Galilean says: The *fearful and faint-hearted* is he that is afraid for the transgressions that he has committed; therefore the Torah has connected all of these so that he might return home because of them [and not be publicly shamed]."[15]

Having clarified the specifics regarding the deferments from active military service, the sages turned to the question of intent. They were evidently troubled by the implications of the biblical stipulations, which in effect exempted a whole range of persons from active service, placing the burden of defending the interests of the people on others, seemingly placing a higher value of the life of those deferred than on those not so privileged. This did not seem tenable and the *Mishnah* invoked what presumably was a longstanding oral tradition in this regard, asserting: "What has been said applies to a discretionary war; but in a mandated war all go forth [to battle], even the bridegroom from his bedroom and the bride from beneath her canopy. R. Judah said: What has been said applies to a mandated war; but in an obligatory war all go forth [to battle], even the bridegroom from his bedroom and the bride from beneath her canopy."[16]

The position favored by the *Mishnah*, presumably that of R. Meir, is that a distinction must be drawn between a discretionary war, that is one decided upon by government, and mandated wars such as those, specified in the Torah, against the pagan nations in the Land of Israel and Amalek on its southern frontiers. Because of the biblical prescription, participation in these wars is considered incumbent upon every member of the nation, whereas a war undertaken at the discretion of the government does not place the same onus of responsibility on the people as the former, thus allowing for the deferments identified in the biblical text. R. Judah, offering a dissenting opinion, essentially saw no difference in this regard between a discretionary and a mandated war, presumably because the decision as to when and under what conditions and circumstances to undertake a mandated war was ultimately a matter of discretion. Surely the Torah was not demanding that Israel go to war when the prospect of success was disproportionate to the loss of life that would be incurred. Instead, R. Judah posited the idea that the only time that everyone was subject to mobilization was when the nation was engaged in a war that was forced upon it, when it was obligated to mobilize and fight in self-defense.

SEDER NEZIKIN

In the rich variety of materials contained in the *Mishnah* there are some collections that defy classification, a classic example of which is *Eduyot*, the seventh tractate in the fourth order, *Nezikin*, the primary content of the latter being concerned with civil and criminal law.

Eduyot or "testimonies" is a collection of unrelated teachings, many of which are repeated elsewhere in the *Mishnah* in their proper context, covering a wide range of subjects. The only apparent linkage to the other tractates in the order seems to be its concern with a single aspect of the halakhic decision-making process, namely the treatment of minority opinions. Perhaps the most prominent feature of the tractate is the recorded differences of opinion among the sages on almost everything, which in itself suggests a didactic purpose that is clearly articulated in the following extract.

Noting the conflicting opinions of the early sages Hillel and Shammai on a number of issues, both of their opinions being rejected by the other sages, the *Mishnah* asks: "Why do they record the opinions of Shammai and Hillel to no purpose [since they do not prevail]? To teach coming generations that one should not be stubborn in his opinion, since even the 'fathers of the world' were not stubborn in their opinion."[17] The point here is not that Shammai and Hillel were prepared to admit they were wrong in their opinions, but that they accepted the judgment of the majority of their peers with regard to how the relevant *halakhah* was to be understood and applied. And, if they who were renowned and revered sages could do this, those of future generations who could not hope to attain their stature should certainly learn to emulate their behavior in this regard.

Next, the *Mishnah* turns to a consideration of the significance of recording minority opinions, and begins by asking: "Why do they record the opinion of the individual along with that of the majority, given that the *halakhah* follows the opinion of the majority? That if a court approves the opinion of the individual it may rely upon him, since a court cannot annul the opinion of another court unless it exceeds it in wisdom and in number; if it exceeded it in wisdom but not in number, or in number but not in wisdom, it cannot annul its opinion."[18] Tradition thus precludes a court from arbitrarily overturning the ruling of a previous court on a particular matter unless it is deemed to be more learned and sagacious in its judgments, with a larger number of assenting jurists, than its predecessor. However, where this is not the case, if there is a recorded minority opinion, the new court may elect to adopt the earlier minority opinion despite its having been rejected by the former court. One important implication of this is that the majority opinion of a court does not in itself establish its eternal validity. Indeed, as the example of R. Eliezer ben Hyrcanus discussed above illustrates, the minority opinion, even if it that of a single individual, may have greater inherent validity than that of an overwhelming majority. The law must follow the majority for practical reasons alone and not because of truth in numbers. However, once a new court is called upon to address the same issue, and there is a valid minority opinion recorded, it is as though the original debate takes place once again, this time with the majority acceding to what was earlier rejected.

Although he does not challenge the rule regarding minority opinions stated above, R. Judah provides an alternate theory of "why they record the opinion of the individual against that of the majority to no purpose," given that it has been rejected. This was done, in his view, "so that if one should say: 'Thus have I received the tradition,' another may say to him: 'You heard it according to so-and-so [against the opinion of the majority].'"[19] From the perspective of R. Judah, recording minority opinions serves to protect the received tradition from corruption. Precisely because it is recorded as the opinion of an individual, no one can claim that he has a tradition that varies from that which has been accepted generally because it can be documented as being a solitary view and therefore not a reflection of an established tradition, which requires the concurring opinion of a majority of the sages.

SEDER KODASHIM

Kodashim (consecrated things) represents one of the more arcane orders of the *Mishnah*, being primarily concerned with the ancient sacrificial rite. *Hullin* (unconsecrated things), the third tractate in the order, is the only one that has been of continuing relevance in Jewish life since the destruction of the Temple in Jerusalem and the termination of the sacrificial rite. In this tractate, in addition to a number of rules related to the sacrificial rite, there are also many of the dietary laws still observed by traditional Jews. The following extract deals with an issue that relates to the sacrificial rite in the Temple but also has contemporary relevance with regard to the matter of treatment of animals. The issue revolves around the biblical rule: *When a bullock, or a sheep, or a goat, is brought forth, then it shall be seven days under the dam; but from the eighth day and thenceforth it may be accepted for an offering made by fire unto the Lord. And whether it be cow or ewe, ye shall not kill it and its young both in one day* (Lev. 22:27–28). Putting aside the intent and rationale behind the injunction, which later commentators attributed to the basic principle of avoiding cruelty to animals, what is at issue here is what should be done if the last stipulation in the injunction, *ye shall not kill it and its young both in one day*, is violated. The *Mishnah* states, in this regard:

> [The rule regarding killing] *it and its young* applies both in the Land [of Israel] and outside the Land, both in the time of the Temple and after the time of the Temple, with regard to unconsecrated beasts and with

regard to consecrated beasts. How is it applied? One who slaughters it
and its offspring, which are unconsecrated, outside [the Temple court-
yard], both of them are valid [*kosher*], but for the second he incurs forty
lashes. [If he should slaughter] consecrated beasts outside [the Temple
courtyard], for the first he is liable to punishment by extirpation, and
both of them are invalid and for each he incurs forty lashes. [If they were]
unconsecrated beasts [and he slaughtered them] within [the Temple
courtyard], both are invalid and for the second he incurs forty lashes.
[If they were] consecrated beasts [and he slaughtered them] within [the
temple courtyard], the first is valid and he is exempt [from punishment
for it], but for the second he incurs forty lashes and it [the beast] is
invalid [as a sacrifice].[20]

The first thing that one will notice about this passage is the number
of bracketed explanatory clauses, without which the translated passage would be meaningless to anyone not already familiar with the
shorthand style of ancient rabbinic writing, a pattern that still prevails
among some modern rabbinic writers. Turning to the substance of the
passage, it asserts that if one violates the rule about slaughtering an
unconsecrated beast, an animal that has not been set aside for the
purpose of ritual sacrifice, and its unconsecrated offspring outside the
Temple courtyard on the same day, the meat of the animals is considered kosher and therefore permitted to be eaten. However, although
the slaughter of the first animal is legitimate, the slaughter of the second
animal is a clear violation of the biblical rule, and for such a violation
the prescribed penalty is corporal punishment.

If, by contrast, both animals were consecrated for sacrificial purposes and they were slaughtered outside the Temple courtyard, they
are both considered invalid for any purpose, sacred or secular, and for
violation of the rules regarding consecration, the perpetrator is subject
to extirpation (*karet*) or death by the divine hand for the improper
slaughter of the first animal. Note that the divine punishment is not held
to apply to the second animal, which, in any case, could not have been
considered a valid sacrifice because doing so would have contravened
the biblical rule prohibiting the slaughter of a beast and its offspring
on the same day. However, because of the violation of the latter rule,
the perpetrator is liable for forty lashes for each of the consecrated animals improperly slaughtered. If one slaughtered both unconsecrated
animals within the Temple courtyard, they are both considered invalid,
presumably because their slaughter in the sacred precincts is considered a sacrilege, and in addition to having his animals declared invalid
for any purpose, the perpetrator is liable to corporal punishment for
the second animal because of his violation of the biblical rule. Finally,
if both were consecrated animals and slaughtered in the Temple courtyard, as appropriate, the first to be slaughtered is considered valid,

and no liability attaches to it. However, the slaughter of the second clearly violates the biblical rule and the animal is therefore considered invalid, while the perpetrator is liable to corporal punishment for his transgression.

SEDER TOHOROT

Tohorot (Cleannesses or Purities), the sixth and final order of the *Mishnah*, deals primarily with issues related to ritual purity, its seventh tractate *Niddah* (The Menstruant) being devoted almost exclusively to the range of issues relating to family and religious life that arise as a result of the natural process of menstruation and the state of ritual impurity that it imposes. However, tucked into a corner of the tractate is a consideration of the important question of when a child is to be considered responsible for his or her actions, specifically with regard to the making of vows, a topic for which there clearly is no biblical source.

> A girl eleven years old and one day—her vows must be examined. A girl twelve years old and a day—her vows are valid; [nonetheless,] they are examined throughout the twelfth year. A boy twelve years old and one day—his vows must be examined. A boy thirteen years old and one day—his vows are valid; [nonetheless,] they are examined throughout the thirteenth year. Before this time, even though they say, "We know before Whom we have vowed," or "for Whom we have dedicated it," their vows are not vows and their dedications are not dedicated. After this time, even though they say, "We do not know before Whom we have vowed," or "for Whom we have dedicated it," their vows are vows and their dedications are dedicated.[21]

The *Mishnah* makes it quite clear here that the age at which children are held conditionally responsible for their actions begins at age twelve for girls and age thirteen for boys, clearly indicating that girls mature earlier than boys and may therefore be held accountable for their actions a year earlier. The twelfth year for girls and the thirteenth for boys are seen as trial periods in which their accountability is conditioned on their level of awareness of the implications of their actions. Once the conditional period has passed, at the onset of the thirteenth year for girls and the fourteenth for boys, they are deemed fully responsible for their actions. Notwithstanding that in modern times, in Western societies, the age of responsibility has been raised from sixteen to twenty-one depending on the kind of responsibility entailed, Jewish tradition continues to place the burden of responsibility on boys and girls at ages thirteen and twelve respectively, as reflected in the modern ceremony

of the Bar and Bat-Mitzvah to commemorate the traditional transition
from childhood to adulthood, at least with respect to Jewish law.

MISHNAH, TOSEFTA, AND BARAITOT

Although the *Mishnah* immediately attained authoritative status in
the Land of Israel because of R. Judah haNasi's patriarchal position,
which was acknowledged by both Jews and the Roman authorities,
it took some time before it gained exclusive acceptance among the
broader community of scholars. Some sages were not convinced that
the halakhic materials excluded from the *Mishnah* were without enduring value and continued to preserve and study them. These excluded
materials, known as *baraitot*, include tanaitic *halakhot* that R. Judah
haNasi excluded from the *Mishnah* as redundant, unnecessary, not
authenticated by tradition, or perhaps because they simply did not fit
his editorial scheme. Many of these *baraitot* were preserved in either
or both of two forms. One form included halakhic material that was
explanatory or illustrative, interpretations of Scripture, or discussion
of rules that were incorporated into the *Mishnah* without comment.
These were preserved in a collection known as the *Tosefta* (Supplement),
compiled by R. Hiyya and R. Oshaya, disciples of R. Judah. The *Tosefta*
is in effect a summarized version of the oral law, constructed according to the methodology employed in the academy of R. Nehemiah, a
disciple of R. Akiba, which was subsequently used as a valued authority for interpreting the *Mishnah*, providing the background of some
of its discussions, and also providing an illustrative narrative of the
world in which the *Mishnah* arose and from which its redactor drew
its material. In addition, many *baraitot* were subsequently reproduced
in the *Gemara*, to be discussed in the next chapter, where later sages
employed the excluded material to assist in explaining the meaning
of assertions in the *Mishnah*. The interrelationship of the *Mishnah*,
Tosefta, and the *baraitot* preserved in the *Gemara* may be seen in the
following examples.

There evidently was a sharp difference of opinion among the early
sages regarding a matter of ritual procedure in connection with the
ceremonial feast (*Seder*) marking the start of the festival of Passover.
Traditionally, the onset of a set festival required a blessing to be pro-
nounced over it. However, tradition also required that four cups of
wine be consumed at the Passover Seder, the first cup at its outset. The
issue was which blessing was to be offered first, that commemorat-
ing the festival or that over the wine. The *Mishnah* dealing with the
issue begins by stating, "They filled the first cup for him," that is for
the one presiding over the ceremony. "Beth Shammai [the disciples

of the sage Shammai] maintain: He recites a blessing for the day and then recites a blessing over the wine; while Beth Hillel [the disciples of the sage Hillel] maintain: He recites a blessing over the wine and then recites a blessing for the day."[22] It is noteworthy that the *Mishnah* does not specify which view is to be followed, even though there is a tradition that says that, with some notable exceptions, the rule generally accords with the view of Hillel. This would seem to leave open the possibility that, as far as R. Judah haNasi was concerned, it made no difference as to which procedure was followed and that the *Mishnah* simply recorded the options.

The *Tosefta*, records the same controversy in a more expansive manner. "Beth Shammai maintains: He recites a blessing for the day and then recites a blessing over the wine, because the day causes the wine to be brought; moreover, the day has already been sanctified, but the wine has not yet come. And Beth Hillel maintains: He recites a blessing over the wine and then recites a blessing for the day, because the wine is what causes the blessing of the day to be said. Another thing: The blessing over the wine is offered routinely, whereas the blessing for the day is not said routinely. And the *halakhah* is in accordance with the Beth Hillel."[23] The *baraita* recorded in the *Tosefta* provides the rationale behind the positions taken by the respective disputants. The disciples of Shammai maintain that the occasion takes precedence because in the natural order of things, the day is already sanctified de facto by the onset of evening even before the wine is poured. Accordingly it is reasonable that that which came first should be blessed first. The disciples of Hillel took the position that the significance of the occasion is not the day per se but what the four cups of wine symbolize and thereby make the day significant. Accordingly, the appropriate order is the blessing over the wine first and then that for the day. The *Tosefta* then adds another reason for giving preference to the view of Beth Hillel, namely that the blessing over wine is something that takes place repeatedly whenever wine is consumed, whereas the holiday comes but once a year. The logic behind this is that something that routinely requires a blessing should be considered of a higher priority than something that is blessed only infrequently. Finally, the *Tosefta* reaffirms what must have been the traditional position that the *Mishnah* elected to omit or perhaps ignore, that the *halakhah* is in accordance with the view of Beth Hillel. In the later *Gemara*, in response to the inconclusive *Mishnah*, the amoraic sages cite verbatim the identical *baraita* recorded in the *Tosefta*, essentially ignoring and tacitly rejecting the open-endedness of the *Mishnah*.[24]

Another example of the interplay between *Mishnah* and *Tosefta* may be seen with regard to the laws of marriage. The *Mishnah* begins its presentation with the assertion: "A woman is acquired [in marriage] in three ways . . . She is acquired by money, by a writ, or by intercourse. 'By money': Beth Shammai maintains, a *denar* or the worth of a *denar*; Beth Hillel maintains, a *perutah* or the worth of a *perutah*. And how much is a *perutah*? An eighth of an Italian *issar*."[25] It will be observed that although the *Mishnah* states the three methods by which a man may legally acquire a wife, it only elaborates on the first, money. Beth Shammai's opinion is that the amount of money that must be paid is a *denar*, which refers to the Roman *denarius*, a fairly substantial amount. Beth Hillel, by contrast, insists that even an insignificant amount such as a *perutah* is sufficient for the purpose of concluding the marriage, a *perutah* being an eighth of an Italian *issar*, which was a tiny fraction of a *denarius*, something of the order of a penny compared to a twenty-dollar bill. However, the *Mishnah* has nothing further to say about either "a writ" or "intercourse" as a vehicle for concluding the marriage. Presumably, it omitted any further discussion of what was meant by these terms because either they were already well known by tradition, or that notwithstanding that those methods were halakhically acceptable, the redactor of the *Mishnah* may have wished to discourage their use, for reasons about which we can only speculate.

The *Tosefta*, on the other hand, has no compunction about considering the application of these various methods to concluding a marriage.

A woman is acquired [in marriage] in three ways . . . She is acquired by money, by a writ, or by intercourse. How is it done 'by money'? If he gave her money or something worth money, and said to her: 'Behold you are consecrated to me, behold you are betrothed to me, behold you are a wife to me,' such a one is consecrated. But if she gave him money or something worth money, and said to him: 'Behold, I am consecrated to you, behold I am betrothed to you, behold I am a wife to you,' such a one is not consecrated. By a writ—one must say it is a writ that is worth a *perutah* for her to be consecrated; she is not consecrated except through something that has the value of a *perutah*, even if it is written on a shard and he gave it to her, even if on an invalid document and he gave it to her, she is consecrated. Through 'intercourse'—[through] any act of sexual relations that is for the sake of marriage, she is consecrated. But if it is not for the sake of marriage, she is not consecrated [to him thereby].[26]

This *baraita*, which one must presume reflects a received tradition, was surely known to the redactor of the *Mishnah* and the omission of the details contained therein regarding the use of "a writ" or "intercourse" as legitimate means of contracting a marriage cannot be accidental. As already suggested, one can only speculate as to why this was done, acknowledging at the same time that, in fact, both controversial methods soon fell into disuse in favor of the use of "money or something worth money," such as a wedding ring. Nonetheless, in their consideration of the *Mishnah*, the amoraic sages of the *Gemara*, while not directly citing the *baraita* in their deliberations, clearly referred to it through paraphrase and a substantial analysis of its provisions and implications.[27]

ETHICS IN THE MISHNAH

In addition to the *Mishnah's* primary concern with providing a compendium of normative *halakhah* covering the obligations between man and God as well as between man and man, what would later be characterized as the religious and the secular aspects of life, a distinction not recognized in Judaism, there also abounded many traditional moral and ethical teachings that did not readily lend themselves to rulemaking. For one thing, rulemaking clearly involves setting the bar of acceptable behavior, so to speak, at a level appropriate for the majority of the people to be able to pass over, whereas moral sensibility may urge that the bar be raised higher for those capable of surmounting it, and for them to do less may be considered improper. Another consideration is that rules tend to be inflexible; too many exceptions will in effect nullify a rule. Moral and ethical considerations, by contrast, may call for diverse principled responses in accordance with varying circumstances.

For reasons that are not entirely clear, the final redactors of the *Mishnah* also elected to compile and include in it a collection of the moral maxims of the sages of Israel in the Hellenistic era of Graeco-Roman domination, the tractate known as *Avot*, which is perhaps the most widely known ancient rabbinic work, even though few are aware that it is actually a mishnaic tractate. It has been suggested by some that the decision to include such a work in the *Mishnah* was made in reaction to the allegations by a growing number of Christians and others that Judaism was so overly focused on legalisms that it essentially ignored morals and ethics; this work would help demonstrate the falsity of such assertions. Whatever the reason, this collection of moral and ethical dicta garnered from a half-millennium of maxims formulated by named teachers (for the most part) is probably the oldest anthology of its kind in literary history.

This unique classic work of rabbinic moral and ethical thought is therefore the only one of the sixty-three tractates in the massive ancient collection of the six orders of *halakhah* or rabbinic legal teachings in the *Mishnah* that does not deal with legal matters. In fact, there is nothing at all of a halakhic character in the work. Moreover, it is noteworthy that this collection of the moral and ethical, as well as some of the spiritual teachings of the sages of the *Mishnah*, the *tannaim*, was placed by the redactor in *Seder Nezikin*, the order of the *Mishnah* that deals with the commercial, criminal, and civil laws of Judaism. Some suggest that this is because the ultimate challenge of Judaic ethics is to provide guidance for dealing with the practical issues of social and economic behavior that are the concern of this subdivision of the *Mishnah*. The third century sage R. Simeon ben Lakish went so far as to consider *Seder Nezikin* to be the order of the *Mishnah* that deals with the matter of "salvation."[28] That is, as explained by one commentator, "Nezikin treats of civil law, knowledge of which saves man (i.e., brings him salvation) from encroaching on his neighbor's rights or allowing his own to be filched away."[29] Presumably, then, the moral and ethical insights and teachings in this tractate would serve as guidance for appropriate decision-making in light of the *halakhah*, although how this would be manifested is not entirely clear. In any case, as suggested, the reason this work was included in this collection at all remains an unsettled question of essentially antiquarian interest to this day.

The tractate *Avot* that is included in the *Mishnah* is one of three versions of the so-called Ethics of the Fathers, which is a partial misnomer because it contains teachings and other matter that do not easily fit under the rubric of ethics, although the largest part of the work is concerned with public as well as private behavior. The other two versions are *Avot deRabbi Natan* I and *Avot deRabbi Natan* II, which are independent source documents from the same period, citing the same early sages as the mishnaic tractate but with some variations and elaboration on their teachings, reflective in some instances of the school of Shammai as opposed to the version in the *Mishnah*, which is the product of the school of Hillel.

According to one of the preeminent modern scholars of these works, the traditions preserved in both *Avot* and the much larger *Avot deRabbi Natan* consist primarily of four ancient collections, albeit modified and amplified over time.[30] The first is a series of maxims formulated between approximately 250 BCE and 20 CE. The second is a series of maxims from the five principal disciples of R. Johanan ben Zakkai in the second half of the first century. The third contains maxims from what apparently was an early (late first–early second century) philosophical society that included the four well-known scholars, R. Akiba ben Joseph, Simeon ben Azzai, Simeon ben Zoma, and Elisha ben Abuya, who also evidently engaged in theosophical speculation. These three collections are presented in the first four chapters of *Avot*, that "preserved those teachings and emphases of the *tannaim* which reflected what most concerned classical Judaism: the claim of high antiquity for the Oral law; the nature and destiny of man; the permanent centrality of Torah; the doctrine of reward and punishment; the approved course for man in his life in this world in expectation of the world to come."[31]

The fourth primary group, which makes up the greatest part of the fifth chapter, is a collection of anonymous maxims collated on the basis of the distinguishing feature of their formulaic openings; statements are introduced by the numbers ten, seven, and four, the numbers serving as mnemonic devices, facilitating memorization of the teachings contained therein. Added to this group are the sayings of three named sages that conclude the original tractate. However, a sixth chapter was added to the mishnaic work in the post-talmudic era for liturgical purposes. A custom had evolved in which the chapters of *Avot* were read and studied on the Sabbath, often during the interval between the afternoon and evening prayers. This custom was especially popular during the six-week period between the festivals of Passover and Shavuot (Pentecost) as a preparation for the latter, which celebrated the giving of the Torah. But, because *Avot* contained only five chapters and there are six Sabbaths between the holidays, another chapter of supplementary statements by the sages was added to the work. The sixth chapter is a collection of sayings in praise of the Torah and the sages that is referred to as *Kinyan Torah* or "Acquisition of Torah," that is also found in the post-talmudic works, *Kallah Rabbati* and *Seder Eliahu Zuta*. Moreover, because of the liturgical practice of reading a chapter or *perek* of *Avot* on the Sabbath, in some communities on every Sabbath from Passover to the week before Rosh Hashanah, the work also became known as *Pirkei Avot* or "Chapters of the Fathers." It should be noted, however, that the use of the translation of the term *avot* as "fathers" here is a matter of contention.

The name of the tractate, understood as meaning "fathers," according to a commonly accepted opinion, derives from the fact that it sets forth "the order of our first fathers generation after generation."[32] Some, however, dispute this explanation because there is a sharp disagreement in the talmudic literature over the use of the term *avot* for this purpose. Thus, on the one hand, in the Babylonian Talmud it is asserted that the sages taught, "The term *avot* is applied only to three," that is, it is applied exclusively to the patriarchs Abraham, Isaac, and Jacob.[33] In the *Tosefta*, on the other hand, there is a reference to the early sages as the "early *avot*."[34] Moreover, the *Mishnah* specifically refers to the sages Hillel and Shammai as "fathers [*avot*] of the world."[35] Pointing out several similar uses of the term in the Jerusalem Talmud, some have concluded that there can be no doubt that the use of the term *avot* to refer to the early sages listed in *Avot* is correct and appropriate.[36] On the other hand, some consider it most appropriate "that the sages of our Law should be referred to in these passages as *Avoth*, for with these sayings they truly act as our 'fathers', providing us, in their discerning wisdom, with the ethical guidance we need to attain the state of perfection ordained for us by God.[37]

Both sides in this scholarly dispute base their opinions on the meaning of "fathers" imputed to the term *avot*. There is, however, an alternate meaning to the term, which is "sources" or an equivalent, that is, which takes the term "fathers" as referring to a point of origin instead of to a particular person. Thus the opening passage of the series of tractates in the *Mishnah* dealing with damages begins with the words, "*arba'a avot nezikin*," which is appropriately rendered as "The four primary causes [*avot*] of injury."[38] Similarly, the sources of impurity are described in the rabbinic literature as *avot hatumot*, and the prototypical categories of work prohibited on the Sabbath are characterized as *avot melakhot*. Accordingly, one eighteenth-century rabbinic authority suggested that the tractate is named *Avot* (sources) for a similar reason.[39] That is, the teachings recorded therein reflect seminal ideas upon which much of the ethical and behavioral thought that is to be found in the literature of Judaism is based.

In any case, liturgical use of the augmented mishnaic tractate led to its reproduction in editions of the traditional prayer book for more than a millennium, and has made it the most accessible and popular tractate in the entire mishnaic corpus. Moreover, because of its subject matter, which deals with the fundamental aspects of life as seen by the ancient sages of Judaism, it is also the treatise best known among non-Jews. The popularity of the tractate has resulted in the very large number of commentaries on the work that have appeared during the course of the last millennium.

The following citation from the work includes several of the popular teachings of R. Judah haNasi, the principal redactor of the *Mishnah*, only the first and last of which will be discussed briefly:[40]

> Rabbi says: "Which is the right course that a person should choose for himself? Any that is an honor to the doer and [brings] him honor from mankind. And be as meticulous with a minor precept as with a major one, since you do not know what the rewards are for the precepts. And calculate the loss [incurred by the performance] of a precept against its reward, and the reward of a transgression against the loss it incurs. Keep in view three things, and you will not come into the grip of transgression: know what is above you—a seeing eye and a hearing ear, and that all your deeds are recorded in a book."[41]

The question with which the sage begins this pericope, "Which is the right course that a person should choose for himself?" is predicated on one of the crucial concepts of Judaism, namely, that man is morally autonomous and endowed with the innate capacity and freedom to make ethical choices. Similarly, R. Judah haNasi is cited elsewhere as having taught: "Which is a right way that a man should choose? Let him love reproof, since as long as there is reproof in the world ease of

mind comes to the world, good and blessing come to the world, and
evil departs from the world."[42]

Some assume that the sage's statement reflects the view that there
may be multiple paths that will in the end lead to eternal felicity, and
that each person is free to choose the path that is most appropriate
to his personality and sensibilities. Also implicit in this is the notion
that although there may be general agreement regarding the virtues
to which man should aspire, his choice of direction must take into consideration actual circumstances and conditions. As a practical matter,
not all virtues are equally desirable at all times. Patience may not be the
appropriate virtue when the situation calls for audacity, nor tolerance in
the face of evil.

The fourth teaching recorded in the *Mishnah*, "Keep in view three
things, and you will not come into the grip of transgression," is a clear
reassertion of the fundamental principle that man, irrespective of
circumstances, retains his moral autonomy and his capacity for free
choice, even though the range of choices may be severely constrained.
The three considerations that R. Judah haNasi is about to set forth are
evidently intended to help a person to view his situation dispassion-
ately and to assist him in setting a morally acceptable course that will
keep him safe from many of life's moral pitfalls.

The notion of coming into the "grip of transgression" may be understood in at least two distinct senses. On the one hand, it can be taken
as an admonition to those who have not transgressed to beware of
the temptations that lead one into sin. On the other hand, it may be
understood as being directed to those who have transgressed, urging
them not to become possessed by sin and not to believe that because
they have transgressed that they are lost and beyond repentance and
redemption. Indeed, to maintain such a view would be in effect to reify
sin as a determinative force.

The key to maintain one's equilibrium in a morally turbulent world
is to "know what is above you—a seeing eye and a hearing ear, and that
all your deeds are recorded in a book." The most common approach to
this teaching understands it as reminding man of divine omniscience,
that all of one's deeds, both in action and in expression, are known as
if they were recorded in a ledger. The notion of a divine account book
would seem to derive from the biblical passage in which Moses pleads
for divine forgiveness of the people's sin, and states, *if not, blot me, I pray
Thee, out of Thy book which Thou hast written* (Ex. 32:32). The idea is
presented more explicitly in the prophetic passage: *And the Lord hear-
kened, and heard, and a book of remembrance was written before Him, for
them that feared the Lord, and that thought upon His name* (Mal. 3:16).

Some see this teaching as postulating three fundamental propositions: a belief in the reality of the divine, a belief in a divine providence

that recompenses man in accordance with his acts, and a belief that one cannot escape the consequences of one's transgressions. The last of these assertions should be understood as stating that a person cannot compensate for transgressions directly through the performance of meritorious acts. This does not mean that such acts are without redemptive value. What it suggests is that a person is punished for his sins and rewarded for observance of the precepts, in accordance with the account balance recorded in the divine ledger. Accordingly, in the final reckoning, the performance of meritorious acts in sufficient number may well tip the balance of merit in one's favor.

The *Mishnah* is a comprehensive work that not only covers the entire range of Jewish law and tradition, but also encompasses, in effect, the intellectual and religious history of the Jewish people from the very beginning to the end of the second century. However, as with virtually all the literature to be discussed in this book, the discovery of the scope and depth of the *Mishnah*'s tersely articulated contents requires intensive study.

Chapter 4

The Talmud

The promulgation of the *Mishnah* as the authoritative compendium of *halakhah* at the close of the second century spurred a dramatic intellectual renaissance among the schools of the Land of Israel and the Diaspora, primarily the Jewish communities in Mesopotamia, still known in the ancient sources as Babylonia, the name it bore at the time of the destruction of the First Temple in the sixth century BCE. Following the death of R. Judah haNasi and the concurrent deterioration of political and economic conditions in the Land of Israel, the comparatively better conditions prevailing in Mesopotamia attracted emigration there that resulted in the emergence of academies of learning that eventually surpassed in importance those of the homeland. This transformation in the Babylonian academic environment was largely due to the work of R. Abba ben Aivu (d. 247), also known as Abba Arikha—"Abba the Tall," who had traveled from Babylonia to complete his education under R. Judah haNasi and received ordination from the venerable sage.

Upon his return to Babylonia, R. Abba, who was acknowledged as an outstanding scholar, became determined to raise the standard of traditional learning there. Unwilling to offend the existing leadership of the Babylonian community, he settled in the small town of Sura, where he established an academy which soon attracted a large number of scholars and students. His influence became so great that he was accorded the popular name of Rav, the teacher *par excellence*, just as his mentor R. Judah haNasi was affectionately known as Rabbi, the rabbi *par excellence*. A younger contemporary of Rav, Samuel ben Abba, also known as Samuel Yarhina'ah ("Samuel the Astronomer), similarly headed an important academy in Nehardea, which was subsequently relocated to Pumbedita. Both academies continued to survive, in one locale or another, for some seven hundred years, well into the period of Muslim domination of the region and long after their sister institutions in the Land of Israel had become defunct. Their founders were revered by later generations and were accorded the honorable titles of "our rabbis in Babylonia" or "our rabbis in the Diaspora."[1]

The availability of a more coherently structured compendium of Oral Torah made it feasible for scholars in both the Land of Israel and Mesopotamia to deal with the vast amount of traditional law and lore in a more systematic way. One result of this was that the focus of their scholarly attention was directed away from the biblical texts, which nonetheless remained the ultimate source of Torah, to critical study and analysis of the *Mishnah*, which incorporated both biblical and extra-biblical teachings. The latter work thus became the preeminent source document for the scholarship that flowered over the next several centuries that is reflected in the compilations of traditional learning that became known by the Hebrew term *Talmud* or by its Aramaic equivalent *Gemara*.[2] As indicated earlier, the sages who engaged in such scholarship after the publication of the *Mishnah* were known as *amoraim*, from the verb *amar*, to speak or interpret, in effect describing them as interpreters of the *Mishnah*.

The *amoraim* studied the teachings of the *Mishnah* intensively, applying many of the analytic techniques previously applied to the biblical texts, and much as contemporary American constitutional lawyers probe the intent and meaning of what the Founders of the republic wrote into the U.S. Constitution, they sought to derive guidance from the *Mishnah* on a wide range of issues that emerged over time that either were not dealt with specifically in the basic document or simply had not arisen in earlier times. As already indicated, in their critical examination of the *Mishnah*, the *amoraim* drew on all the relevant material they could lay their hands on, especially the teachings being incorporated into the major works of *midrash halakhah* as well as the *baraitot* that were subsequently recorded in the *Tosefta* and other unpublished collections of normative teachings and exposition that were still available in the rabbinical academies. They used these materials to challenge, amplify, and explicate the generally terse statements of the *Mishnah*, ultimately producing a vast body of scholarly work that became known affectionately as "the sea of Talmud," which one had to learn to navigate in order to have a successful voyage through it.

The Talmud, however, is also more than a commentary on the *Mishnah*. As one of the great modern talmudists puts it:

> It is a conglomerate of law, legend, and philosophy, a blend of unique logic and shrewd pragmatism, of history and science, anecdotes and humor.

It is a collection of paradoxes: its framework is orderly and logical, every word and term subjected to meticulous editing, completed centuries after the actual work of composition came to an end; yet it is still based on free association, on a harnessing together of diverse ideas reminiscent of the modern stream-of-consciousness novel. Although its main objective is to interpret and comment on a book of law, it is, simultaneously, a work of art that goes beyond legislation and its practical application. And although the Talmud is, to this day, the primary source of Jewish law, it cannot be cited as an authority for purposes of ruling.[3]

What this suggests is that the discussions recorded in the Talmud may inform decision-making on halakhic issues but are not in themselves determinative of those decisions. Subsequent decisors in every age must assume responsibility for the appropriate application of halakhic principles and rules in accordance with or notwithstanding prevailing contemporary conditions.

The sages of the Talmud approached their intellectual task of probing the depths of the Oral Torah without regard to whether the issue they were dealing with had immediate practical relevance. They considered every aspect of life and thought that had any connection with Torah to be worthy of study and analysis. The question of practical relevance or value is never raised in the Talmud. Indeed, it is not unusual to find protracted in-depth analyses and debates even regarding halakhic positions or views that had been rejected and were of no legislative import. "When the talmudic sage examined an ancient tradition, he perceived it, above all, as a reality in itself, and whether binding on him or not, it was part of his world and could not be dismissed. When the scholars discuss a rejected idea or source, their attitude resembles that of a scientist contemplating an organism that has become extinct... but this fact does not detract from its interest for the scientist as a subject of study."[4] In other words, they treated study of Torah not as a means to an end, but as an end in itself; the search for knowledge and understanding for its own sake was for them an act of faith, a religious imperative. Nonetheless, as will be seen, not all parts of the mishnaic corpus were addressed with equal vigor and intensity.

As it turned out, for reasons that are primarily social and economic, the academies in the Land of Israel and those in Mesopotamia devoted much of their attention to those parts of the mishnaic corpus that had particular practical relevance for the prevailing circumstances in which each community found itself. For instance, the community in the Land of Israel was more involved in agriculture than the communities of Mesopotamia, where commerce played a greater role in their economy. The result of this was that the volume of material related to *Nezikin*, the order of the *Mishnah* devoted primarily to civil law and related matters and secondarily to criminal law, produced in the

Mesopotamian academies dwarfed that produced in the academies of the Land of Israel. By contrast, many of the traditional laws that dealt with matters that had relevance only in the Land of Israel, where they continued to be observed long after the destruction of the Temple, evidently were of little immediate interest to the sages in the Mesopotamian academies, where they did not become subjects of intense study and analysis.

As a result of these circumstances, neither version of the Talmud deals fully with the sixty-three tractates of the *Mishnah*, the Babylonian Talmud containing a *Gemara* to thirty-six of the tractates and the Jerusalem Talmud to thirty-nine. The Babylonian Talmud does not have a *Gemara* to any of the tractates in *Zeraim*, the first order of the *Mishnah*, with the exception of the tractate *Berakhot*, which deals with matters relating to prayer and is placed in *Zeraim* as a matter of convenience rather than because of its affinity to the primary subject matter of the other tractates in the order. It may well be the case that *Berakhot* was made the first tractate in the *Mishnah* to emphasize the importance of standardized prayer as a vehicle for assuring communal cohesion in the face of the challenges of alien domination of and dispersion from the Land of Israel. Similarly, the Babylonian Talmud has a *Gemara* to only nine of the eleven tractates of the order *Kodashim*, which deals primarily with the Temple and the sacrificial rite. It also has no *Gemara* to any tractate in the entire order of *Tohorot*, which deals mainly with issues of ritual purity, except for the tractate *Niddah*, which focuses on issues relating to menstruation and its concomitant issues concerning ritual purity, many of which continued to be relevant to Jewish family life irrespective of the cessation of the Temple rites.

Somewhat surprisingly, in the Jerusalem Talmud there is no *Gemara* at all to the order of *Kodashim*, and none to *Tohorot*, with the exception of three chapters of the tractate *Niddah*. Two plausible reasons may be suggested to account for this anomaly. One is that there was a body of amoraic literature devoted to these topics but it was lost as a result of the chaotic state of the Jewish community in the Land of Israel under Byzantine rule. Alternatively, the absence of the relevant material might be explained as a consequence of the deepening despair over the loss of the Temple and with it all semblance and hope of national autonomy. This loss was something that the sages of the Land of Israel were made painfully aware of daily, and perhaps they did not want to expend valuable time on subjects that were becoming increasingly remote from reality when there were other topics of greater immediate relevance to explore.

There was in fact a notable difference in the political climates in which the sages had to do their work in Mesopotamia and in the Land of Israel respectively. In Mesopotamia, the Persian overlords had little interest in the communal or religious life of its Jewish communities, and therefore allowed Jewish academic life to thrive undisturbed for the most part. This resulted in a continuity of traditional leadership that was absent in the Land of Israel, which early in the fourth century had become part of the Christian Byzantine Empire, whose official church had vital theological interests at stake in the stubborn perseverance of the rabbinic tradition. This resulted in practical problems for the sages in the Land of Israel that their contemporary coreligionists in Mesopotamia, generally speaking, did not experience.

In 351, following an abortive revolt against the provincial Byzantine commander Gallus, a campaign of suppression was undertaken against the Jews of Tiberias, Sepphoris, and Lydda, which were the seats of the primary academies of Jewish learning in the country. The persecutions and troubles continued and intensified, with the patriarchate becoming defunct in 421, the year that the academy of Tiberias closed its doors. Although Torah study continued among the sages in smaller and sometimes clandestine conventicles, the political climate was no longer conducive to creative scholarship. It was apparent by the middle of the fourth century that it was essential to gather and consolidate whatever scholarly talmudic materials were available if the intellectual work of some three centuries were not to be lost, an effort that was undertaken and brought to completion by the end of the century. In the meanwhile, however, the increasingly desperate situation of the sages may have resulted in the actual loss of substantial amounts of scholarly work, accounting in part for the disparity in volume between the material collected and published by the *amoraim* in the Land of Israel and the much larger amount collected and published in Mesopotamia. As a consequence of these factors and other differences in the focus of scholars in these centers of Jewish life, the body of work produced by them reflected those areas of study of greater immediate relevance to them, marking significant differences between the Talmud or *Gemara* of the Land of Israel and that of Babylonia, not only in volume but also in content.

An additional factor distinguishing the two compendiums is that there are some occasionally significant differences between the texts of the *Mishnah* as they appear in the Babylonian and Jerusalem editions of the Talmud, presumably the result of the use of different manuscripts in the two communities. How this came about is uncertain, a plausible theory being that R. Judah haNasi issued more than a single edition of his *Mishnah*, later editions reflecting emendations or even retractions of particular halakhic positions promulgated in earlier versions. The final edition of his *Mishnah* was sent to Babylonia where it became the basis for the deliberations of the *amoraim*. In the Land of Israel, however, where earlier editions of the *Mishnah* were still widely available, the debate over the wording of the final edition continued, and in a few instances later sages decided to revise the *Mishnah* in favor of an earlier rendition. These changes were never incorporated into the ostensibly final version on which the work of the Babylonian *amoraim* was predicated. As a result, the version of the *Mishnah* found in the Jerusalem Talmud is different in a number of halakhic positions than in the version found in the Babylonian Talmud, which was held by later rabbinical authorities to mirror the final views of R. Judah haNasi on all issues more closely.[5]

The Talmud (*Gemara*) of the Land of Israel, known in Hebrew as the *Talmud Yerushalmi* and in English as the Jerusalem Talmud, even though it was not compiled in Jerusalem, or the *Talmud de-Eretz Yisrael* rendered in English as the Palestinian Talmud, was compiled at about the end of the fourth century. The Talmud of the Babylonian sages, known in Hebrew as the *Talmud Bavli* and in English as the Babylonian Talmud, was compiled at about the end of the fifth century. Because of its later composition, the Babylonian Talmud has been generally regarded as the more authoritative source for the further development of *halakhah*.

Not surprisingly, there was a good deal of interaction between the sages of Mesopotamia and those of the Land of Israel and it is not unusual to find the scholars of one of the Talmuds mentioned or cited, sometimes prominently, in the other Talmud. It should also be noted that although the term Talmud actually refers to the *Gemara* of the *amoraic* sages, the published editions of their works all incorporate the *Mishnah* for purpose of reference. This practice has led to the misleading notion that the Talmud is a composite of *Mishnah* and *Gemara*, whereas within the work itself the term Talmud, when referring to a body of learning, is always used as the equivalent of *Gemara*.

Although the original language of both versions of the Talmud is Aramaic, the language in common use throughout the region, there are some significant differences between the dialects employed by the scholars of the Land of Israel and those of Mesopotamia. The Babylonian Talmud is written in Eastern Aramaic, with a considerable admixture of Hebrew, while the Jerusalem Talmud is written in Western Aramaic with the admixture of a substantial number of words from the Greek dialect commonly spoken in Syria and Palestine, many of which are severely corrupted and difficult to comprehend. There is also a significant difference in the quality of editing between the two versions. The Jerusalem Talmud was put together in great haste, under great pressure, and was never properly edited, making it very difficult to study. By comparison, the Babylonian Talmud was edited and reedited over a considerable amount of time, making it far more accessible. Because of this, the examples of the Talmud discussed in this chapter are drawn primarily from the latter rather than the former.

Although both versions take the same general approach to the analysis of the *Mishnah*, what perhaps most distinguishes the two bodies of literature is that the Babylonian Talmud also contains a great deal of material that deals with the explication and homiletic interpretation of Scripture, something that is present in much smaller amounts in the Jerusalem Talmud, which helps account for the much larger volume of the former, and perhaps explains in part the greater popularity and acknowledged authority of the Babylonian Talmud. By contrast, in the Land of Israel, the Talmud was for the most part limited to halakhic matters, and the large amount of Scripture commentary and homiletic interpretation attributed to the sages went into the various compilations of *midrash aggadah*, which will be discussed in the next chapter. In the Babylonian Talmud the non-halakhic material, the *aggadah*, constitutes about two-thirds of the whole, whereas in the Jerusalem Talmud it only characterizes about one-sixth of the whole.

The general approach taken in the *Gemara* with regard to its halakhic content consists of four basic elements: (1) A critical reading of the precise language of the *Mishnah*, explaining its choice of words, explicating the rule under consideration, and illustrating it through an example; (2) Elaborating on the meaning of the rule and considering the reason for it; (3) Discussing the secondary and possibly unanticipated implications or consequences of its applications; (4) Reviewing the opinions of contending scholars with regard to the halakhic rule, and considering the record of prior case law as it would be affected by differing interpretations of the mishnaic rule. The approach of the *amoraim* to analysis of the *Mishnah* involves four modes of analytic criticism that are surprisingly modern, indeed contemporary, in spirit. These are rational criticism of the tradition and responses to questions raised; historical criticism of the sources on which the mishnaic rulings are based; philological and literary criticism of the halakhic formulations; and critical evaluation of the *halakhah* as applied in practice.[6] In addition to its critical analysis of the *Mishnah*, the *Gemara* also raises theoretical questions of law not associated with any particular passage in the *Mishnah*, performs exegesis of biblical statements unrelated to the *Mishnah*, makes a variety of purportedly historical statements, and relates illustrative stories and legends about earlier and contemporary sages and their disciples.

THE TALMUDIC *SUGYA*

Bearing in mind the distinctions between the contents of the two compendiums, and putting aside for later consideration the large amount of non-halakhic material found in both, the critical components of the

Gemara that deal with the *Mishnah* and its implications are found in relatively discrete units of discourse, each referred to as a *sugya*, which make up the bulk of the halakhic material to be found in the Talmud. As a general proposition, it may be said that the central underlying theme of the *sugya*, as one modern talmudist put it, "is not analysis, not originality, not creativity, but consistency. The quest for consistency is the overriding imperative of the Talmud itself and of all the rabbinic commentaries that develop its concepts. This quest mandates that all superficial inconsistencies must be resolved and thereby gives rise to the great surge of analysis, logic, original thought, and sheer genius that characterize Talmudic scholarship."[7] In pursuing this quest for consistency, the sages of the Talmud subject every law, rule, or statement intended to serve as the basis for *halakhah* to intense, indeed, sometimes excruciatingly detailed analysis to determine whether it is consistent with all other related teachings, precepts, and rulings in the written Torah as well as in the oral traditions reflected in the *Mishnah* and the related *baraitot* or teachings excluded from the latter. Any inconsistencies that cannot be reconciled must at the least be explained. The issues raised in the *sugya* also must be vetted rigorously from the standpoint of logic and the accepted hermeneutic rules of biblical exegesis. With regard to the fundamental role logic plays in the deliberations of the sages, the following example recorded in the Talmud, which often is the student's first introduction to the *Gemara* in traditional rabbinical academies or seminaries, displays the critical reasoning that is typical of the analytic approach to the text that is common to the work as a whole.

The first hypothetical case set forth in the mishnaic pericope under consideration concerns two litigants that might appear before a court, both in actual possession of an object, whose original ownership cannot be determined, that each claims to have found. The qualification that both are in possession of the object is important in the case at hand because if only one person possessed it and another claimed it, the one in actual possession would have a stronger claim and other legal principles would be involved in the adjudication of the disputed claims. The second hypothetical case concerns two litigants, one of whom claims sole right to the object and the other claims that it was found by both simultaneously and that half of its value should by right be his. In both cases, a basic premise is that there are no witnesses to the event that could testify on behalf of either of the litigants. The *Mishnah* states:

> Two hold a garment. One of them says, "I found it," and the other says, "I found it"; One of them says, "it is all mine," and the other says "it is all mine," then the one shall swear that his share in it is not less than half,

and the other shall swear that his share in it is not less than half, and
[the value of the garment] shall be divided between them. If one says, "it
is all mine," and the other says, "half of it is mine," he who says "it is all
mine" shall swear that his share in it is not less than three quarters, and
he who says, "half of it is mine" shall swear that his share in it is not less
than a quarter. The former then receives three quarters [of the value of
the garment] and the latter receives one quarter.[8]

In the first instance, the obviously logical disposition of the case where
there are two competing absolute claims to a found object, and where
there are no witnesses, is to divide it equally between the two claimants, the requirement for each to swear to the veracity of his claim
presumably intended as a deterrent to making a false claim. Because
both claims cannot be true at the same time, the oath is worded in a
way to deal with this problem: each swears that at a minimum, given
the possibility that they may actually have found the object simultaneously, his share is no less than half of its value, although each might
believe that he was really entitled to the whole of its value.

In the second instance postulated in the *Mishnah*, the case is to be
adjudicated quite differently. Here, one claims that he found the object
and that it belongs to him, while the other implicitly claims that they
found it together and that half its value should therefore be his. The
logical disposition of the case takes into consideration that the second
claimant, by arguing for only half the value implicitly concedes half
the value of the object to the other claimant, effectively denying any
claim to that portion of the value of the object, thereby removing it
from any further contention. Having thus disposed of the question of
ownership of half the value of the object, the dispute now turns to the
disposition of the remaining half of the value of the object, which both
claimants argue should entirely be theirs. Following the logic of the
first case, where two litigants make absolute claims, and there are no
witnesses to testify that they found the object together and simultaneously, the only reasonable solution is to divide equally between them
the value of what is in contention. Accordingly, the one who made the
consistently absolute claim would receive three-quarters of the total
value of the object and the one who claimed only half would receive
only a quarter of the total.

The logic of the mishnaic rulings was considered so self-evident that the
sages of the *Gemara* did not even bother to discuss it. What they did discuss were the possible further implications of the wording of the cases.
They raised a number of questions regarding the way the case is set
forth in the *Mishnah*. For one thing, they were troubled by the apparent
redundancy: "One of them says, 'I found it,' and the other says, 'I found it';
One of them says, 'it is all mine, and the other says 'it is all mine.'"

Surely one plea would have been sufficient!—It is only one plea: One says
"I found it and [therefore] it is all mine," and the other says "I found it,
and [therefore] it is all mine!" But why not just state "I found it," and it will
be understood that the intention is to claim the whole garment?—The
term "I found it" might have been explained as denoting "I saw it," the
mere seeing [of the garment] entitling him to claim it as his possession
[even though the other claimant may have taken hold of it first]. Therefore the plea "it is all mine" is added, so as to make clear that seeing
alone does not constitute a claim ... But even so, would it not have been
sufficient to state "it is all mine" without the plea of "I found it"? Had
[the *Mishnah*] stated only the plea "it is all mine" I might have said that
elsewhere [in the Talmud] the term "found" is used to mean ["seen,"
and the conclusion would have been drawn] that mere sight constitutes
a claim to possession. For this reason the *Mishnah* states first "I found
it" and then "it is all mine," so that we may gather from the additional
clause that mere sight does not constitute a claim to possession.[9]

This first argument raised in the *Gemara* with regard to the wording
of the claim is thus shown to have important legal implications, both
for the case at issue as well as in other unrelated instances. The sages
therefore concluded that the seemingly obvious redundancy of the
wording of the *Mishnah* is quite deliberate and highly significant for
equitable dispute resolution. The question and response style of the
argument is quite typical of talmudic analysis, which takes some getting used to, but is actually a highly economical way of saying what
needs to be said about the matter in as concise a manner as possible.
The remainder of the *Gemara*'s analysis of the cited mishnaic pericope
and its implications, which constitutes a *sugya*, consumes some seven
double-sided folio pages, the full exposition of which would require a
sizeable monograph.

Although any one *sugya* may vary in a number of ways from others,
it is possible to suggest that, in general, the *sugya* conforms to a discernible basic structure, which in rather oversimplified outline is as follows.
A comprehensive *sugya* will typically incorporate as many as seven discrete elements. It begins with (1) a *Statement* of the *halakhah*, which is
followed by (2) a *Question* about the halakhic statement, followed by
(3) a *Response* to question, followed by (4) a *Challenge* to the response,
which evokes (5) a *Rebuttal* of the challenge, followed by the pointing
out of (6) a *Problem* with the rebuttal, the *sugya* reaching its conclusion
with (7) a *Resolution* of the problem. An illustration of a brief and relatively uncomplicated *sugya* found in the tractate *Baba Kamma* of the
Babylonian Talmud that reflects these elements follows.[10]

(1—Statement) The *Mishnah* states: "If a man stole [an ox or a sheep]
according to the evidence of two witnesses, and killed or sold it according to their evidence or that of two others, he must make fourfold or

fivefold restitution."[11] This statement of the *halakhah* appears rather straightforward, incorporating the elements of two specific biblical stipulations. The first states: *If a man steal an ox, or a sheep, and kill it, or sell it, he shall pay five oxen for an ox, and four sheep for a sheep* (Ex. 21:37). The second asserts, *At the mouth of two witnesses, or at the mouth of three witnesses, shall a matter be established* (Deut. 19:15).

(2—Question) The *Gemara* raises a question reflecting the concern that, although the rule asserted in the *Mishnah* appears to be consistent with the biblical texts, it also appears to be inconsistent with the authoritative opinion of R. Akiba regarding the meaning and application of the second cited biblical text. The following argument regarding this concern is presented in the *Gemara*, the implications of which will likely not be self-evident to a reader inexperienced with navigating one's way through rabbinic texts. Indeed, it might strike the novice as fairly incomprehensible but will be seen to be quite reasonable and logical to the more experienced student of Talmud. The *Gemara* asks:

> Are we to say that the *Mishnah* is not in accordance with R. Akiba? For how could it be in accordance with R. Akiba who said that [the biblical term] *matter* implies "not half a matter"? As it has been taught: R. Jose said: "When my father Halafta went to R. Johanan b. Nuri to learn Torah, or as others say when R. Johanan b. Nuri went to my father Halafta, he said to him: Suppose a man had the use of a piece of land for one year as testified by two witnesses, and for a second year as testified by two other witnesses, and for a third year as testified by still two other witnesses, what is the position?—He replied: 'This is a proper usucaption [it constitutes a valid title].' Whereupon the other rejoined: 'I also say the same, but R. Akiba joins issue on the matter for R. Akiba used to say: [Scripture states] *A matter* [implying] 'but not half a matter.'"[12]

What is at issue here is R. Akiba's understanding of the biblical stipulation that *at the mouth of two witnesses, or at the mouth of three witnesses, shall a matter be established*. His understanding is that the witnesses to *a matter* must be witnesses to the "entire matter," whereas in the statement of the *Mishnah*, the stealing of the animal may be attested to by one set of witnesses, and the slaughter or selling of it attested to by a different set of witnesses. Applying R. Akiba's reasoning to this case, we would have to consider each pair of witnesses as able to attest only to "half a matter," a circumstance that would not satisfy the biblical requirement for conviction and imposition of the stipulated penalty. Similarly, in the case of the use of a piece of land brought up in the discussion by R. Jose, three sets of witnesses, each able to attest that a person made use of a piece of land for a single year, were, according to the sages Halafta and R. Johanan b. Nuri, able to satisfy the rule that a person must demonstrate three years of undisturbed possession of a piece of land to establish a presumptive title to it. However, according to R. Akiba, the attestations of the witnesses would be insufficient to establish presumptive title because none of the witnesses could attest to the person's continuous possession of the land for the required three consecutive years.

(3—Response) With regard to the question raised by the *Gemara* concerning the consistency of the *Mishnah* with the teaching of R. Akiba, the sage Abaye offers the following response:

> Abaye, however, said: You may even say that this is in accordance with R. Akiba. For would R. Akiba not agree in a case where two witnesses state that a certain person had betrothed a woman and two other witnesses testify that another person has subsequently had intercourse with her, that though the evidence regarding the intercourse presupposes the evidence regarding the betrothal [in order to become relevant], nevertheless, since the evidence of betrothal does not presuppose the evidence of intercourse, each testimony should be considered a matter [complete in itself]? So also here, though the evidence regarding the slaughter presupposes the evidence regarding the theft [if it is to be relevant] nevertheless since the evidence regarding the theft does not presuppose the evidence regarding the slaughter, each testimony should be considered a "matter" [complete in itself].

Abaye suggests that the position of R. Akiba with regard to the matter at hand has been misconstrued and that there is no inconsistency to be reconciled. He draws an analogy to the case where two witnesses can attest that a betrothal took place, making the woman legally married, even though the marriage, which in Jewish tradition takes place in two distinct stages, has not yet been consummated. If another pair of witnesses testifies that a person other than her husband subsequently had been intimate with her, both adulterer and adulteress become subject to the severe biblical penalty for such a transgression, which is considered a capital crime (Lev. 20:10). Abaye argues that R. Akiba would surely agree with this position, notwithstanding that the act of betrothal in itself does not presuppose consummation of the marriage between the betrothed, because betrothal alone establishes the basis for a subsequent act of sexual intimacy with another man to be considered adultery. Similarly, the slaughter or selling of an animal becomes criminal only if it presupposes that the person committing the act is not the legal owner of the animal, whereas stealing the animal does not necessarily presuppose that it will be slaughtered or sold. Accordingly, Abaye maintains, R. Akiba would agree that in each case, the evidence of the different witnesses would be considered complete and valid.

(4—Challenge) Testing the validity of Abaye's response, the sages raised a new challenge regarding the applicability of R. Akiba's assertion that the biblical term *a matter* does not imply "half a matter." It is pointed out that the majority of the sages would agree that the evidence given independently by three sets of witnesses, each testifying that a person occupied a piece of land for one of three consecutive years, to be adequate to establish a presumptive title to it, a position that would appear to reject the validity of R. Akiba's dictum. The *Gemara* thus asks: "But according to the Rabbis what will this term *matter* [implying] 'but not half a matter' exclude?" That is, is R. Akiba's stated understanding of the biblical term *a matter* to be simply ignored, something that seems highly unlikely? And if one argues that it does not apply to the issue at hand, to what situation would it apply?

(5—Rebuttal) In rebuttal to the challenge raised, the *Gemara* asserts: "It will exclude a case where one witness testified that there was one hair on her back and the other states that there was one hair in front." That is, R. Akiba's understanding of *a matter* but "not half a matter" would be held to apply to a case where witnesses are called upon to testify as to whether a girl has reached puberty, and thus acquired majority legal status. According to another text in the *Mishnah*: "If a girl [being twelve years and one day old] has grown two [pubic] hairs she is subject to all the commands prescribed in the Torah, and she may perform *halizah* or contract levirate marriage."[13] In the case under consideration, each witness testified only to the presence of a single hair. Accordingly, such testimony would be discounted as "half a matter."

(6—Problem) However, the sages found a problem with this explanation, which seemed to trivialize the view of R. Akiba. They argued: "But [since each hair is testified to by one witness], would this not be both half a matter and half a testimony?" That is, it seems rather self-evident that this sort of testimony is insufficient since the witnesses are not testifying to the same thing, and as a result it does not meet the biblical requirement that *At the mouth of two witnesses, or at the mouth of three witnesses, shall a matter be established*.

(7—Resolution) Accordingly, the *Gemara* concludes the *sugya* with the following resolution of the problem: "[We must say] therefore that it excludes a case where two witnesses testify that there was one hair on her back and two other witnesses state that there was one hair in front, as in this case the one set [of witnesses] testify that she was still a minor and the others similarly testify that she was still a minor." That is, R. Akiba's reading of the biblical requirement for establishing a legal fact by two or more witnesses would exclude a case such as the determination of female puberty, where both sets of witnesses are able to testify only to half of what is required. Although no other example of the application of R. Akiba's understanding of the biblical requirement for establishing *a matter* is offered here, its validity is reaffirmed and found to be consistent with the *Mishnah*, as explained by Abaye.

As may be seen in this comparatively brief *sugya*, the analysis is rather complex as well as both far-reaching and exhaustive, moving easily from a halakhic ruling dealing with the theft and subsequent slaughter or selling of an ox or sheep to one concerned with establishing squatter's rights to real property and then to another concerned with establishing a legal status of adulthood for a pubescent female child. Moreover, it will have been noted that the actual intent and meaning of the talmudic passages is often quite incomprehensible unless elaborated and explained, a consideration that makes independent study of the *Gemara* extremely difficult at best for beginners.

SEMANTIC ANALYSIS

The following extract from part of a unit of talmudic discourse found in the Babylonian Talmud, tractate *Kiddushin*, reflects a rather different approach to consideration of a halakhic ruling in the *Mishnah*, focusing more sharply on the semantics of the statement and its implications. The case in point is the rule concerning the contracting of a marriage, discussed in part briefly in the preceding chapter. The *Mishnah* states: "A woman is acquired [in marriage] in three ways and acquires her freedom in two. She is acquired by money, by deed, or by intercourse . . .And she acquires her freedom by divorce or by her husband's death."[14]

In considering this statement, the *Gemara* is struck by the passive voice in which it is phrased and the absence of any direct reference to the husband. Accordingly, it begins to probe for the reasons behind the seemingly somewhat awkward formulation.[15] "'A woman is acquired.' Why does he [the anonymous sage] state here, 'A woman is acquired,' whereas he elsewhere teaches 'A man can betroth [a woman] etc.?'"[16] That is, for the sake of consistency the sage should have used the same assertive formulation here, or, if for some reason it was important to state the proposition in a passive voice, it could have stated, "A woman is betrothed." The question, of course is rhetorical, and the *Gemara* proceeds to offer an explanation.

> Because he wishes to state "Money"; and how do we know that money effects betrothal? By deriving the meaning of "taking" from the field of Ephron: Here it is written, *If any man take a wife* [Deut. 22:13]; and there it is written, *I will give thee money for the field: take it of me* [Gen. 23:13]. Moreover, "taking" is designated acquisition, for it is written, *the field which Abraham acquired* [Gen. 49:30]; alternatively, *men shall acquire fields for money* [Jer. 32:44]; therefore, he teaches, "A woman is acquired."

The complex argument of this terse passage is that the mishnaic for-mulation, "A woman is acquired," is necessary to establish the prin-ciple that money may be used to contract a marriage, and the way this is done is by use of the hermeneutic rule of *gezerah shavah*, whereby the use of the same term in two different biblical passages indicates that their laws or connotations are similar. In this case, the key term is "taking." In the case of Abraham, who was purchasing the field of Machpelah as a gravesite, the transfer of ownership of the property took place through the acceptance by the seller of a monetary pay-ment, *I will give thee money for the field: take it of me*, so too in the case of a marriage, *If any man take a wife*, the "taking" or acquisition is accomplished through her acceptance of a monetary payment by which she becomes exclusively consecrated to her husband. Accord-ingly, "A woman is acquired . . . by money."

However, this analysis does not explain why it later states, "A man can betroth [a woman]." As the *Gemara* puts it: "Then let him state there, 'A man acquires [a woman].'—He [the sage] first employs bibli-cal phraseology, but subsequently the rabbinic idiom. What does the rabbinic term connote? —That he [the husband] interdicts her to all [men] as *hekdesh* [something that is forbidden for secular use]." The rationale employed by the *Gemara* to explain the distinction between "A woman is acquired" and "A man can betroth," is that the first is a reflection of the biblical verses that speak of acquisition, as explained above, whereas the later usage of betrothal reflects the rabbinic notion underlying the very concept of *kiddushin* or marriage. To betroth means to consecrate a woman exclusively to her husband, the betrothal transforming her into *hekdesh*, thus placing her in a special category of sanctity that precludes access to her by any male other than her husband. Although this would explain why it later states, "A man can betroth," it does not explain why the idea of acquisition is stated here passively as "A woman is acquired."

> But why not teach here, "A man acquires"?—Because he desires to teach the second clause, "and acquires her freedom," which refers to her [the woman], he therefore teaches the first clause likewise with reference to her. Then let him state, "A man acquires . . . and makes [her] acquire."—Because there is the husband's death where it is not he who frees her, but it is Heaven who confers [her freedom] on her. Alternatively, were it taught "he acquires," I might have thought, even against her will, hence it is stated "A woman is acquired," implying only with her consent, but not without.

In the first part of this response, the *Gemara* effectively sets up a "straw man" in its explanation that the statement in the *Mishnah* is striving for literary consistency and therefore couches the first clause in terms of the woman in order to be symmetrical with the second clause which similarly refers to the woman, an argument it immediately dismisses out of hand. It then raises the possibility of framing both clauses in terms of the man rather than the woman, "A man acquires . . . and makes [her] acquire." This possibility is also dismissed because although the second clause would apply in the case of divorce, it would be irrelevant in the case of the husband's death since it is not he but the divine hand that grants her freedom. There still remains an option that is not mentioned in the *Gemara*, "A man acquires a woman . . . and a woman acquires her freedom," which is effectively precluded by the alternate explanation that the statement of the *Mishnah* is framed in terms of the woman in order to emphasize the issue of consent.

COMPARISON OF THE TWO TALMUDS

There are occasions when the *Gemaras* of the Babylonian and Jerusalem Talmuds discuss and comment on a particular mishnaic stipulation but differ significantly in how they understand its implications. The following example, drawn from the Jerusalem Talmud, tractate *Berakhot*, is an instance in which a matter of *halakhah* is derived and affirmed, but is not even mentioned in the discussion found in the Babylonian Talmud. Because of the cryptic manner in which the discussion is recorded in the Jerusalem Talmud, it will be presented here discursively rather than verbatim. The mishnaic text under consideration is one that specifies the points of disagreement between the academies of Hillel and Shammai with regard to ritual matters connected with the order of recitation of blessings at the meals marking the onset of the Sabbath or a holiday. The essence of the disagreement between the schools is the same as discussed toward the end of the preceding chapter with regard to the sanctification of the holiday of Passover, namely, whether the blessing over wine should precede the blessing over the occasion.

The *Gemara* in the Babylonian Talmud makes the same case as recorded in the preceding chapter of this book, but in the course of the discussion also cites a *baraita*, which states, "When one goes into his house on the outgoing of Sabbath, he says blessings over wine and light and spices and then he says the *havdalah*," the benediction marking the transition from sanctified time to the secular, following the order of prayer affirmed by Beth [the school of] Hillel.[17] In the course of discussing this in the Jerusalem Talmud, the *Gemara* cites the opinion supportive of Beth Hillel in the name of R. Yose as well as the opposing view of R. Mana, who makes a strong argument in favor of the opinion held by Beth Shammai, at least with specific regard to the order of the *havdalah* ritual. R. Mana makes the case that Beth Hillel's position is based in part on the argument presented in the *Tosefta*, with regard to the Passover Seder, that Beth Hillel maintains: "He recites a blessing over the wine and then recites a blessing for the day, because the wine is what causes the blessing of the day to be said."[18] That is, the disciples of Hillel took the position that the significance of the occasion is not the day per se, as is the case with the Sabbath, but the essence of what is symbolized by the required four cups of wine, namely, the process of national redemption from adversity; it is therefore the latter that lends special significance to the occasion. Accordingly, the appropriate order is the blessing over the wine first and then that for the holiday. R. Mana therefore concluded that if the same logic were applied to the order of the *havdalah* rite, one should argue that the ending of the Sabbath is not a function of the blessing over wine—the day ends when it ends. On the contrary, it is the ending of the Sabbath or the holiday, including that of Passover, which provides the occasion for another blessing over wine. The implication of all this is that the appropriate order for the *havdalah* service is the reverse of the *Kiddush* or sanctification service that takes place at the onset of the occasion.

The Jerusalem Talmud then goes on to state that R. Zeira, a Babylonian sage who emigrated to the Land of Israel and is one of those most frequently cited in both Talmuds, inferred from the arguments presented by both R. Yose and R. Mana that the *havdalah* service at the end of the occasion might be performed without wine, since it obviously is a secondary element of the rite, but that the *kiddush* at the outset of the occasion may be recited only over wine. Indeed, R. Zeira is cited as having stated that the *havdalah* service might even be performed over beer, but that we are required to go from one place to another, if necessary, for the sake of hearing the *Kiddush*, the blessing of sanctification of the occasion, made over wine.[19]

As these several examples indicate quite clearly, the Talmud is indeed an intellectual sea in which one can easily get lost without the assistance of a seasoned navigator. Although complete and partial editions of the Talmud are presently available in English translation, some of which are accompanied by substantial explanatory notes, self-study of its complex arguments remains a formidable challenge for novices. Nevertheless, those willing to make the effort required to enter its waters will discover insights into the intellectual world of rabbinic Judaism that are unavailable to those content never to leave the shore and must rely exclusively on second-hand reports about its currents and depths.

It should be noted that there is a massive body of rabbinic literature related to the Talmud, commentaries and elaborations, that will not be discussed in this book for two reasons: first, because virtually none of this literature has been translated thus making it inaccessible to anyone without the required ability to read and comprehend rabbinic Hebrew and idiom, and second because it presupposes more than a casual acquaintance with the Talmud. In other words, this literature, for the most part, is designed and intended for specialists and those aspiring to become talmudic scholars.

Chapter 5

Midrash Aggadah

As indicated in the preceding chapters, the literature dealing with matters related to *halakhah* was accompanied by a much larger body of material devoted to a range of non-halakhic concerns that defined the cultural milieu that provided the context within which the halakhic corpus evolved. Perhaps first and foremost among such concerns was the need to comprehend the biblical narrative and its implications, theological, cultural, and historical for the people of Israel. Post-exilic Israel was deeply affected by the cultural currents flowing through the ancient Middle East, especially from Zoroastrian Persia and the Hellenism introduced into the region by the Macedonian conquest and its further entrenchment by Roman domination of the Land of Israel, a situation that was further exacerbated by the emergence of Christianity and the challenges it posed to traditional Jewish teachings. As a result, a great volume of material relating to biblical interpretation came into being that not only dealt with the straightforward meaning of the biblical texts but which also sought to draw out more elusive sub-texts from the biblical writings. Following the Muslim conquest, greater Jewish interest began to be shown in the apocalyptic and pseudepigraphic literature of the Second Temple period, which was disregarded by the earlier sages, primarily because of their controversial polemical use by the Christians. As a result, the literature of the period witnessed an upsurge of interest in contentious subjects such as angels and demons, the Garden of Eden, and the throes of perdition.

The literature produced during this long period of history is far-ranging in scope, covering serious analysis and commentary on the biblical texts as well as some controversial forays into diverse esoteric subjects such as mysticism, magic, and astrology, as well as folk medicine. As indicated in the preceding chapter, a good deal of this material is to be found in the Babylonian Talmud alongside profound analyses of halakhic issues, and an even greater amount in a variety of compilations produced primarily in the Land of Israel in addition to a substantial amount of such material to be found in the Jerusalem Talmud. This type of non-halakhic material is broadly categorized as *midrash aggadah*, the freewheeling counterpart to the more structured *midrash halakhah* discussed earlier. It is noteworthy that a not very successful attempt was made to systematize *midrash aggadah* through the articulation of a set of hermeneutic rules of exegesis similar to those of Hillel and R. Ishmael, developed for the *midrash halakhah*. In a work attributed to the sage R. Eliezer b. R. Jose the Galilean, no less than thirty-two rules of exegesis were set forth for aggadic interpretation, but the extent to which this cumbersome mass of rules was applied in practice is unclear. In any case, as one noted scholar observed, "the Haggadic Midrash continued to express the ideas, aspirations, hopes, fears, and collective thoughts of the people of Israel in successive generations. Many of the thoughts in the Haggadic Midrash were due to poetic inspiration, and these were often ahead of their times. In this sense they were prophetic, and in respect of function they continued the prophetic tradition, though formally and chronologically they were the direct descendants of the Scriptures, children of their verses, souls of their soul."[1]

In the pages that follow, some representative examples of *midrash aggadah* will be drawn from a number of the major works that are included under this rubric and will be accompanied by a brief discussion of each that will point out what may not be apparent to a reader unfamiliar with the peculiarities of rabbinic writing.

THE PASSOVER HAGGADAH

Perhaps the most familiar example of *midrash aggadah* is that found in the work known as the Passover Haggadah, the recitation of which constitutes the principal focus of the annual Passover Seder ritual. One of the principal requirements of the Seder is the retelling of the story of the exodus from Egypt, which is what is being commemorated and celebrated. Moreover, in their desire to enhance consideration of the story of the exodus and its critical role in the formation of Judaism, the ancient sages assigned special importance to the elaboration of the story indicating that in this case, contrary to their tradition of stating things concisely, more is better. That is, the more extended the presentation and discussion in commemoration of the exodus, the greater the merit of the participants. Accordingly, the Haggadah, which in its present form reflects the accretions of texts over a very long period, includes a number of texts that seem clearly designed to provoke analysis and discussion. One of these texts is an ancient aggadic *midrash* that elaborates on the following biblical passage relating to the redemptive exodus from Egypt:

> A wandering Aramaean was my father, and he went down into Egypt, and sojourned there, few in number; and he became there a nation, great, mighty, and populous. And the Egyptians dealt ill with us, and afflicted us, and laid upon us hard bondage. And we cried unto the Lord, the God of our fathers, and the Lord heard our voice, and saw our affliction, and our toil, and our oppression. And the Lord brought us forth out of Egypt with a mighty hand, and with an outstretched arm, and with great terribleness, and with signs, and with wonders (Deut. 26:5–8).

A modern authority on the subject has characterized the midrashic exposition of this passage as the oldest in all of rabbinic literature, dating to the latter half of the third century or the first half of the second century BCE. It is suggested that the biblical passage was chosen for purposes of the Seder because it was well known even to those who had limited access to the biblical texts. The cited verses constituted part of the confessional recited each year by pilgrims bringing offerings of the first fruits to the Temple in accordance with the biblical prescription (Deut. 26:1–11).[2] The midrashic exposition of the passage illustrates quite effectively how the sages approached the biblical texts in search of deeper meanings that could only be derived by probing beneath the surface of the simple sense of the texts.[3] As is the case with virtually all of classical rabbinic writing, it is difficult to comprehend what is being said or alluded to in this exposition without significant experience with such texts or without clarifying annotations of the rabbinic assertions. The passage in the Haggadah begins:

> Go forth and learn what Laban the Aramaean sought to do to our patriarch Jacob. For Pharaoh only issued a decree [of death] against the males, whereas Laban sought to uproot the whole, as it is said: *An Aramaean sought to destroy my father. And he [Jacob] went down into Egypt and sojourned there, few in number; and he became there a nation, great, mighty, and populous* (Deut. 26:5).

A cursory glance at any standard translation of the Hebrew Scriptures will reveal that something is amiss here. Instead of the usual rendering of the opening clause of the biblical citation, *Arami oved avi*, as, *A wandering Aramaean was my father*, the aggadist chooses to read the unvoweled Hebrew text as stating, *Arami ibed avi*, "an Aramaean

sought to destroy my father," to make a homiletic point, although it is
not entirely clear what that point is, provoking a debate among commentators over the legitimacy of such a non-Masoretic reading that
has lasted for a millennium until this very day without resolution. Following this introductory statement, the aggadist begins to expound,
through annotation and the introduction of supportive biblical prooftexts, the meaning and significance of each of the clauses of the cited
biblical verse. The purpose of all this seems intended to elaborate on
Israel's experience of persecution in the Egyptian Diaspora and thereby
to emphasize the magnanimity of the divine redemption in which it
culminated, beyond the cursory information provided by the biblical
text, thus illustrating the divine *quid* for which Israel's debt of obedi-
ence to the divine word is its *pro quo*.

> *And he went down into Egypt*—Compelled by the [divine] word.

The aggadist appears to assert that Jacob's descent to Egypt was "compelled by the [divine] word," even though there is nothing in the biblical
narrative to suggest any such thing. Indeed, the statement that Jacob
went down [yarad] into Egypt clearly suggests that he did so on his own
volition, in contrast to the case with Joseph, who *was brought down
[hurad] to Egypt* (Gen. 39:1). However, it may be that the intended reference is not to the word given to Jacob, but rather to Abraham. In this
case, the statement in the Haggadah takes on a new cogency. During
the enactment of the critical covenant God and Abraham, the latter
is told that his descendants will experience subjugation in a foreign
land for four hundred years before they are redeemed and given the
land of Cisjordan as their inheritance (Gen. 15:13–14). Presumably, it
is this divine "word" that is considered by the aggadist as historically
compelling. The story of Joseph and his brothers would thus serve as a
stage setting for the drama that ultimately led to bringing all of Jacob's
descendants into that foreign land, and it is perhaps in this sense that
Jacob's descent into Egypt is considered by the aggadist as having been
"compelled by the [divine] word."

> *And sojourned there*—This teaches that the patriarch Jacob did not go
> down to Egypt to settle, but only to sojourn there. As it is said: *And they
> said unto Pharaoh: To sojourn in the land are we come; for there is no
> pasture for thy servants flocks; for the famine is sore in the land of Canaan.
> Now therefore, we pray thee, let thy servants dwell in the land of Goshen*
> (Gen. 47:4).

The midrashic exposition next makes the important observation that
the descent of Jacob and his family to Egypt did not constitute emigration from their home in Cisjordan. As merely temporary sojourners in

Egypt, they did not forfeit their claims to their patrimony in Cisjordan, to which they always intended to return. The rationale for their sojourn in Egypt is given in the prooftext adduced by the aggadist, which asserts that they were driven to seek temporary refuge in Egypt because of the severity of the famine that ravaged their homeland.

The aggadist then proceeds to expound the meaning and implications of the next clauses in the biblical verse (Deut. 26:5).

> Few in number—As it is said: *Thy fathers went down into Egypt with three score and ten [seventy] persons; and now the Lord thy God hath made thee as the stars of heaven for multitude* (Deut. 10:22).

In the stable agricultural environment of Egypt, the Israelites were able to raise large families. As a result, although they were merely a handful when they first arrived, by the time they left two centuries later that small group had been transformed into a substantial population. In support of this proposition, the aggadist presents a biblical prooftext that portrays the dramatic growth in numbers experienced by Israel in Egypt.

> And he became there a nation—This teaches that Israel was distinguishable there.

The children of Israel not only increased their numbers dramatically; they also began to take on the characteristics of a nation. The aggadist suggests that the biblical clause about Israel's becoming a nation "teaches that Israel was distinguishable there." That is, the culture of the Israelites, as a collectivity, differed markedly from that of the host nation, and was easily discernible. This, in effect, set the Israelites apart, further reinforcing their distinctiveness.

> Great, mighty—As it is said: *And the children of Israel were fruitful, and increased abundantly, and multiplied, and waxed exceeding mighty; and the land was filled with them* (Ex. 1:7).

The explication of the biblical terms *great* and *mighty* in the exposition appears, in essence, to be nothing more than a repetition of the interpretation given earlier for the phrase *few in number*. Here, however, an alternate prooftext is provided that is of special relevance because it too uses the word *atzum* (*mighty*) to describe the phenomenal population growth of the Israelites in Egypt.

> And populous—As it is said: *I cause thee to increase, even as the growth of the field. And thou didst increase and grow up, and thou camest to excellent beauty: thy breasts were fashioned, and thy hair was grown; yet thou wast naked and bare* (Ezek. 16:7).

The aggadist expounds the biblical term *populous* by providing another prooftext that employs the word. This time, the choice fell on a prophetic passage that also describes the rapid growth in population of the Israelites. *I cause thee to increase, even as the growth of the field.* This verse is chosen because the Hebrew term for "populous" (*rav*) is closely related, etymologically and phonetically, to the word used by the prophet for "increase" (*revavah*). The aggadist thus employs the technique of play on words to expound the text.

However, by citing the complete passage from Ezekiel, rather than just the portion relevant to the word play, a new thought that bears on the Exodus and its consequences is introduced. Employing the image of Israel as a young maiden growing to maturity, the prophet laments, *yet you were naked and bare.* This passage has been understood as suggesting that even though Israel blossomed and grew physically in Egypt, it remained spiritually and morally immature prior to the exodus, which served as a turning point in the evolution of the nation.

Having completed the explication of the first biblical verse in the exposition of the story of the redemption, as required at the Passover Seder in accordance with the rule set down in the *Mishnah*, the aggadist proceeds to expound the meaning and implications of the second verse:

> And the Egyptians dealt ill with us, and afflicted us, and laid upon us hard bondage (Deut. 26:6).

> And the Egyptians dealt ill with us—As it is said: Come, let us deal wisely with them, lest they multiply, and it come to pass, that, when there befalleth us any war, they also join themselves unto our enemies, and fight against us, and get them up out of the land (Ex. 1:10).

The aggadist takes the statement, *And the Egyptians dealt ill with us*, as referring to the policy adopted by the Egyptian government of progressively diminishing the civic status of the Israelites to that of a persecuted underclass. As evidence of this, it cites the biblical passage (Ex. 1:10), which portrays a new pharaoh as voicing doubts about the prospective loyalty of the Israelite residents in Egypt during anticipated times of crisis.

> And afflicted us—As it is said: Therefore did they set over them taskmasters to afflict them with their burdens. And they built for Pharaoh store-cities, Pithom and Raamses (Ex. 1:11).

As part of its campaign of discrimination against the Israelites, the Egyptian authorities imposed on them the responsibility of carrying out a massive public works program under Egyptian supervision. This is depicted in the prooftext, which is cited as evidence of the *affliction* suffered by the Israelites in Egypt. Presumably, the burden of the public works program would progressively impoverish the Israelite community, which would be increasingly restricted in its ability to maintain a successful agricultural and pastoral economy because of the drain on its human resources.

> *And laid upon us hard bondage*—As it is said: *And the Egyptians made the children of Israel to serve with rigor* (Ex. 1:13).

As evidence of the *hard bondage* imposed upon the Israelites in Egypt, the aggadist invokes the prooftext that asserts the Israelites were forced to serve the Egyptians *with rigor* (*befarekh*). Having completed the explication of the second biblical verse in the exposition of the story of the redemption, the aggadist proceeds to expound the meaning and implications of the third verse:

> *And we cried unto the Lord, the God of our fathers, and the Lord heard our voice, and saw our affliction, and our toil, and our oppression* (Deut. 26:7).
>
> *And we cried unto the Lord, the God of our fathers*—As it is said: *And it came to pass in the course of those many days that the king of Egypt died; and the children of Israel sighed by reason of the bondage, and they cried, and their cry came up unto God by reason of the bondage* (Ex. 2:23).

Once again, evidence is provided from another biblical prooftext involving the cry of the people to heaven for help to assist in explicating the text of Deuteronomy. The passage chosen is one that describes the despair of the Israelites as they await the installation of a new Egyptian regime following the death of the reigning pharaoh. Presumably, they were concerned that the new pharaoh was unlikely to be more humane than his predecessor, causing them to cry out to their God for help at this critical juncture.

> *And the Lord heard our voice*—As it is said: *And God heard their groaning, and God remembered His covenant with Abraham, with Isaac, and with Jacob* (Ex. 2:24).

The people are reassured of God's continuing response to the outcry of the children of Israel. Once again, the aggadist presents a parallel biblical prooftext that deals with God's being made aware of the suffering of the children of Israel. However, this prooftext goes beyond merely being aware of the anguish and suffering of the Israelites; it also invokes the divine commitment to their redemption as evidenced by its reference to the covenant made with the patriarchs, the time for the fulfillment of which was now at hand.

> *And saw our affliction*—This refers to setting aside social norms. As it is said: *And God saw the children of Israel, and God took cognizance of them* (Ex. 2:25).

In characterizing the *affliction* experienced by the Israelites, the aggadist draws on a parallel biblical verse, which also employs the word *saw*. However, the aggadist also makes a prefatory statement that the clause being explicated "refers to setting aside social norms," a euphemism that is commonly understood as referring to the disruption of normal marital relations. This notion is made more explicit in the halakhic midrash, *Sifre on Deuteronomy*, where a connection is made between the phrase, *and saw our affliction*, and the text that describes the pharaoh's instructions to the midwives concerning how they were to deal with the infants born to the Israelites.[4] They were told *ye shall look upon the birthstool* (Ex. 1:16), to determine the sex of the newborn. In other words, the *affliction* of the Israelites was the fear of having male children, which were to be disposed of immediately. This fear led them to desist from connubial relations.

The idea of *affliction* connoting a disruption of the normal order of marital relations is quite evident in the biblical text that deals with the punishment meted out in the case of an improper relationship with a betrothed woman. In such a case, the male is punished *because he hath humbled his neighbor's wife* (Deut. 22:24). The Hebrew word translated as *humbled* is from the same root as the word used for *affliction*. Thus, the Talmud also interprets the phrase, *and saw our affliction*, as "the enforced abstinence from marital intercourse," using the same Hebrew euphemism as the aggadist.[5]

> *And our toil*—This refers to the sons. As it is said: [*And Pharaoh charged all his people, saying:*] *Every son that is born ye shall cast into the river, and every daughter ye shall save alive* (Ex. 3:9).

In explicating the meaning of the phrase *our toil* (*amalenu*) in the biblical text, the aggadist suggests that the phrase *our toil* refers to the drowning of all newborn males, in accordance with Pharaoh's instructions to the midwives (Ex. 1:22). In this case, the aggadist deviates from his previous methodology and employs a prooftext that does not have any linguistic elements in common with the phrase he is explicating. If there is something that might tie the phrase being parsed and the prooftext together, what that might be remains a mystery. That is, unless one assumes that "toil" is not the appropriate translation of the Hebrew word.

In that case, the aggadist would be employing verbal sleight of hand to confuse matters and provoke discussion. The biblical word under consideration is normally understood to mean "toil" or "labor," and it seems clear that it is used in the source text of Deut. 26:7 in this sense. However, the same Hebrew word may also be used to convey the idea of "misery" or "suffering." If the aggadist chooses to understand the word in this latter sense, then the substantive if not the linguistic connection to the prooftext becomes evident. The statement in the Haggadah would then be translated as, *"And our misery*—This refers to the [newborn] sons. As it is said: *Every son that is born ye shall cast into the river, and every daughter ye shall save alive."* The prospective murder of the newborn males would certainly have been a basis for the misery of the Israelites. Moreover, that misery would have been compounded by the realization that their newborn females will be unable to find mates among their own people, ultimately leading to the effective annihilation of the children of Israel as a distinct people.

> *And our oppression*—This refers to duress. As it is said: *Moreover I have seen the oppression wherewith the Egyptians oppress them* (Ex. 3:9).

In explicating the final clause of the verse, *and our oppression*, the aggadist turns to a straightforward exposition and explains it by reference to a parallel prooftext, dealing with the situation of the Israelites in Egypt, which employs the term for "oppression" (*lahatz*) twice in the same sentence.

Having expounded several biblical verses that deal with the circumstances leading to the necessity of redemption and the Exodus, the aggadist now turns to an exposition of a text that deals with the divine intervention that brought the latter about.

> *And the Lord brought us forth out of Egypt with a mighty hand, and with an outstretched arm, and with great terribleness, and with signs, and with wonders* (Deut. 26:8).
>
> *And the Lord brought us forth out of Egypt*—Not by means of a messenger, and not by means of a seraph, and not by means of an agent, but by the Holy One, blessed is He, in his glory and by Himself. As it is said: *For I will go through the land of Egypt in that night, and will smite all the first-born in the land of Egypt, both man and beast; and against all the gods of Egypt I will execute judgments: I am the Lord* (Ex. 12:12).

The aggadist focuses his exposition on the immediate divine role in the exodus, and points out that the biblical text states explicitly that it was the Lord Himself who intervened to release Israel from its captivity in Egypt. Moreover, he emphasizes that the divine intervention was personal and direct, and "not by means of a messenger, not by means of a seraph, and not by means of an agent." As evidence for this contention, the aggadist introduces a prooftext that explicitly specifies the direct involvement of God in the slaying of the first-born of Egypt. *For I will go through the land of Egypt in that night, and will smite all the first-born in the land of Egypt . . . and against all the gods of Egypt I will execute judgments: I am the Lord* (Ex. 12:12). Perhaps because of the importance of the prooftext for the Passover story, the aggadist deviates from his routine and provides a separate exposition of the prooftext.

> *For I will go through the land of Egypt in that night*—I and not a messenger—*and will smite all the first-born in the land of Egypt*—I and not a seraph—*and against all the gods of Egypt I will execute judgments*—I and not the agent—*I am the Lord*—I am He and no other.

In expounding the significance of this prooftext, the aggadist repeatedly emphasizes the use of the first person singular in the biblical text, which demonstrates the divine intent to take the necessary actions without the use of intermediaries. Presumably, by the reference to "the agent" (ha'shaliah), the aggadist is referring to Moses, whose role in the Exodus is thereby clearly subordinated to that of the direct divine intervention.

The exposition of the prooftext concludes with the statement, "*I am the Lord*—I am He and no other." That is, when God uses the personal pronoun, I, it means that God alone is involved. Indeed, in the view of the sages, it would constitute a sacrilege of the first order to consider the actions of any created thing, including man, in association with the divine. They taught, "Whosoever associates the name of God with something else is uprooted from the world."[6]

Following this brief digression, the aggadist returns to the exposition of the text of Deut. 26:8.

> *With a mighty hand*—This refers to the murrain. As it is said: *Behold, the hand of the Lord is upon thy cattle which are in the field, upon the horses, upon the asses, upon the camels, upon the herds, and upon the flocks; there shall be a very grievous murrain* (Ex. 9:3).

In explicating the meaning of with a mighty hand, the aggadist sought an appropriate biblical prooftext that focused on the use of the word hand. He chose the cited passage, which refers to the fifth of the ten plagues, the murrain that afflicted the cattle and other livestock of Egypt.

> *And with an outstretched arm*—This refers to the sword. As it is said: *A drawn sword in his hand stretched out over Jerusalem* (I Chron. 21:16).

In explicating the phrase, *with an outstretched arm*, the aggadist sought a prooftext containing the word "outstretched," and settled on the indicated verse, only part of which is cited. The full text reads: *And David lifted up his eyes, and saw the angel of the Lord standing between the earth and the heaven, having a drawn sword in his hand stretched out over Jerusalem* (I Chron. 21:16). On the basis of the parallelism, the aggadist concluded that the phrase, *with an outstretched arm*, refers to the use of a sword, given that that is what the prooftext is talking about.

> *And with great terribleness*—This refers to the revelation of the Divine Presence. As it is said: *Or hath God assayed to go and take Him a nation from the midst of another nation, by trials, by signs, and by wonders, and by war, and by a mighty hand, and by an outstretched arm, and by great terrors, according to all that the Lord your God did for you in Egypt before thine eyes* (Deut. 4:34).

In explicating the clause, *and with great terribleness [terror]*, the aggadist sought a prooftext that used the same wording. He thus presents a parallel passage that deals directly with the divine role in the exodus, in which God caused *great terrors*. The aggadist understands this as indicating the "revelation of the Divine Presence" in Israel's history. Nonetheless, the equation of *great terribleness* and "revelation of the Divine Presence" seems somewhat strained. To deal with this problem, many commentators over the centuries have concluded that the aggadist employed an alternate reading of the biblical text that yielded the equation he articulates. Thus, rather than *uvemorah gadol* or *great terribleness*, as the Masoretic text of the Bible has it, he read the unvoweled text as *uvemareh gadol* or "great vision," yielding "revelation of the Divine Presence."[7]

> *And with signs*—This refers to the rod. As it is said: *And thou shalt take in thy hand this rod, wherewith thou shalt do the signs* (Ex. 4:17).

In keeping with his theme, the aggadist suggests that the clause, *and with signs*, refers to those supra-natural acts performed by Moses and Aaron by use of the *rod*. The prooftext presented makes it clear that the *rod* serves as a divine instrument. In other words, the aggadist is emphasizing that even where Moses was directly involved in the events of the exodus, he was always acting in the capacity of an agent or instrument through which the divine will was made manifest.

> *And with wonders*—This refers to the blood. As it is said: *And I will show wonders in the heavens and in the earth, blood, and fire, and pillars of smoke* (Joel 3:3).

The aggadist connects the clause, *and with wonders*, with the plague of *blood* that afflicted Egypt's water supply (Ex. 7:19). A suitable prooftext is produced from the prophet Joel. However, an exploration of the context in which this prophetic statement is made will indicate that it bears no connection whatever to the story of the Exodus. Joel is speaking of the apocalyptic portents that will precede the coming day of the judgment of mankind. Nonetheless, the aggadist chooses to link it with the Exodus, possibly suggesting that there is a symbolic connection between the two events, the beginning of Israel's history in the Exodus and the end of history as such in the coming messianic age.

COMPILATIONS OF *MIDRASH AGGADAH*

Aside from the large volume of aggadic material present in the Talmuds, there are a substantial number of separate collections of *midrash aggadah* that have been published over the centuries since talmudic times. In general, these compilations reflect two basic types of aggadic *midrash*—exegetic and homiletic. Compilations of exegetic *midrash aggadah* tend to deal with a complete book of the *TaNaKH*, providing commentary on every chapter, every verse, and sometimes every word of the text. Works of homiletic *midrash aggadah* tend to be of two types: (a) a *midrash* to a book of the Torah in which only the first verse (or verses) of the weekly portion read in the synagogue is expounded; (b) a *midrash* based only on the biblical and prophetic readings for special Sabbaths and Festivals in which only the first verses are expounded. Both types of homiletic *midrash aggadah* are also distinguished from the exegetic by each chapter or section focusing on a single topic.

The following three examples are drawn from the voluminous anthology known as *Midrash Rabbah* (The Great *Midrash*), which includes collections of midrashic commentary on each of the five books of the Torah and the five scrolls, Song of Songs, Ruth, Lamentations, Ecclesiastes, and Esther. Of these, the collection on the book of Genesis is held to be the oldest; it is generally considered as having been finalized for the most part in the form in which we have it shortly after the redaction of the Jerusalem Talmud. Similarly, the work on Lamentations, cited below, is also held to have originated in the fourth century. The other works in the multi-volume anthology were completed in the form they now appear over a period of centuries, the volume on the book of Numbers, also cited below, perhaps first being finalized as late as the twelfth century. The extent to which the statements and perspectives attributed in these works to the sages of a period long before the compilations were completed are accurate reflections of the teachings of those so named is an issue about which there is little consensus. There is no question, however, that the perspectives cited in these works do clearly fit within the framework of classical Judaic thought and are therefore to be considered valid representations of the views of the ancient sages.

MIDRASH RABBAH: GENESIS

A classic example of exegetic *midrash aggadah* is the massive compilation of *midrash* on the book of Genesis known as *Bereshit Rabbah* or *Midrash Rabbah: Genesis*. The following excerpt is typical of the style of this genre. Commenting on the very first sentence in Scripture, *In the beginning God created the heaven and the earth*, the work records a controversy between the schools of Shammai and Hillel regarding the order in which the creation took place:[8]

> The Academy of Shammai maintain that the heaven was created first and the earth afterward, while the Academy of Hillel maintain that the earth was created first and the heaven afterward. Each provides a rationale for their argument. In the view of the Academy of Shammai . . . this is comparable to the case of a king who first made his throne and then his footstool, for it is written, *The heaven is My throne, and the earth is My footstool* (Isa. 46:1). In the view of the Academy of Hillel this is comparable to a king who builds a palace; after building the lower portion he builds the upper, for it is written, *In the day that the Lord God made earth and heaven* (Gen. 2:4).

The controversy between the two schools of thought over the order of creation is not an argument over the simple meaning of the biblical text, a seemingly inconsequential point. However, the disagreement may also be understood as one that could have profound theological and philosophical implications. By according priority in the divine scheme of creation to heaven, the Academy of Shammai may be implicitly suggesting that the primary concern of the Torah is with bringing man closer to heaven, in effect denigrating its concern with the world of man. The Academy of Hillel, by according priority to the earth in the order of creation may be understood as implicitly suggesting that the primary concern of the Torah is in fact with the world of man and bringing heaven closer to man, that is, helping man to lead a heaven-inspired existence.

Alternatively, it has been suggested that the dispute is actually over the question of whether an ideal creation preceded the physical, a doctrine popular in Hellenistic-Jewish circles of the time. The import of this doctrine is that it is predicated on the notion of there having been an intermediate step between the divine will and the bringing of the world into existence, a notion that fostered belief in the existence of intermediary beings between God and man. The Academy of Shammai may thus be understood as maintaining that heaven, being created first, served as the ideal plan for the creation of the earth, heaven thus serving as an intermediary between God and the world. The Academy of Hillel, by insisting that the earth was created first, effectively rejects the idea of there being any intermediary between the world and its creator, that is, between man and God.[9]

Although the academies of Hillel and Shammai did not survive the destruction of the Temple and the Judean state in the first century, their controversy over this issue continued to resonate among the sages for at least another century. However, the weight of rabbinic opinion clearly began to shift in favor of the position of the Academy of Hillel, if for no other reason than the fact that it was the descendants of Hillel who constituted the rabbinic dynasty that served as religious leaders of the community in the Land of Israel for nearly two centuries. The midrashic pericope under consideration thus continues with further arguments in support of the opinion of the Academy of Hillel.

> R. Judah bar Ilai said: Even Scripture supports the Academy of Hillel, viz. *Of old Thou didst lay the foundations of the earth*, which is followed by, *And the heavens are the work of Thy hands* (Ps. 102:26). R. Hanin said: From the very text (Gen. 1:1), which [appears to] support the Academy of Shammai, the Academy of Hillel refute them, viz. *And the earth was* [the biblical term *hayyetah* translated as *was* being read as the pluperfect *had been*] (Gen. 2:1), meaning that it had already existed [prior to heaven].

Nonetheless, there were also sages who were uncomfortable with the idea of dismissing the opinion of the earlier members of the Academy of Shammai and sought to find a compromise position between the two schools. Accordingly, the midrash records the opinions of two such sages:

> R. Johanan, citing the sages, said: As regards creation, heaven was first; as regards completion, earth was first. R. Tanhuma said: I will posit the grounds [for this opinion]: as regards creation heaven was first, as it is written, *In the beginning God created the heaven*; whereas in respect of the completion earth took precedence, for it is written, *In the day that the Lord God made earth and heaven* (Gen. 2:4)

These sages argued that the advocates of both academies were correct in their views but, in effect, were speaking about different stages in the overall creation process, even though it would seem that the actual positions taken by the two schools on the question, as cited above, hardly seem to lend any support to this attempt at conciliation. A more potent and ultimately more successful attempt to put an end to the controversy once and for all argued that the entire issue was pointless and without merit.

> R. Simeon b. Yohai observed: I am amazed that the fathers of the world [the sages] engage in controversy over the order of creation. I say that both were created [simultaneously] like a pot and its lid, as it is written, *When I call unto them* [heaven and earth], *they stand up together* (Isa. 48:13). R. Eleazar b. R. Simeon commented: If my father's view is correct, why is the earth sometimes given precedence over the heaven, and sometimes heaven over earth? This is only to teach that they are equal to each other.

There is also more than meets the eye in the assertion of R. Simeon and the amplification of his opinion given by his son, who not only seems to dismiss the disagreement of the two academies out of hand but at the same time also makes an important theological statement. In essence, what these sages are saying is that there is no order of precedence between heaven and earth and to choose one over the other is to distort the divine intent. By implication, then, the sages may be understood as arguing that for as long as one is alive, one must find the appropriate balance between the spiritual and the material since both are divine creations.

MIDRASH RABBAH: NUMBERS

Although this work is included in the collection known as *Midrash Rabbah*, it is of a very different nature than *Midrash Rabbah: Genesis* discussed above. Whereas the latter is an example of exegetic midrash, this work is an example of homiletic midrash, in which the aggadist essentially employs a biblical verse as a hook upon which to hang the homily he wishes to convey to anyone prepared to listen. The work begins with a series of homilies based on the first verse of the biblical book, *And the Lord spoke unto Moses in the wilderness of Sinai* (Num. 1:1). The following is the seventh homily in the collection, which the aggadist begins with a question about the biblical text.

> *Why in the wilderness of Sinai?* Our sages have inferred from this that the Torah was given to the accompaniment of three things, fire, water, and wilderness. "Fire"; from where is this derived? From the text, *Now Mount Sinai was altogether on smoke, because the Lord descended upon it in fire* (Ex. 19:18). And "water"; from where is this derived? For it is said: *The heavens also dropped, yea the clouds dropped water* (Judg. 5:4). And "wilderness"; from where is it derived? From the text, *And the Lord spoke unto Moses in the wilderness of Sinai.* Why was the Torah given

with the accompaniment of these three things? To indicate that just as these are freely available to all humankind, so too are the words of the Torah freely available; as it is said: *Ho, every one that thirsteth, come ye for water* (Isa. 55:1).[10]

The point of the homily, of course, is that the essential guidance of the Torah for man and society is available to anyone who wishes to follow the divinely prescribed path to the good life. Israel's role in this regard is not only to live in accordance with it but also to serve as its trustee for all humankind. The prooftext for this is the statement from Isaiah, in which all who thirst are invited to come for water, the latter term serving as a metaphor for the Torah.

MIDRASH RABBAH: LAMENTATIONS

Some midrashic works are introduced with one or more proems or preambles designed to catch and stimulate the attention of their intended audiences. Typical of such a device is one of the numerous proems that take up some sixty pages in English translation that are attached to *Ekhah Rabbah* or *Midrash Rabbah: Lamentations*, a collection of midrashic expositions of the biblical book traditionally attributed to Jeremiah that bemoans the destruction of Jerusalem and the Temple. Setting the stage for the midrashic consideration of the biblical book,

> R. Abba b. Kahana opened his discourse with the text, *Who is the wise man, that he may understand this?* (Jer. 9:11). R. Simeon b. Yohai taught: If you behold cities uprooted from their site in the land of Israel, know that the inhabitants failed to pay the fees of the instructors in Bible and Mishnah; as it is said, *Wherefore is the land perished? . . . And the Lord saith: because they have forsaken My law* (Jer. 9:11–12).[11]

In this brief excerpt from a much longer proem, the sage sets forth a restatement of the traditional prophetic philosophy of history, namely, that when Israel is faithful to the Torah, the divine hand will shield them from the vicissitudes of politics and history. Accordingly, the very ruins of cities in the land of Israel serve as testimony to the neglect of Torah. Having thus set the stage, the Midrash proceeds to discuss the book of Lamentations, *Ekhah*, which derives its Hebrew name from the first word of the biblical text.

> *How (Ekhah) doth the city sit solitary* (Lam. 1:1). Three uttered prophecies using the word *ekhah*, viz. Moses, Isaiah, and Jeremiah. Moses said: *How can I myself alone bear your cumbrance* (Deut. 1:12). Isaiah said: *How is the faithful city become a harlot* (Isa. 1:21). Jeremiah said: *How doth the city sit solitary*. R. Levi said: It may be likened to a matron who

had three groomsmen: one beheld her in her happiness, a second beheld her in her infidelity, and the third beheld her in her disgrace. Similarly, Moses beheld Israel in their glory and happiness and exclaimed: *How can I myself alone bear your cumbrance*. Isaiah beheld them in their infidelity and exclaimed: *How is the faithful city become a harlot*. Jeremiah beheld them in their disgrace and exclaimed: *How doth the city sit solitary*.[12]

In this homily the aggadist describes the fate of Jerusalem lamented by the biblical writer as the result of a continuous process of regression from the time of Moses, when the disharmony in the society made the burden of assuring justice too onerous for Moses to deal with alone, to that of Jeremiah, when the Israelite state and its institutions were destroyed unnecessarily because of the gross arrogance and moral turpitude of its leaders. The implication of all this being that the final outcome was avoidable, if only Israel had been more steadfast in trust, faith, and moral integrity. The point, of course, is that it is not sufficient to bemoan the past; true contrition requires that the errors of the past be corrected if there is to be hope for a better future.

MIDRASH TANHUMA

Another popular compilation of homiletic *midrash* on the entire Pentateuch is known as *Midrash Tanhuma*, incorporating the name of Tanhuma bar Abba, a prolific aggadist of the fourth century who is cited frequently in the book. Although some of the material in the work, which has been published in two versions, is undoubtedly of earlier origin, the book itself was probably compiled no earlier than the late eighth or early ninth century, as it contains material that clearly can be assigned to that period. In the following sample passage, an anonymous aggadist attempts to deal with the popular question as to why the story of the creation of the world begins with the second letter of the Hebrew alphabet rather than the first, which would seem more appropriate to the story of a beginning.

Why did He commence the account of the creation of the universe with the letter *bet* rather than with the letter *alef*, which is the first letter of the alphabet? He did so because the *alef* is the first letter of the word arur ("cursed"), while the *bet* is the first letter of the word *barukh* ("blessed"). The Holy One, blessed be He, said: "I will begin the account of the creation of the universe with the letter that symbolizes a blessing." But even though the account of that which was created begins with a letter symbolizing blessedness, mankind angers its Creator. How much angrier would mankind have made Him if the creation narrative had commenced with the letter that symbolizes a curse.[13]

In this exposition, the aggadist deftly achieves two purposes, the first being an attempt at a plausible explanation of what had long been considered an anomaly in the biblical text, the second registering a homiletic thrust against the ingratitude of man toward God for the blessings one enjoys in life, perhaps beginning with life itself.

MIDRASH ON PROVERBS

This compilation, which was put in its final form sometime between the ninth and eleventh centuries, is an especially interesting work that combines exegetic and homiletic expositions of the wide variety of issues raised by the biblical book to which it is devoted. Among these is a brief discussion that reflects the deeply nationalistic spirit of many of the sages in the wake of the destruction of the state in the first century and the disastrous consequences of the Bar-Kokhba revolt against Roman rule in the first third of the second century. At that point, with a shrinking Jewish population in the Land of Israel and an increasing one in the lands of the Diaspora, especially Mesopotamia, where the academies of rabbinic learning were flourishing, some of the Palestinian sages expressed their concern about the apparent lessening of the importance of the biblical homeland in indirect ways that clearly challenged the ultimate significance of the growing Diaspora communities. The following passage from the *Midrash on Proverbs* deals with this issue, hinging its argument on an interpretation of the biblical adage, *Better a dry crust with peace, than a house full of feasting with strife* (Prov. 17:1).[14]

> R. Johanan said: *Better a dry crust with peace*—this refers to the Land of Israel, for even if one eats but bread and salt but is resident there, he is assured of life in the world to come; *than a house full of feasting with strife*—this refers to the other lands, which are full of violence and robbery.

The proposition offered by R. Johanan is extraordinary in that it asserts that, notwithstanding its pollution over much of its history by corrupt rulers both domestic and foreign, the land itself has redemptive power, and is able to assure its residents of a place in the world to come. The implication, of course, is that even under adverse conditions this alone makes living in the Land of Israel of greater ultimate value than a materially more satisfactory life in the world beyond its borders, which is also full of violence and robbery but without redemptive value. In another citation from the same sage, corroborated by others as well, the redemptive quality of the land is further elaborated.

> R. Johanan said: Anyone who walks four cubits in the Land of Israel is assured of life in the world to come. R. Levi said: Anyone who lives in the Land of Israel even for a single hour and dies there is assured of life

in the world to come. What is the prooftext for this assertion? *And doth make expiation for the land of His people* (Deut. 32:43). R. Nehemiah said [with regard to this text]: The Land of Israel atones for the sins of its dead.

With regard to R. Johanan's assertion that "anyone who walks four cubits in the Land of Israel is assured of life in the world to come," it needs to be pointed out that the phrase "walks four cubits" has special meaning in rabbinic law, and its use here should be understood in that context. Four cubits, or six feet, represents the outer limit of private space in the public domain. The notion of walking four cubits has particular relevance with regard to the laws of the Sabbath, when one is forbidden to carry or transport objects from private space into the public domain. In other words, one might carry an object out of one's house for a distance up to four cubits without violating the Sabbath in public, which is considered a very serious transgression. R. Johanan appears to be saying here that a person who walks four cubits and enters into the public and thereby desecrates the Sabbath in public, if this desecration takes place in the Land of Israel, that desecrator will nonetheless be assured a place in the world to come because of the redemptive value of the land itself, whereas such automatic expiation would not take place outside the land.

R. Levi takes the point a stage farther by addressing the question of whether there are particular residence requirements before the redemptive quality of the land takes effect. He asserts that a single hour of residence in the land prior to death is sufficient to bring one within its redemptive embrace, and provides a biblical prooftext in support of the proposition, which R. Nehemiah clearly interprets as affirming that the land itself atones for the sins of those who are interred there. These assertions leave open the troubling question of what happens to those Jews who continue to live in the Diaspora, where the land has no redemptive qualities or value.

> R. Zebida asked: What would you do with all of the righteous people who died outside of the Land of Israel? Therefore one must say that the Land of Israel atones for its dead, and with regard to the righteous outside the land, the Holy One, blessed is He, will command the ministering angels to bring the righteous who died abroad through tunnels to the Land of Israel, where atonement will be made for them, as it is said, "And I will purify them upon their land."

R. Zebida, as a Mesopotamian sage, is particularly troubled by these assertions since he and his colleagues did not live in the Land of Israel and relocating for the sole purpose of dying there was impracticable for most. Moreover, he also appears to have been a disciple of R. Huna, the religious leader of Mesopotamian Jewry at the time of the completion of the *Mishnah*, the Mesopotamian counterpart of R. Judah haNasi. R. Huna died in Mesopotamia but was buried in the Land of Israel, reportedly the first sage of the Diaspora to be so interred, and would therefore have satisfied R. Nehemiah's stipulation that "the Land of Israel atones for the sins of its dead." However, R. Zebida could not accept the proposition that there was no future for the righteous of the Diaspora unless they arranged to die or at least to be buried in the Land of Israel, and he therefore proposed an incredible solution to the dilemma, presumably intended as a rebuff to the position articulated by R. Johanan. That suggesting such a fantastic solution was deemed necessary, even though it may have been done tongue-in-cheek, makes it clear that among the Mesopotamian sages, the religious-nationalist teaching of R. Johanan struck a raw nerve. The presentation of the issue addressed in this passage is by no means unique; it is also dealt with in numerous other places in the Talmud and the midrashic literature, where it is elaborated on from a number of perspectives, all focusing on the question of the centrality of the Land of Israel in Judaic thought and tradition.

The notion of bones rattling through tunnels from the Diaspora to the Land of Israel that was elaborated on and espoused by those Mesopotamian sages seeking to justify their continued living in the Diaspora on religious grounds, subsequently found a good deal of resonance among many simple people of faith during the Middle Ages and later, even though it became a common practice that persists to this very day for many who could manage it to have their bodies transported to the Land of Israel for burial.[15] It is also noteworthy that the prooftext ostensibly adduced by R. Zebida does not in fact exist in Scripture and may be a scribal error. Although scholars have offered a number of suggestions as to what actual biblical verse the sage intended to refer, none is compelling.

In addition to the compilations discussed above, there is also a genre in the *midrash aggadah* in which an entire work is attributed to a single author or editor, sometimes a sage of a much earlier period and in one case even an ancient prophet. As a rule, the actual authors or redactors of these works as well as their time of composition have remained contentious and subjects of lively scholarly debate. What is clear is that these works tend to grapple with a large number of concerns about belief, faith, and morals, albeit expressed in terms of scriptural commentary and interpretation.

TANNA DEBE ELIYAHU

This work, the core of which is attributed by some to the prophet Elijah, has been dated by various scholars to a time between the third and tenth centuries. It is a large work that is organized topically, in no obvious order, around issues of significant interest and concern. The passage below comes from a chapter devoted to the question of why God tolerates evil in His world.

> Blessed is the "Place" [i.e., God], blessed be He, who knows at the beginning what will be at the end, and can tell from the outset what the outcome will be before anything is done, who knows what was done and what will be done. Nonetheless, He chooses to perceive the good and chooses not to perceive the evil, and is thus rich and content with his portion.

In these few words, the author of the paragraph sets forth, explicitly and implicitly, several important assertions. One is that God is omniscient, all knowing, and able to perceive the entirety of an event from outset to outcome before a first step is taken, a notion that would place divine "knowing" outside the dimension of time. That is, for this to be reasonable or even possible from a human perspective, God would have to be able to see the continuum of past, present, and future simultaneously, which is conceivable only if time does not exist for God. At the same time, the aggadist implicitly asserts that man is free to make moral choices about his actions, something that is necessary if some are to be seen as good and others as evil. The clear implication of all this is that divine omniscience is somehow not determinative, God knowing what a person will do does not require that he in fact does it, a paradox that sages and philosophers throughout the centuries will expend much ink in trying to rationalize, but which is nonetheless a core belief in Judaism. Finally, the aggadist suggests that the answer to the question of why God tolerates evil in the world is that God chooses to see the good in the world and to be content with that, and by so doing be as one who is rich, in accordance with the adage of the early sage Ben Zoma, "Who is rich, one who is content with his portion."[16] However, this still leaves the question of why God chooses not to perceive the evil that men do, which the aggadist seeks to explain in the following paragraph.

> In His wisdom and with His understanding God created the world and prepared it [for man]. Afterward, He created Adam in it and caused him to lie prone before Him. And He scrutinized [what would come of him] throughout all the generations and foresaw that his descendents would provoke His anger. He said: If I hold mankind to account for its misdeeds the world will not endure. It is therefore incumbent upon Me to pass over such misdeeds. And, indeed, this is what He did. And from where may you know for yourself that this is the case? When Israel was in the wilderness, they befouled themselves with their misdeeds, but God passed over what they had done, as it is said: *The Lord passed by [va-ya'avor] before him* (Ex. 34:6). Do not read *va-ya'avor* [passed], but *va-ya'avir* [made pass]; this teaches that He made pass all their evil from before Him. Know that this was so.[17]

The aggadist's answer is that man is presumed to be innately endowed with free will, and must therefore be given the opportunity to exercise it without constraint, ultimately to be held accountable for his actions. However, the volume of his misdeeds was so great that if he were to have been held to strict account for them from the outset, mankind would not have been able to endure. Accordingly, God found it expedient, for the sake of His creation, to allow man the leeway to continue to err if he so chose, the accounting for his misdeeds presumably to take place beyond the arena of history. This, of course, touches on one of the most difficult issues in Jewish theology, the vindication of divine justice with regard to man.

PESIKTA DERAB KAHANA

This is a compilation of discourses, homilies, and interpretive comments formulated over a period of more than four centuries that were inspired by the readings from the Torah during the synagogue service on special Sabbaths, the festivals, and other special days. The work is ascribed to R. Kahana, who is assumed to have completed it sometime during the fifth century, and is organized in discrete sections that follow the order of the special readings assigned for the entire year. Each such section is designated as a *piska*, the Aramaic term *pesikta* in the title of the work being a cognate form of the word, meaning section or share. The following selection from the work is inspired by the biblical reading assigned to the festival of *Shavuot* or Pentecost, which commemorates the revelation of the Torah on Mount Sinai.

The first discourse in the *piska* begins with a discussion by the late-third- or early-fourth-century sage R. Judah bar Simon of the consideration that every society must have some rules of conduct in order to assure security and stability. Israel received its guidance in this regard with the giving of the Torah, but what of primeval man? Did not the earliest societies have such basic rules, and if they did, from where did such rules originate? The sages maintained that God in fact issued such basic rules for all mankind, six to Adam at the outset of creation and a seventh to Noah after the Deluge and the effective rebirth of human society. These rules have been known through history as the Noahide Laws. However, the following passage only mentions but does not elaborate on the seventh of these rules; its primary focus being on the six rules commanded to Adam. The brief discourse on this point attempts to demonstrate that all six are intimated in the biblical verse containing the introduction to God's command to Adam regarding how he was to conduct himself in the Garden of Eden.

> Adam was given six commands: to refrain from idolatry, to refrain from blasphemy, to establish a legal system, to refrain from bloodshed, to refrain from improper sexual relationships, and to refrain from robbery. All of these are intimated in a single verse, *And the Lord God commanded the man, saying: Of every tree of the garden thou mayest freely eat* (Gen. 2:16).

In explaining how the six commands are derived from this one verse, R. Judah proceeds in a typically midrashic way to parse the individual words of the biblical sentence by analogy to their use elsewhere. I will not quote the *Pesikta* directly because the argument it presents would be incomprehensible to those unfamiliar with rabbinic writing without extensive annotation. The sage takes the Hebrew word *vaye' tzav*, translated as *commanded*, to refer to a command to refrain from idolatry, connecting it to the use of the word *tzav* by the prophet Hosea, who said: *Oppressed is Ephraim, crushed in his right; because he willingly walked after tzav* [translated as "filth" but generally understood as referring to idolatry] (Hos. 5:11). The use of the four-lettered divine name *YHVH*, the Tetragrammaton, rendered as *Lord* in the verse is taken as implying the command to refrain from blasphemy, because of the text, *He that blasphemeth the name of the Lord, he shall surely be put to death* (Lev. 24:16). The divine name *Elohim*, rendered as *God* in the verse, is taken as implying the command to establish a legal system because of the text, *Thou shalt not revile God* (Ex. 22:27), one of a number of instances where the word *Elohim* refers to judges or persons with God-like authority rather than to God. The use of the term *man* in the verse is taken as implying the command to refrain from bloodshed, because of the text, *Whoso sheddeth man's blood, by man shall his blood be shed* (Ex. 9:6). The use of the term *saying* in the verse is taken as implying the command to refrain from improper sexual relationships, because of the use of the term by the prophet Jeremiah . . . *saying: If a man put away his wife, and she go from him, and become another man's, may he return to her again? Will not that land be greatly polluted* (Jer. 3:1). In other words, according to Mosaic Law, a man may not remarry his divorced wife if she had relations with another man in the interim between the divorce and the remarriage—such a relationship being deemed improper and immoral, as is a long list of relationships deemed illicit by the Torah. Finally, the words, *of every tree of the garden thou mayest freely eat*, are taken as implying the commandment to refrain from robbery, that is, seizing that which belongs to another. The prooftext adduced in support of this contention is problematic because the precise wording does not correspond to anything in Scripture. However, scholars have suggested that the reference may actually be to the very next verse (Gen. 2:17), which enjoins against eating of

the tree of the knowledge of good and evil and to do so would constitute robbery, taking that which belongs to another.[18]

What lay behind the convoluted analysis of texts in this passage?
One should be wary of simply taking it as a word game and thereby
trivializing it. It is rather a typically midrashic way of dealing with
a very serious question, namely, the relation between the laws of
Israel, which are grounded in divine authority, and the laws of the
nations that are not. In effect, the sage is grappling with the problem of
natural law—the assumption that there are laws inherent in human
nature that provide the basic guidelines for human conduct, which is
one explanation for the fact that all societies have some laws, without
which social life would be impossible. The sage is here arguing that
those basic laws assumed by many to be inherent in nature, are in
themselves divinely ordained to enable societies to function at a base
level, and that these are the six commandments given to Adam, and
the seventh given to Noah, *Only flesh with the life thereof, which is the
blood thereof, shall ye not eat* (Gen. 9:4), making up the seven so-called
Noahide Laws.

PESIKTA RABBATI

Pesikta Rabbati is another collection similar in purpose and organization as the *Pesikta deRab Kahana*, and is perhaps influenced by it to
the extent that in some editions it is known as *Pesikta Rabbati deRab
Kahana*, even though this attribution is widely assumed to be pseudepigraphic. The work was probably completed no earlier than the ninth
century and focuses on the teachings of the sages of the Land of Israel
who thrived in the third, fourth, and fifth centuries. Fortunately for the
reader, the redactor of the work does not use a great deal of rabbinic
"shorthand," and the discourses are easily comprehensible. The following passage deals with an attempt to comprehend the significance
of some of the divinely imposed requirements on Israel in light of commonly held perceptions of the nature of God, primarily His transcen-
dence and incorporeality.

> R. Judah bar Simon said in the name of R. Johanan: Moses heard three
> things from the Divine Power that startled him and caused him to recoil.
> [First,] when He said: *And let them make Me a sanctuary, that I may
> dwell among them* (Ex. 25:8), [Moses asked the Holy One, blessed be He:
> Master of universes, behold, not even the heavens can contain Thee,
> and yet Thou sayest: *Let them make Me a sanctuary*. Thereupon the Holy
> One, blessed be He, reassured Moses][19]: Moses, it is not as you think;
> although the sanctuary will be twenty boards in the north, twenty boards

in the south and eight in the west, I shall descend below and contract My presence between them, as it is said, *And there I will meet with thee* (Ex. 25:22).

[Second,] when the Israelites sinned and God said: *They shall give every man a ransom for his soul* (Ex. 30:12), Moses asked: Master of the universes, who can give a ransom for his soul? *No man can by any means redeem his brother, nor give to God a ransom for him—for too costly is the redemption of their soul, and must be let alone for ever, etc.* (Ps. 49:8–9). The Holy One, blessed be He, said to him: It is not as you think, but *This they shall give* [. . . *half a shekel for an offering to the Lord*] (Ex. 30:13), that is, they shall give only as much as this . . .

[Third,] when He said: *My food . . . of a sweet savor unto Me, shall ye observe to offer unto Me in its due season* (Num. 28:2). Moses asked the Holy One, blessed be He: Master of the universes, if I were to bring all the beasts of the earth, would they be sufficient for a single offering? Or would all the trees of the world be sufficient for a single altar fire? For it is written, *And Lebanon is not sufficient for altar fire, nor the beasts thereof sufficient for burnt offerings* (Isa. 40:16). The Holy One, blessed be He, reassured Moses: It is not as you think, but only *he-lambs of the first year without blemish, two day by day* (Num. 28:3). Not even two at a time, but one *in the morning, and the other lamb shalt thou offer at dusk* (Num. 28:4).

R. Huna said in the name of Rab: The verse that says, [in effect,] Almighty, we have not found Thee out, *O excellent in power* (Job 37:23), means that we cannot discover the full power of the Holy One, blessed be He, for the Holy One, blessed be He, does not come with onerous demands on Israel. And when Moses heard this he began praising Israel, saying: *Happy is the people that is in such a case, yea, happy is the people whose God is the Lord* (Ps. 144:15).[20]

There are several important points that are expressed in this midrashic exposition. First, from a theological perspective, it argues most clearly that God is both transcendent and immanent and can therefore transform a structure made of boards into a sacred space to house his contracted presence, if He but chooses to do so. The notion of voluntary contraction of the divine presence will play a critical role in the medieval Kabbalah, where it is employed to explain how it is possible, if God is everywhere, that the world could come into being and occupy space that is already occupied by God. Second, it suggests quite emphatically, albeit implicitly, that God has no need of gifts from man, and that the sacrificial requirements are for man's benefit rather than God's, essentially providing a means by which man can demonstrate his loyalty through the voluntary sacrifice of something of tangible value to him. Indeed, if God had need of the sacrifices, there would not be enough animals in the world that could possibly fill such a need. Finally, it points out that the requests or demands that God makes of man are not of an onerous nature, and are not seen as such by those who are truly members of the faith community.

PIRKE DERABBI ELIEZER

This work, translated as *The Chapters of Rabbi Eliezer the Great*, is attributed to the sage R. Eliezer b. Hyrcanus who lived in the last half of the first century and the early part of the second century, but scholarly estimates of when the work was completed tend to place it either in the late eighth or early ninth century. The actual author or compiler of the work remains one of the many such mysteries in the rabbinic literature.

Pirke deRabbi Eliezer is not designed as an aggadic exposition of specific biblical verses but rather elaborates primarily on selected episodes in the biblical narratives. The work constitutes a veritable treasure house of material dealing not only with the elaboration of the biblical accounts but also with elements of rabbinic mystical thought, including chapters on the calendar and astronomy, not found elsewhere to the same extent in the earlier rabbinic literature, as well as other issues, all of which accounts for the frequent references to the work in later rabbinic writing. The passage selected for consideration here deals with the classical doctrine of the two paths, of good and evil, of life and death, which is of course an affirmation of the critical belief in free will and that, regardless of external circumstances and constraints, man always has the moral freedom to choose the path of the good. In addition, however, the passage also touches on an important societal issue. We present here only the first part of the lengthy exposition, that dealing with the good, the section dealing with the evil requiring extensive annotation to make it fully comprehensible.

> Rabbi Eliezer said: I heard with my own ears the Lord of hosts speaking. Of what did he speak? *See, I have set before thee this day life and good, and death and evil* (Deut. 30:15). The Holy One, blessed be He, said: Behold, these two ways have I given to Israel, one of good and one of evil; that of good is that of life, that of evil is that of death. That of the good has two paths, one of righteousness and one of lovingkindness, and Elijah, be he remembered for good, is placed between them. When a person comes to enter, Elijah cries out *Open ye the gates, that the righteous nation that keepeth faithfulness may enter in* (Isa. 26:2). Samuel the prophet stood between these two paths and asked: By which path shall I go? If I go by the path of lovingkindness, the path of righteousness is better than it; if I go by the path of righteousness, the path of lovingkindness is better than it. However, I call on heaven and earth to be my witnesses that I will not leave either but will take both. The Holy One,

blessed be He, said to him: Samuel! You have placed yourself between these two good paths. By your life! I will even give you three good gifts. This is to teach you that everyone who desires and does righteousness and acts of lovingkindness shall inherit three good gifts, and they are life, righteousness, and honor, as it is said: *He that followeth after righteousness and mercy [lovingkindness] findeth life, prosperity and honor* (Prov. 21:21).[21]

It is not entirely clear just what the aggadist has in mind with this passage, and some traditional commentators have interpreted it as a conflict between pursuing the spiritual path of those things that are between man and his Maker and the mundane path of dealing with those matters that are between man and man. The moral to be taught is presumed to be that God desires that we do both. I will suggest an alternative reading of the passage, noting that the aggadist deals with the terms *hesed* (lovingkindness or mercy) and *tzedakah* (righteousness), both of which, in addition to their simple meanings in biblical Hebrew, also have special meanings in rabbinic usage that might be applied here to reach a different sense of what the aggadist is getting at. *Tzedakah*, in rabbinic usage refers particularly to the obligation to provide care for those who are unable to help themselves, whereas *hesed* refers to the voluntary acts that a person does to help others, over and above what he is biblically obligated to do. The first is a matter of *tzedek* or justice, whereas *hesed* or *gemilut hasadim* (the "acts of lovingkindness" specifically referred to by the aggadist) is a matter of philanthropy or charity. The choice between the two good paths is therefore that of doing what one is morally obligated to do and doing that which goes beyond obligation to that which is motivated by love of one's fellow man. The prophet Samuel's refusal to choose between them, but to pursue both simultaneously is considered exemplary. Why? The reason is because, as viewed from the rabbinic perspective, although philanthropy is considered highly laudable, charity alone cannot satisfy the biblical concern for the welfare of the poor and downtrodden. What is biblically required is an obligatory tithe among other impositions on income to alleviate the poverty of those unable to help themselves, in effect a system of poor taxes. Only once these obligations are satisfied is there an appropriate and highly valued role for philanthropy. Accordingly, Samuel refused to follow only the path of *tzedakah*, but insisted on also following the path of *hesed*, and according to the aggadist, his refusal to choose between them was considered most meritorious and deserving of special divine reward.

Chapter 6

Law Codes and Related Literature

In general, the idea of codification originally referred to the reduction to writing of laws, rules, or regulations that previously existed only in oral form. The idea of codification was subsequently expanded to deal with the need to eliminate or at least reduce the shortcomings that resulted from the proliferation of legal provisions found in different literary sources, the inconsistent styles of legal directives, and the gradual emergence of conflicting legal norms. A code came to constitute the authoritative source for locating laws, and its directives had the effect of abrogating any other provision of the law that preceded or was inconsistent with it.

In Jewish law, the process of codification ran into serious opposition, because the principle that a code abrogates any inconsistent rule of earlier date was neither accepted nor applied within the system of *halakhah*. Traditionally, anyone empowered to render legal decisions, that is, to serve as a *posek* or decisor with regard to issues of *halakhah*, required proper authorization. In Roman times, the issuance of such authorization was the privilege of the Sanhedrin or rabbinic high court, until the Roman occupation government outlawed the practice of ordination in the aftermath of the Bar-Kokhba rebellion in the early second century. From that point on, anyone who had been properly ordained was able to confer ordination on his own worthy disciples, a practice that led to a degree of inconsistency in halakhic decision-making between different communities. Although the practice of ordination in the traditional sense came to an end sometime between the fourth and eleventh century, individuals acknowledged as expert in *halakhah* were nonetheless accorded popular authority to serve as decisors to meet the practical needs of the community. As a result, occasionally significant differences arose between the traditions followed by different communities and sometimes even different congregations within a community, and there was a natural reluctance to accept any attempt to codify halakhic practice if it did not conform to the traditions of a particular community. Indeed, to this day, there are significant differences in some religious practices between the Ashkenazic and Sephardic communities, especially but not exclusively with regard to foods that may or may not be eaten during the festival of Passover. Nonetheless, there was always a felt need for some form of codification, as evidenced by the promulgation of the *Mishnah* as a compendium of *halakhah* at the end of the second century.

Codification of Jewish law took three literary forms: (1) books devoted to the collection of normative formulations drawn from halakhic discussions and analyses, each formulation being preceded by a brief discussion of the talmudic sources on which it is based; (2) books devoted to the collection of settled *halakhah*, in which the normative conclusions are stated without discussion of the sources from which they were derived; and (3) books that are a combination of the first two forms.

The earliest known attempts at codification following the publication of the *Mishnah* took place in the eighth century. It is not entirely clear what precipitated the evident need for such works, but one may speculate that it was out of concerns about ensuring the continued integrity of the Jewish communities that arose as a result of the Arab conquest of the region and the proselytizing fervor inspired by Islam. Ahai of Shabha (680–752), a senior scholar in the famous rabbinical academy of Pumbedita in Mesopotamia, produced the first of these works under the title of *Sheiltot* or Questions, the first book written after the completion of the Talmud to be attributed to its actual author. The work, the full title of which in the printed editions is the *Sheiltot deRab Ahai Gaon*, is multifaceted and unique in Judaic literature. Although the book contains a good deal of homiletic material, it is not considered a midrashic work because of the preponderance of its halakhic content. Unlike most of the later attempts at codification, it is not organized as an orderly arrangement by subject matter for easy reference, nor does it consistently follow the order of the sections into which the Torah is divided. The methodological approach adopted by the author is to attempt to connect the halakhic decisions it records to sources in the Torah, sometimes grounding them in the biblical narrative rather than in biblical precept. The title of the work derives from the fact that each of its units of discourse is a response to a substantive question raised by the author. There is some agreement among scholars that the various sections of the *Sheiltot*, which were composed in Aramaic rather than Hebrew, were originally prepared and delivered as sermons in the synagogue of the academy on the Sabbath and other occasions. This conclusion was reached in large measure because the complexity of the material is such that only the more scholarly worshippers who attended services at the academy would be likely to readily follow and fully comprehend the presentations.

On a personal note regarding the author, although he is referred to as Ahai Gaon, the honorific "Gaon" is accorded to him because of his profound scholarship. The title of Gaon, however, was formally accorded to the deans of the Mesopotamian academies at Pumbedita and Sura, the bearer of the title becoming in effect one of the two highest *religious* authorities in the land, as opposed to the *Resh Galuta* or Exilarch who served as the official political leader of the Jewish community in Mesopotamia. In the case of Ahai, when the position of Gaon at Pumbedita became vacant about 750, for reasons that are unknown but most likely were related to the state of communal politics, he was bypassed for the highly coveted position and, to add insult to injury, the Exilarch appointed one of Ahai's disciples in his place. Enraged at the affront, Ahai left the country and relocated to the Land of Israel, where he died two years later. It is not known with any certainty whether the *Sheiltot* was put in its final form in Mesopotamia or in the Land of Israel.

A few years later, Yehudai ben Nahman, another scholar from the academy at Pumbedita who had been appointed as Gaon of the academy at Sura, serving in that position from about 757 to 761, published another attempt at codification of the *halakhah*, the *Halakhot Pesukot* or "Decided *Halakhah*." The work was arranged according to both subject matter and the relevant talmudic tractates, the halakhic conclusion being preceded by a brief synopsis of the sources, but without discussion of how or why the recorded decision was made. It is important to note that the *Halakhot Pesukot* included only those rules and regulations that had practical relevance at the time and place, thus essentially ignoring a substantial body of legal material that only had relevance in the Land of Israel and only when the Temple in Jerusalem existed and was functional. As a result, the large number of biblical precepts and extra-biblical traditions regarding the sacrificial rite, the Jubilee Year, and other matters were treated with benign neglect. This editorial decision set a precedent that was followed by almost all subsequent halakhists who confined their work of codification exclusively to those rules and regulations that were applicable in practice at the time and place in which they lived. In addition, Yehudai Gaon based the decisions he recorded exclusively on those derived from the Babylonian Talmud as well as the traditions of the immediately preceding generations of scholars, without any consideration of alternate opinions or providing any rationale for discounting them. This approach to codification did not go over well among the scholars of the Land of

Israel, where there was opposition to accepting Yehudai Gaon's halakhic authority. Nonetheless, the influence of Yehudai and his work were such that the Babylonian Talmud subsequently became the ultimate rabbinic authority for rendering halakhic decisions, overriding any differing conclusions drawn from the Jerusalem Talmud, although some later codifiers did take the opinions cited in the latter into consideration in their work.

Several decades later, about 825, the *Halakhot Gedolot* ("Large Halakhot") appeared, a similar work of codification attributed by many to Simeon Kayyara of Basra who lived in the eighth century. The authorship and dating of the work is an ongoing subject of scholarly contention, some suggesting that it actually preceded the composition of the *Halakhot Pesukot* of Yehudai Gaon, the latter work being based in part on the former. In any case, the *Halakhot Gedolot* provides a systematic and comprehensive summary of the legal materials found in the Talmud, stating the general principle first and then the details of the precept. It is noteworthy that the work, by contrast with the *Halakhot Pesukot*, also includes some rules and regulations that were no longer observed following the destruction of the Temple. It also represents another marker in the development of the literature of Judaism in that it is the first rabbinic work to contain an introduction, in which it enumerated, for the first time, the 613 precepts of Judaism mentioned in the Talmud, 365 negative and 248 positive, classifying them according to the degree of punishment their transgression incurred as well as other commonalities. This enumeration served as the basis for a whole genre of literature dealing with the identification and elaboration of those precepts, to be discussed below.

Although these early codifications served the practical needs of the communities spread throughout the Diaspora, and became popular references and handbooks of the laws and practices of Judaism, their very convenience also served as a cause of concern among some of the rabbinic authorities. It was feared, often with justification, that excessive reliance on such handbooks might cause people to turn away from study of the sources upon which they were based, something that was considered counterproductive and ultimately dangerous to the halakhic process, which was predicated on the sources and not on epitomes of those source documents. As a result of this growing concern, no further attempts at comprehensive codification were undertaken for about two centuries.

By the mid-eleventh century, however, Mesopotamia was no longer the preeminent center of Jewish life in the Diaspora, its great academies having long entered into a period of decline as an increasingly large number of Jewish communities emerged in Europe and North Africa. Disconnected from the once prestigious and authoritative

Mesopotamian academies, the increasing variations in customs and practices in the widespread religiously autonomous communities generated concern about the long-range effects of such incompatibilities. A new sense of need emerged for the codification of the *halakhah* as a means of assuring basic commonality between the various communities, and a number of efforts by prominent religious authorities were undertaken in this regard.

Isaac ben Jacob Alfasi (1013–1103), who was twenty-five years old when Hai Gaon (939–1038) the last head of the Pumbedita academy died, undertook to fill the resulting gap in halakhic authority. After a period of study in Kairouan, Tunisia, Alfasi settled in Fez, Morocco (thus accounting for his geographical surname), where he remained until 1088, when he was forced to flee to Spain, spending his remaining years in Lucena, where he became the head of its rabbinical seminary. The code that he composed, the *Sefer haHalakhot*, became one of the most important and enduring halakhic works, and is still studied by scholars to this day. The work appears to have been modeled after the much earlier *Halakhot Gedolot* but is far superior to it in both volume and content.

The design of the work was intended to achieve two aims: first, to extract and compile all the halakhic material in the Talmud that had contemporary relevance but omitting material of only academic interest, ascertaining the halakhic decision where there were opposing views, and thereby providing a compendium of *halakhah* for ready reference; second, to prepare an epitome of the relevant tractates of the Talmud, only twenty-four of which are considered in the work, to facilitate their study. Alfasi provides a synopsis of the talmudic discussion of the *halakhah* at issue, renders a decision on numerous halakhic problems that had been matters of contention, often citing the Jerusalem Talmud in his decisions, but giving precedence to the Babylonian Talmud when the positions of the two Talmuds are found to conflict. He also makes extensive use of the three earlier codifications mentioned above. Later generations accepted Alfasi's work as decisive and binding, and it overshadowed all other works written during the next hundred years.

It was only in the twelfth century that a new form of work on the *halakhah*, the book of decisions, was introduced by Maimonides (1135–1204). Born and raised in Cordoba, Spain, at age thirteen he was forced to flee religious persecution with his family to North Africa, settling in Fez in 1160, and finally in Fostat near Cairo where he was appointed as a physician to the sultan in 1185. In his massive work, the *Mishneh Torah*, completed in 1180, Maimonides presented a concise statement of the *halakhah*, written in lucid Hebrew and modeled after the style and language of the *Mishnah*, without any discussion of opposing opinions or sources. Like the *Mishnah*, it dealt with the full range of Jewish law and not only with that which applied in the time and place that he lived. However, unlike the *Mishnah*, Maimonides's work was arranged more systematically in fifteen books by topic and did not follow the order of the tractates in the *Mishnah* and Talmud. It was a code of law in the truest sense, a handbook that was written in a style that made it readily accessible to anyone with a working knowledge of Hebrew. A clear example of this is Maimonides's codification of the *halakhah* as it applied to problems of assuring social justice in Jewish society in which he delineated more than two hundred provisions detailing the rules concerning assuring the welfare of the poor and those unable to fend for themselves. With regard to the obligation to meet the needs of the impoverished, he emphasized, "It is our duty to be more careful in the performance of the precept of almsgiving than in that of any other positive precept, for almsgiving is the mark of the righteous man." In discussing the matter of philanthropy, he delineated eight degrees of giving, in descending order of significance for both donor and recipient.

> The highest degree, than which there is none higher, is one who upholds the hand of an Israelite reduced to poverty by handing him a gift or a loan, or who enters into partnership with him, or who finds work for him, in order to strengthen his hand so that he should have no need to beg from others . . .
>
> Below this is one who gives alms to the poor in such a way that he does not know to whom he has given, nor does the poor person know from whom he has received. This constitutes the fulfillment of a religious obligation for its own sake . . .
>
> Below this is one who knows to whom he is giving, while the poor person does not know from whom he has received. . . .
>
> Below this is the case where the poor person knows from whom he has received, while the donor does not know to whom he gave . . .
>
> Below this is one who gives to the poor person before being asked.
>
> Below this is one who gives to the poor after being asked.
>
> Below this is one who gives to the poor person less than is appropriate, but with a friendly countenance.
>
> Below this is one who gives to the poor with a frown.[1]

Maimonides explained why he had undertaken the composition of the *Mishneh Torah* in his introduction to the work:

> In our days severe vicissitudes prevail, and all feel the pressure of hard times. The wisdom of our wise men has disappeared; the understanding of our prudent men is hidden. Hence the commentaries of the Geonim and their compilations of laws and responsa, which they took care to make clear, have in our times become hard to understand, so that only a few individuals fully understand them. Needless to add, such is the case in

regard to the Talmud itself—the Babylonian as well as the Jerusalem—the *Sifra, the Sifre*, and the *Tosefta*, all of which require, for their comprehension, a broad mind, a wise soul, and considerable study, after which one might learn from them the correct way to determine what is forbidden, what is permitted, as well as other rules of the Torah. On these grounds, I, Moses, the son of Maimon the Sephardi, bestirred myself, and relying on the help of God, blessed be He, and intently studied all these works with a view toward compiling from them everything concerning that which is forbidden or permitted, impure and pure, and the other laws of the Torah, all stated in plain language and terse style so that the entire Oral Torah might systematically become known to all without citing difficulties and disagreements . . . so that no one should have a need to refer to any other work with regard to any of the laws of Israel.[2]

As it turned out, Maimonides succeeded in carrying out his intent to the extent that there was a strong reaction against the *Mishneh Torah* from many contemporary rabbis and scholars who were concerned that the work would effectively supplant the Talmud because of its accessibility. This triggered a controversy that went on for centuries, with a host of commentators rising in support of Maimonides against his opponents and detractors. The net result of the controversy was a proliferation of literature that effectively nullified Maimonides's original intent and caused a great deal of confusion about what was the accepted *halakhah*.

The next major work of codification of the *halakhah*, the *Piskei haRosh*, was undertaken by Asher ben Jehiel (c. 1250–1327). Asher was the acknowledged leader of German Jewry but felt compelled to leave Germany in 1303 and relocate to Spain where he remained for the rest of his life, becoming the rabbi of Toledo in 1305. His composition was modeled after the work of Alfasi, identifying conflicting opinions and then rendering his own decisions, which were accepted as binding, and often preferred to those of Maimonides. The *Piskei haRosh* follows the order of the tractates of the Talmud and an epitome of the work prepared by the author's son may be found appended to many large editions of the Babylonian Talmud.

In addition to the works described thus far, a rich and extensive halakhic literature was produced in Germany and France during the twelfth and thirteenth centuries in a variety of forms, including thousands of responses issued by rabbinic authorities to halakhic questions addressed to them, which will be discussed below. These responsa were in effect judicial opinions that established new precedents in Jewish law that dealt with the changing realities of Jewish life in a frequently inhospitable environment, and they had to be taken into account by any competent decisor, as they do to this very day. As a result, it was no longer feasible to rely solely on halakhic codes that reflected the realities of an earlier period. Having concluded that "reasoning had become faulty, controversy had increased, opinions had multiplied, so that there is no halakhic ruling which is free from differences of opinion,"[3] Jacob ben Asher (c. 1270–1340), who succeeded his father Asher ben Yehiel as rabbi of Toledo, undertook the compilation of a new code of *halakhah* that took into account prevailing customs and the decisions rendered in the responsa literature as well as in the more ancient sources.

His major halakhic work was organized in four sections and is known as the *Arba'ah Turim* ("Four Columns"). Section 1, *Orah Hayyim*, contains 697 chapters dealing with matters pertaining to daily life including prayers, blessings, the Sabbath, festivals, and fasts. Section 2, *Yoreh De'ah*, contains 403 chapters on dietary laws, ritual purity, circumcision and mourning, as well as on usury and idolatry. Section 3, *Even haEzer*, contains 178 chapters on laws affecting women, including marriage, divorce, levirate marriage, and marriage contracts. Section 4, *Hoshen Mishpat*, contains 427 chapters on civil law and procedure and interpersonal relations. The comprehensiveness and simple style of the work set a new standard for codes of halakhah. *Arba'ah Turim* is essentially a combined book of *halakhah* and book of decisions. The author presents the substance of the individual rules and regulations in terse form, without citing sources, then concisely cites the differing opinions of post-Talmud scholars on the *halakhah* under consideration, and concludes by rendering his decision on the issue. As a general rule, Jacob ben Asher codified the *halakhah* in accordance with the decisions of Alfasi, and where this was disputed by Maimonides or other decisors, he accepted the opinion of his father, as the latest competent authority.

During the two centuries following Jacob ben Asher, a series of decisive events profoundly influenced Jewish life, beginning with the Black Death (1348–1350), the intensified persecution of German Jewry and that of Spanish Jewry, the latter culminating in the expulsion from Spain in 1492. This resulted in the mass migration of Jewish communities and the establishment of new centers such as that of the German Jews in Poland, and of the Spanish Jews in the Middle East. The turmoil in Jewish life raised a host of halakhic issues relating to the diverse practices of the host communities and the newcomers, creating problems that cried for resolution, and for which the code of Jacob ben Asher did not provide the necessary answers. It was Joseph Caro (1488–1575), who undertook the challenge of compiling a new comprehensive code of *halakhah*. Caro was probably born in Spain and taken by his family to Portugal after the expulsion of 1492, and then to Turkey after the expulsion of the Jews from Portugal in 1497. He remained in Turkish territory for some forty years, living in Istanbul, Adrianople, Nikopol, and Salonika before moving to Safed in 1536.

Caro envisioned a comprehensive work consisting of two parts, different in form and content, but complementary in achieving a common purpose. The first part of his code, *Beth Yosef* ("House of Joseph"), was intended to include all the halakhic material available at the time, taking note of the opinions expressed in the post-Talmudic literature up to his day, and citing the work of thirty-two of the most distinguished halakhic scholars, whom he specifically mentions by name. To avoid repetition of the material already compiled by Jacob ben Asher in the *Abra'ah Turim*, Caro keyed the *Beth Yosef* to the latter, to which it is appended in most published editions of the earlier work. The second part of the code, the *Shulhan Arukh* ("Prepared Table") was intended to be a book of decisions that would assure that there would be a common *halakhah* for all members of the Jewish community anywhere. To achieve this, he followed an original method for determining the applicable rule. Whenever Alfasi, Maimonides, and Asher ben Yehiel dealt with a particular matter, as a general rule the decision would follow the majority of the three. If only two of the three had considered the matter and differed, five additional authorities were consulted and the law decided according to the majority. If none of the three earlier codifiers considered the matter, the law was decided in accordance with a majority of the five authorities.

In preparing the *Shulhan Arukh*, Caro basically adopted the model set by Jacob ben Asher and produced a code that was even briefer than the latter's or that of Maimonides. It should be noted, parenthetically, that although the codes of Maimonides, Jacob ben Asher, and Joseph Caro are relatively concise, their modern printed editions, especially those of Jacob ben Asher and Joseph Caro, are prodigious in size because of the many subsequent critical commentaries, glosses, and other scholarly materials keyed to the text that were added to the printed pages.

The *Shulhan Arukh*, with some subsequent additions, became the definitive code of Jewish law that remains in effect till the present day. The additions were incorporated directly into the body of Caro's text to make it more comprehensive. This was necessary because some of the traditional practices of the Ashkenazic community differed from the primarily Sephardic practices reflected in the code. The halakhic annotations regarding these different customs and practices were prepared by Moses Isserles (1525 or 1530–1572), a major Ashkenazic rabbinic authority, and are known in the printed texts of the *Shulhan Arukh*, somewhat humorously, as the *Mappah*, that is, as the "Tablecloth" covering the "Prepared Table." The addition of the *Mappah*, which also reflects a number of instances in which Isserles rejects the opinion of Caro on a particular *halakhah* and renders a conflicting opinion, made the *Shulhan Arukh* acceptable as the preeminent source code of *halakhah* to both the Ashkenazi and Sephardi communities, an acceptance that was not realized fully until a century later because of the traditional opposition to codes as detrimental to the study of original sources.

For the more than four centuries since the publication of the *Shulhan Arukh* there has been no subsequently prepared code recognized as authoritative covering the entire range of applicable *halakhah*. However, this is not because no new issues have arisen that are not dealt with in the classic work. On the contrary, it has been observed that more than half of the halakhic rules specified in the *Shulhan Arukh* have undergone reinterpretation, glossing, and augmentation, and that many thousands of responsa have been written and collected over the centuries, all of which must be taken into account by those rendering halakhic decisions. The single notable exception to this generalization is the *Arukh haShulhan* ("Arrangement of the Table") of Jehiel Michal Epstein (1829–1908) of Belarus. Epstein explained that just as Maimonides saw a need to compose the *Mishneh Torah* and Joseph Caro the *Shulhan Arukh*, so he too saw the need to bring the latter work up to date, incorporating halakhic rulings made over the centuries since its publication. However, although the work is considered authoritative, it does not carry the same weight as the *Shulhan Arukh*.

The primary reason for the lack of other attempts at codification on the scale of the classic works discussed above would appear to be historical, namely, the effects of Jewish emancipation at the end of the eighteenth century, which led to the disruption of traditional Jewish society. With emancipation came the dissolution of the traditional organization of the Jewish communities, accompanied by a decline in religious observance, the introduction of secular culture and the challenge of growing assimilation into the host society, all of which militated against the compilation of new comprehensive codes, the relevance of which was questionable, and in any case of low priority among the issues confronting Judaism in the modern era. For the traditional elements in Jewish society the challenges brought by emancipation called for increased focus on those halakhic matters that were of immediate interest and concern for preserving the traditional way of life. Accordingly, a number of codes were in fact produced in the eighteenth and nineteenth centuries that focused on the issues of daily life, bringing up to date those matters considered in the relevant parts of the *Shulhan Arukh*, but virtually ignoring more than a third of the material contained in the latter. Some of the better known of these works are the *Shulhan Arukh* of Schneur Zalman of Lyady (1784–1812), the *Hayyei Adam* and *Hokhmat Adam* of Abraham Danzig (1748–1820), and the popular *Kitzur Shulhan Arukh* of Solomon Ganzfried (1804–1886), the latter still in common use among traditional Jews to this day.

ENUMERATIONS OF THE PRECEPTS

There is a passage in the Babylonian Talmud that spurred the emergence of a genre of halakhic literature closely related to the codes discussed above. The text reads: "R. Simlai explained, 613 precepts were revealed unto Moses at Sinai, 365 prohibitive precepts, like the days of the solar year, and 248 positive precepts corresponding to the number of limbs in the human body."[4] As a corollary to the codifications of *halakhah* that began in the eighth century, compilations of the 613 precepts also soon began to appear in two forms, as liturgical poems some of which were incorporated into the synagogue liturgy, and as books of precepts that not only listed the precepts but also provided accompanying expositions.

Since antiquity, rabbinic homilists have viewed the Torah as the amplification of the Ten Commandments and, this being the case, the 613 precepts were similarly related to the Ten Commandments, the homilists noting that the Decalogue consists of 613 letters. This equation of the 613 precepts to the Decalogue gave rise to a type of literature called *Azharot* ("Warnings"), liturgical poems that take each statement of the Decalogue to refer to a group of precepts, or each letter of the Decalogue to refer to a particular precept, and to list them accordingly. Although it is believed that the name *Azharot* is derived from the first word of an early liturgical poem of this type, it has also been noted that the name *Azharot* is used because its numerical equivalent is 613, bearing in mind that Hebrew letters all have numerical values.

Azharot were introduced into the liturgy after the recitation of the Decalogue as part of the liturgy was stopped in talmudic times for polemical reasons, the *azharot* serving the same purpose but in both disguised fashion and in greater detail. *Azharot* are found in the liturgies of the communities in the Land of Israel, Babylonia, Spain, Italy, Provence, and Byzantium, however, the authors of many of the earliest *azharot* remain unknown and most are based on the enumerations of the 613 precepts that are to be found in the Introduction to the *Halakhot Gedolot*, discussed above. The earliest composer of *azharot* whose name is known with any certainty is Saadia Gaon (882–942), who incorporated them into the prayer book he compiled in two forms. Subsequently, numerous *azharot* were composed by some of the outstanding poets of the medieval period.

The *azharot* were recited primarily on the festival of Shavuot or Pentecost because the holiday commemorates the revelation of the Decalogue, although similar liturgical poems were prepared for other religious occasions as well. Although *azharot* may be found in some Ashkenazi prayer books they are rarely if ever actually recited as part of the liturgy. By contrast, in the Sephardic and Yemenite rites, the *azharot* of Solomon ibn Gabirol (c. 1027–1057) are read in the synagogue on Shavuot. In those communities outside the Land of Israel, where the festival is celebrated for two days, the *azharot* referring to the positive precepts are recited on the first day, and those referring to the negative precepts are recited on the second day.

It is noteworthy that there is also a long history of rabbinic opposition to compositions of *azharot*, primarily because some of their authors were merely poets rather than scholars who wrote poetry and in some instances wrote of the precepts in a manner inconsistent with traditionally accepted perspectives.

The first and by far the most important book of precepts that enumerated and explained all 613 precepts, specifying the biblical source for each, was the *Sefer haMitzvot* ("Book of the Precepts") of Maimonides, which he composed in Arabic prior to his monumental *Mishneh Torah*. His avowed purpose in writing it was to ensure that he did not omit anything in composing his massive halakhic work, the *Sefer haMitzvot* thus serving as an outline for the larger effort. The work is divided into two parts, dealing with the positive and negative precepts respectively, each part being arranged topically. The *Sefer haMitzvot* also complements the *Mishneh Torah* in that the author merely states the *halakhah* in the latter work without any indication of sources or the reasoning behind his decisions. In discussing the basic precepts of the Torah in the former work, Maimonides lays bare his entire reasoning process that he applied in the latter work. This may be seen in the following extract from the discussion in *Sefer haMitzvot* regarding "regulating our conduct by the stars," in which Maimonides not only deals with the matter of horoscopes but also extrapolates from the precept more far-reaching implications.

> By this prohibition we are forbidden to regulate our conduct by the stars: that is, we are not to say, "This day is auspicious for a certain enterprise, and we will undertake it," or "This day is inauspicious for a certain enterprise, and we will refrain from it." This prohibition is contained in His words (exalted be He), *There shall not be found among you . . . an observer of clouds (me'onen or soothsayer)* [Deut. 18:10], and is repeated in His words, *Neither shall ye practice . . . soothsaying (te'onenu)* [Lev. 19:26], on which the *Sifra* says . . . this refers to those who pronounce times [auspicious or otherwise]—the word *te'onenu* being derived from *onah* (meaning time or period). That is to say, there shall not be found among you a soothsayer who decides that one time is auspicious and another is inauspicious. . . .
>
> This prohibition covers also deceit by optical illusion. The Sages say: *Me'onen*: this refers to one who deceives by optical illusion: this covers a large number of tricks accomplished by sleight of hand, which deceive men into thinking that they see things that do not exist . . . All tricks of

this kind are forbidden . . . and cause very great harm by making that which could not possibly exist appear possible to fools, women and children, and thus accustoming them to accept impossibilities as possible.[5]

The idea of this kind of book of precepts soon caught on and numerous works enumerating and explaining the precepts began to appear, some of them, such as the *Sefer Mitzvot Gadol* ("The Great Book of Precepts") of Moses ben Jacob of Coucy (thirteenth century), are based on Maimonides's *Mishneh Torah*, which is cited profusely throughout the work. However, the work is also augmented by a rich variety of other sources that made the large work highly popular among medieval scholars and decisors, causing it to be one of the first Hebrew books to be printed. The work effectively doubled as a book of precepts and one in which halakhic decisions were rendered. In this work, when there was a controversy between the rulings of Maimonides and distinguished Franco-German scholars, Moses of Coucy ruled in favor of the latter. One of the motivating factors behind Moses' work was the decree of Gregory IX (1242) banning the Talmud. His work was intended to serve as a means of study and decision-making until the ban was lifted, and remained one of the best-known textbooks of *halakhah* for a long time.

The work of Moses of Coucy inspired another contemporary French scholar, Isaac ben Joseph of Corbeil (d. 1280), to undertake the writing of a more popular work, the *Sefer Mitzvot Katan* ("The Small Book of Precepts"), one designed for the masses in place of the massive book of the former, which was designed to meet the needs of the scholarly community. He did this by omitting the extensive halakhic discussions in the earlier work and providing a concise compendium of *halakhah* to which he added ethical homilies, parables, and legendary materials. Evidently intending that the book be read through during the course of a week, he divided the precepts into seven "Pillars," corresponding to the days of the week. The book was published in a printed version for the first time in Constantinople in 1510, and republished numerous times since.

Another book of precepts of enduring value appeared at the end of the thirteenth century, the *Sefer haHinukh* ("Book of Education"), whose author is unknown, although some attribute it to Aaron ben Joseph haLevi of Barcelona (c. 1235–1300). Although the work is based on Maimonides's enumeration of the precepts, the book differs from the latter's *Sefer haMitzvot* in both objective and scope. Thus, whereas Maimonides's work deals exclusively with the halakhic aspects of the precepts, the primary objective of the *Sefer haHinukh* is to understand the religious and ethical roots of the precepts, their spiritual quality, and how they further the welfare of the individual and the community, an approach that makes the work an essential source for the study of *halakhah* and the philosophy of Judaism. Editorially, the book differs from its predecessors in that it lists the precepts in the order in which they appear in the biblical texts.

The approach taken in the book is to divide the exposition of each of the precepts into four parts, the first consisting of a discussion of the nature of the precept, its source in the Torah, and how it was understood by the sages of the Talmud. The second part concerns itself with a consideration of what might be the underlying reason for the precept. The third part deals with the specific rules entailed in the precept as derived from the Talmud and other sources. Finally, it discusses the practical questions of where, when, and to whom the precept applies, and the penalty for transgression. The following brief passage is the first of the precepts listed in the *Sefer haHinukh*, which is the positive obligation to propagate the species, and in which the four elements of each discussion may be clearly seen.

Referring to the first section of Genesis, it states: "There is one positive precept in it, and that is the precept of propagation, as it is said, *And God blessed them; and God said to them: Be fruitful and multiply* [Gen. 1:28]." Turning to the rationale for the precept, the author states: "The root of this precept is that the world should be populated, for God desires it to be so, as it is written: *He created it not a waste, He formed it to be inhabited* [Isa. 45:18]. It therefore constitutes a major precept because of which all other precepts can be fulfilled, for the world was given to mankind and not to the ministering angels." Turning to the specific rules concerning the precept, he writes: "With regard to the precept, when a person is obligated to be engaged in it, and how many offspring he should have before he is released from it, and from what other precepts he is relieved in order to fulfill this one, and other specifics are elucidated in the talmudic tractate *Yevamot*, chapter 6, and in tractate *Berakhot* [25b end]." Finally, with regard to when and where the precept applies, he writes: "It is applicable everywhere and at all times, and a man is obligated to arrange for someone who is appropriate for it, and the time is that which our sages of blessed memory set forth for marriage [age eighteen for men]. However, this precept does not encumber women, and he who dismisses it, dismisses a positive precept, and his punishment will be very severe because he demonstrates that he does not desire to fulfill the divine wish to populate His world."[6]

Although no new original compilations of the precepts have been authored since the medieval period, numerous works have appeared in many languages that explore, elaborate upon, and popularize the classical works for a contemporary audience because of their continuing relevance for Judaic thought and practice.

RESPONSA

As implicitly suggested earlier, written codes can only reflect the state of the *halakhah* up until the moment of writing, after which they become static documents in a dynamic environment where change is incessant and new issues constantly arise to which the written codes do not offer clear guidance, even to those scholars to whom they are accessible. As such issues arose over the centuries, it became a common practice to refer such issues orally or in writing to an acknowledged halakhic authority and ask how one should respond in a given situation, and for the halakhic decisor to render an opinion based on his knowledge of the sources and his ability to extrapolate from them, in effect expanding or otherwise modifying the application of existing *halakhah* in practice. Collections of thousands upon thousands of such queries and responses (*sheilot uteshuvot*) constitute the voluminous responsa literature that is presently undergoing computerization at Bar Ilan University in Israel.

Such queries and responses, of course, are not modern phenomena and are to be found recorded in the Talmud. However, the origin of responsa as a distinct literary genre dates to eighth-century Mesopotamia. The Jews of the Diaspora, who were becoming ever more dispersed as a consequence of the turmoil and dislocations accompanying the Islamic wars of conquest, and the increasing decline in popular familiarity with the Aramaic language of the Talmud, turned to the scholars of the renowned Mesopotamian academies for explanations of the ancient texts, for guidance and decisions with regard to the disputes that arose between local scholars, and issues for which there were no known precedents. During the period from 850 to 1050, tens of thousands of responsa from the Mesopotamian scholars were written, but only a small portion of these were collated and published in booklets, quite unsystematically, making it difficult to discern authorship.

Some of these early responsa have been printed in collections such as *Teshuvot haGeonim: Shaarei Teshuvah* ("Responsa of the Geonim: Gates of Repentance") from which the following freely translated anonymous example is drawn.

Query: Is it lawful, in the case of a person who has a bad reputation or is accused of committing a transgression, to cause that person to swear as to whether or not he committed such a transgression, and if he admitted it under oath, to inflict corporal punishment; or, should he be considered free of guilt under the principle that a rational person will not make himself out to be evil?

Response: It is unlawful to cause a person to swear as to whether or not he committed a transgression, but if it becomes clear to the court that he did so, he should be punished in accordance with his misdeed, and he should be made to swear that he will not repeat it, as it is written: *And I contended with them, and cursed them and smote certain of them* . . . and *made them swear by God* [that they would not repeat their misdeeds] (Neh. 13:25).[7]

The query was obviously precipitated by a conflict of opinion as to whether or not a suspect can be induced to confess to his own detriment by demanding that he swear by God to his innocence. The response reaffirms the halakhic position that the burden of proof is always on the accuser and that not only may a confession not be coerced but even a voluntary admission is unacceptable as evidence. However, once it is independently established that a transgression has been committed, appropriate punishment should be meted out and only then should one be made to swear that he would not repeat the offense, an appropriate biblical prooftext for the latter being the ancient words of Nehemiah, uttered in his capacity as the Persian-appointed governor of Judea.

From medieval times to the present there has been a constant production of responsa and of published volumes of responsa from every corner of the world where Jews are to be found. The prodigious amount of responsa produced by some halakhic authorities has led to the publication of books of responsa from individual rabbis in addition to collections from multiple sources. In contemporary times, notwithstanding the emergence of different trends in Judaism, Orthodox, Reform, Conservative, and Reconstructionist, the production of responsa in each movement continues to flourish unabated, frequently using the identical traditional sources to support the opinions rendered therein. The one common characteristic of modern responsa is that they tend to be lengthy, each a study in legal history, primarily because of the need to establish the authority for a decision after due consideration of the major earlier sources that dealt with some aspect of the issue. Thus, while the early responsum cited above is extremely brief, one may rest assured that a contemporary response to the identical question would probably read like an extended essay on the topic. In other words, the modern decisor must often undertake the same kind of legal research, examining precedents and the reasons behind them, that goes into a competent constitutional court judge's opinion. An example of this is the response to a query about naming a child prepared by Jacob Z. Lauterbach, a Reform rabbi, which consumes forty-two pages and eighty-five footnotes, that reviews the entire gamut of relevant halakhic literature. After considering the various opinions of rabbis through the ages, he ultimately concludes that, "while it is proper to follow the custom established by the community or the group, it actually makes no difference what names we give to children. For no matter what name a person is given by others, what ultimately counts is the name which he makes for himself by his actions and his conduct."[8]

There are, however, some issues that do not entail in-depth historical analysis but rather contemporary scientific knowledge. An example of this kind of responsa may be seen in the answer to a query directed to Isaac Klein, a Conservative rabbi, which deals with the Jewish dietary law that stipulates that only fish that have fins and scales are considered kosher and suitable for consumption.

Question: Are turbot, lumpfish, and mahi-mahi kosher fish?

Answer: Turbot is of the family teleosts to which belong most of the kosher fish. In the Fishery Leaflet 531 issued by the Bureau of Fisheries it is listed as a kosher fish. It is so because it is covered with cycloid scales. (Prof. Carl Gans, Chairman, Department of Zoology, University of Michigan). Hence we consider turbot kosher.

Lumpfish. In *Fishes of the Atlantic Coast of Canada*, by A.H. Levin and W.B. Scott, it is indicated that Lumpfish probably does not have scales. Prof. Carl Gans indicated to me that in a monograph on Lumpfish in 1911 (in German) by Albrecht Hase it is stated that the Lumpfish has scales but these are like the scales found on sharks rather than on teleosts. Hence, we would consider Lumpfish forbidden.

Mahi-Mahi was questioned because it was unclear whether it is in the porpoise or the dolphin family. The Marine Fisheries Service gives this information. Mahi-mahi is the Hawaiian common name of the dolphin-fish *Coryphaena hippurus* which has fins and scales although the scales are very small. *Fishery Leaflet 531* of the Bureau lists it among the fish that have fins and scales. Hence we consider mahi-mahi as kosher.[9]

Responsa sometimes deal with truly heartbreaking questions, an example of which concerns the principle of Jewish law that if a woman has voluntarily committed adultery, her husband may no longer live with her once he becomes aware of the fact. However, if she were forced to commit adultery, the restriction on the husband is inapplicable. Shortly after the German defeat in 1945, a young man and woman, who had been separated and lost all their children in the Holocaust, reunited to attempt to rebuild their lives and start a new family, when the husband discovered to his horror and dismay that there was a tattoo on his wife's arm which read, "Prostitute for the Armies of Hitler." The husband was concerned that the presence of the tattoo might be misconstrued as suggesting that his wife may have willingly served as a prostitute, and inquired as to whether it was permitted under Jewish law for him to live with his wife once again.

In his response, Rabbi Ephraim Oshry, a survivor of the Kovno ghetto, reviewed all the relevant classic sources and concluded from the facts of the case: "There is not the slightest shadow of suspicion that she might have been seduced into voluntary intercourse with the Germans, since she herself saw what they had done to her fellow Jews, men, women, and children, murdered and slaughtered without mercy or compassion. Certainly these oppressors were so disgusting, abominable, and detestable in her eyes that it is inconceivable they could have seduced her." He therefore decreed, "It is therefore the *din* [legal ruling] that this unfortunate, and all her sisters whose bitter fate it was to be seized for such shameful purpose, are permitted to their husbands . . . and there is not the slightest reason to forbid them to their husbands." With regard to the tattoo on the woman's arm, he wrote further: "I am of the opinion, therefore, that there is no need to attempt to efface the tattoo; on the contrary, it should be viewed not as a sign of shame and disgrace, but rather as a sign of honor and strength, to show how we suffered for the sanctification of His blessed name."[10]

Chapter 7

Bible Commentaries

The Hebrew Scriptures, and most especially the Torah, the five books of Moses, are the ultimate source and point of reference of Judaism. There are, however, some serious problems of comprehension when one considers writings dating back centuries, let alone millennia. Although it may be maintained, as Judaism does, that the words of Scripture have eternal meaning and significance, it seems self-evident that those writings, to have survived the generation in which they first appeared, would of necessity had to be comprehensible to their readers. It seems safe to suggest that if this had not been the case, those writings would have been ignored, and failing to be copied they would have soon disappeared. The problem for any subsequent reader is that language is dynamic and the meaning of words in one era may have very different connotations in another. The implication of this is that if one reads a passage of the Hebrew Bible, it may not mean the same thing in Modern Hebrew as it did in Biblical Hebrew, even though the words literally may be the same. The same situation was confronted by the scholars of the talmudic era, for whom their Hebrew usage and vocabulary differed in some respects from that used in the biblical writings.

Moreover, it is not only a question of the meaning attached to the individual words but also their connotation, that is, the idea that the words are being used to convey to the reader. How does one determine the meaning of a biblical word or phrase that does not appear self-evident in the context in which it is found? The usual method of doing so is by analogy to its use in other texts where its meaning is unambiguous, or by its similarity to words in cognate languages. Although this approach is by no means certain or flawless, it does represent an attempt to understand the text objectively, that is, what it conveyed to the reader of the period in which it was written. An alternative approach to the biblical texts is more subjective in nature, namely, that of asserting what the text is attempting to convey to its reader by its choice of language, not only by what it actually states but also by what it may be understood as implying. These two alternate approaches, the objective or straightforward reading of the text, called the *peshat* and the subjective interpretive reading called *derash* in Hebrew respectively, can lead to very different understandings of the scriptural word.

The ancient sages were well aware of the intellectual dangers inherent in the subjective approach to the texts, that might not only involve *exegesis*, drawing out the author's ideas from the text but also *eisegesis*, reading one's own ideas into the text. To prevent distorting the biblical text by failing to be appropriately circumspect in applying the subjective approach, they adopted the interpretive principle that although one may infer subtexts from a particular word or passage, the text itself never loses its objective meaning. In other words, they accepted the notion that a biblical text might contain layers of meaning that might be extruded from it in addition to its objective meaning, but not in place of it.

In a sense, the objective approach is historical in that it conveyed a particular meaning to the audience to which it was originally addressed, the subjective approach is ahistorical, divorced from time and place, and perhaps containing a message for future generations. The interplay of these alternate approaches can also produce incompatible results that can be troublesome, especially when the biblical texts being interpreted are legal in nature or have normative implications. The following is an example of this problem drawn from the *Mishnah* and the Talmud.

There is a rule specified in the *Mishnah* with regard to normative practice on the Sabbath: "A man may not go out with a sword or a bow or a shield or a club or a spear; and if he went out he is liable to a Sin-offering. R. Eliezer says: They are his adornments. But the sages say they are nothing but shameful, for it is said: *And they shall beat their swords into plowshares, and their spears into pruning-hooks*" (Isa. 2:4).[1] The ruling, which reflects the majority opinion, is justified on the basis of the cited prooftext. The question that is raised subsequently in the Talmud is on what basis did R. Eliezer assert that the weapons should be considered as part of one's dress? The rationale supplied by later sages is that his opinion is based on the biblical verse, *Gird thy sword upon thy thigh, O mighty one, Thy glory and Thy majesty* (Ps. 45:4), which would appear to consider the sword as an adornment. However, another sage challenged this assumption, arguing that the word "sword" in this text is a metaphor for "the words of the Torah," that is, for learning, which is Israel's weapon. The response to this challenge was, "A verse cannot depart from its plain meaning."[2] In other words, treating the word "sword" in this context as a metaphor for homiletic purposes cannot override its plain sense as the basis for a halakhic opinion.

As this example illustrates, there is an abundance of biblical commentary imbedded in the Talmud, where biblical prooftexts abound in support of one position or another, some of them deviating sharply from the plain sense of the text as written. Over time, in the post-talmudic period, as comprehension of even the plain sense of the biblical texts became cloudy as knowledge of Biblical Hebrew declined in favor of the Rabbinic Hebrew of the medieval period, the need for interpretation of the texts increased to the extent that freestanding commentaries on Scripture began to appear. Another factor that precipitated this development was the emergence of Karaism, a movement that rejected the concept of an Oral Torah and therefore took a literalist approach to the reading of the biblical texts. This in turn put pressure on traditionalist scholars to carefully parse the language and grammar employed in the texts in order to be in a position to challenge Karaite readings of Scripture.

SAADIA GAON AND OTHER EARLY COMMENTATORS

One of the early leading figures in this effort was Saadia Gaon (892–942), head of the academy of Sura in Babylonia, who translated the Torah and several books of the Prophets and Hagiographa into Arabic, and included a substantial amount of commentary into the translation. He evidently also wrote separate commentaries on parts of the *TaNaKH* that are cited in various medieval commentaries and other manuscripts, many of which have relatively recently been aggregated, translated into Hebrew, and published. Saadia and the Mesopotamian scholars who followed him took the objective approach (*peshat*) to expositing the meaning of the biblical texts. A later dean of the Sura academy, Samuel ben Hofni Gaon (d. 1013), a prolific writer little of whose work has survived, wrote a commentary on the Torah in Arabic, some of which, primarily on Genesis, has also recently been translated into Hebrew and published. Samuel ben Hofni was more extreme than his illustrious predecessor in his objective approach to the biblical texts, asserting that no meaning might be attributed to a biblical text that exceeded the bounds of reason. He is cited frequently in some of the other medieval commentaries discussed below. Another scholar of the period, Hananel ben Hushiel (c. 965–1055), head of the academy of Kairouan in Tunisia, similarly took the position that one should not place confidence in interpretations that reason rejects.

His commentaries on the Torah, written in Hebrew, are known only from their being cited from no longer extant manuscripts in other medieval works, and have also relatively recently been collated from these sources and published.

Although biblical commentary continued to be pursued in North Africa and Spain following the closing of the Mesopotamian academies, the next major development in this regard took place in France. One of the earliest commentators on the biblical writings in France was Menahem ben Helbo (eleventh century), who wrote commentaries in Hebrew on the books of the Prophets and the Hagiographa, but not on the Torah. Although none of his books are extant, fragments of his work are found in other medieval commentaries. He was, moreover, the first commentator in France to focus on *peshat*, although he also included some homiletic interpretations in his work. He appears to have lived in Provence for a time, and the Arabic and Provençal form of French words that appear in the commentaries of the next and by far more important commentator attest to the influence of his seminal work.

RASHI

The perhaps most influential commentator on the biblical texts in all of Jewish history is Solomon ben Isaac (1040–1105), better known by the acronym Rashi, who was born and spent most of his adult life in Troyes, after attending the important academies in Mainz and Worms. It is also noteworthy that Rashi was not a professional scholar, but seems to have earned his living from viticulture, having been given a vineyard from which to support himself and his family. Rashi wrote Hebrew commentaries on most of the Bible, and it appears that all of his known writings have survived and his commentary on the Torah was first translated into English between 1929 and 1934, and a new translation has recently been published. Rashi's commentary is the first known Hebrew work to have been printed in 1475, and since then most editions of the Hebrew Bible designed for Jewish use have included it.

The dominant characteristic of his commentary is its presentation of both literal and midrashic interpretations, his selection of the latter being those closest to the literal. Rashi, who was both a linguist and philologist, focused his commentary on meticulous analysis of the language of the texts, although he did not clearly take note of the distinctions between biblical and mishnaic Hebrew. He often resorted to the use of vernacular French to explain difficult words and phrases, and more than a thousand of such instances are to be found in his work. His writing style is to be as brief as possible and is frequently terse to the point of incomprehension, explaining difficult problems with a word or simply a hint, presupposing that his reader has the background to understand his meaning. This is one of the factors that led to more than 200 super-commentaries on his commentary having been written over the centuries.

For purposes of comparison both in terms of style and content, the following example of Rashi's approach will focus on part of his understanding of the first verse in the Torah, as will the examples of the commentaries of the subsequent commentators discussed in this chapter. The verse, which speaks of the creation of the universe, states in Hebrew, *Be'reshit bara Elohim et ha'shamayim ve'et ha'aretz*, which I will not translate into English at this point because both its literal meaning and intent are matters of controversy.

Rashi begins his commentary by exclaiming: "This verse says nothing if not 'Expound me!'" thus acknowledging that its meaning is by no means self-evident. He then proceeds to provide a homiletic interpretation of the first word *be'reshit* "as our rabbis of blessed memory expounded it, on behalf of the Torah, which is called *reshit darko* (*the beginning of His way*) [Prov. 8:22], and for Israel, who are called *reshit tevuato* (*His first-fruits of the increase*) [Jer. 2:3]." From this standpoint the verse might be understood as saying, "For the sake of the Torah and Israel God created the heaven and the earth." However, Rashi goes on

> If you wish to explain it according to its simple meaning (*peshat*), explain it thus: In the beginning of the creation of the heavens and the earth . . . The purpose of the verse is not to teach the order of Creation by saying that these came first, for if this is what it intended to teach it should have stated *Ba'rishonah bara et ha'shamayim* (At first He created the heavens), because there is no instance of the word *reshit* in Scripture that is not attached to the word that follows it, such as *Be'reshit mamlekhut Yehoiakim* (In the beginning of the reign of Jehoiakim) [Jer. 26:1], etc.... Here too you should say that the phrase *Be'reshit bara Elohim etc.* should be understood as "in the beginning of creating."

He then goes on to present a lengthy argument as to why translating the verse as *In the beginning God created the heaven and the earth*, the translation used in most English bibles for many centuries, and thereby establishing the order of creation, will entangle one in a number of textual difficulties later on.[3]

RASHBAM

The next important commentator following Rashi was his grandson Samuel ben Meir (from c. 1080–1085 to c. 1174), known by the acronym Rashbam, who was born in Ramerupt in Champagne in northern France.

Like his grandfather, he also earned his livelihood from viticulture, supplemented by sheep farming. Rashbam studied under his grandfather, with whom he frequently disagreed, and rejected the validity of many of his commentaries. He was a devotee of the objective approach to the biblical texts, although he occasionally refers to a midrashic explanation if it is consistent with the literal meaning of the text, and strongly attacked some earlier commentaries that wandered from the *peshat*, including some of those of his grandfather, referring to some of them as "nonsense" and "twisted explanations." He was of course well aware that the sages of the Talmud often used midrashic explanations of the biblical texts in the halakhic process, to which he was unhesitatingly committed, by basing their rulings on redundancies in the biblical texts in accordance with the hermeneutical rules by which they expounded the Torah. Confronted but undaunted by this problem, he made his position abundantly clear. "Let every sensible person know and understand that although they are of primary importance I have not come to explain the *halakhot* . . . derived as they are from textual redundancies. They can be partly found in the commentaries of Rabbi Solomon, my maternal grandfather. My aim is to interpret the literal meaning of Scripture."[4] Rashbam seems to have written commentaries on the entire *TaNaKH*, most of which succumbed to the vicissitudes of medieval history. The primary exceptions to this being his commentary on the Torah, a substantial portion of which was found in a truncated manuscript, and some fragments from his works that are cited in later commentaries.

In his commentary on the first verse of Genesis, Rashbam strongly affirms the position of Rashi, rejecting out of hand the reading which would render it as though it stated *"Ba'rishonah bara et ha'shamayim* (At first He created the heavens)," and repeats much of his grandfather's commentary in this regard, concluding that it should be read as though it stated *"Be'tehilat briat shamayim va'aretz* (At the outset of the creation of heaven and earth)." He suggests that the reason the text says this is to make us aware that the natural world as we know it was not created at once "in the beginning," but rather over a course of six days, thereby emphasizing the importance of the Sabbath, the seventh day on which God ceased from further creative activity, and therefore, by implication, the first day on which the world as we know it was already complete.

IBN EZRA

Abraham ibn Ezra (1089–1164), a contemporary of Rashbam, was born in Tudela, Spain, was by any account a remarkable individual, both secular and religious poet, Hebrew grammarian, physician, astronomer, philosopher, and biblical commentator. Little is known of his life before 1140, when he left Spain for Rome, other than that he was chronically impoverished, formed a close bond with the philosopher–poet Judah Halevi, and that he visited Morocco, Algeria, and Tunisia. It was in Rome, at the age of 51, that he began his exegetical activity that continued throughout the rest of his life as he wandered from Rome to Lucca, Mantua, and Verona, leaving Italy in 1147 for France, visiting Narbonne and Béziers in Provence, and Rouen and Dreux in the north. In 1158 he moved to London, reappearing in Narbonne in 1161, after which little is known of him, legend having it that he moved to the Land of Israel. During this long period of wandering he never ceased writing, in Hebrew, preferring to compose short works that were more compatible with his life style than longer ones. It seems quite likely that Ibn Ezra wrote commentaries on all the books of the *TaNaKH*, notwithstanding that there are no extant copies of his commentaries on the Early Prophets, Chronicles, Proverbs, Jeremiah, Ezekiel, and Ezra and Nehemiah.

From his works it becomes clear that Ibn Ezra was devoutly religious, brilliant, sharp-witted and sharp-tongued, and possessed of a sophisticated sense of humor, all of which are reflected in his introduction to his commentary on the Pentateuch, which the author named the *Sefer ha'Yashar* (Book of the Upright). The work begins with a poetic preface, which rhymes in the Hebrew.

> Invoking the name of the Great and Awe-inspiring God,
> I begin to explain the meaning of the Torah.
> I beseech thee, O God of my father Abraham,
> Deal kindly with thy servant Abraham.
> And from the salvation of thy face, may help come
> To the son of thy maid servant who is named Ben Ezra.
> This *Book of Jashar*, composed by Abraham the poet,
> Is bound by the ropes of grammar.
> The eyes of the intelligent will find it fit.
> All who take hold of it will be glad.
> The above mentioned Abraham the Spaniard says:
> Those who comment on the Torah do so in one of five ways.[5]

Ibn Ezra then proceeds to enumerate and sharply criticize the various types of commentators and their approaches, using the simile of truth as a dot in a circle. The first approach to biblical interpretation is one which ranges far from the text and may be compared to the periphery of the circle, which when one follows it only brings one back to the staring point, never penetrating into the circle itself. The second approach is that of distortion, those who deviate from tradition and interpret the biblical text in accordance with what they want it to say, based largely on their ignorance of Hebrew grammar and syntax. Such believe they have penetrated the circle and reached the dot at its center, but actually have no idea where it is. The third approach is one of darkness and gloom, and lies entirely outside the circle. Those who adopt this approach invent secret meanings to everything found in Scripture and consider the teachings and laws of the Torah as riddles to be solved. In Ibn Ezra's opinion, this approach is unworthy of serious consideration and is like groping in the dark for that which is clear in the light of day. The fourth approach is close to the mark, relying on midrashic exposition of the texts. However, Ibn Ezra asks, since most of these interpretations are already contained within the classical literature of the sages, why do contemporary writers bother to repeat in their works that which already exists? He points out that in fact some midrashic explanations are consistent with the literal meaning of the text; however, many such explanations are not and should not be taken at face value as actually explaining the biblical text. The fifth approach is the one that Ibn Ezra asserts he will follow, that of understanding every word in the text in accordance with grammar and explaining each word of which the meaning is uncertain the first time it appears.

In his commentary on the first verse of Genesis, Ibn Ezra essentially takes the same position as both Rashi and Rashbam, namely, that the word *be'reshit* is in the construct form and that it should be read not as *In the beginning*, but as *In the beginning of*. However, in his commentary on the second word of the verse, *bara*, ordinarily translated as "created," Ibn Ezra introduces an alternative understanding of the term, based on a complex grammatical analysis that suggests "The meaning of *bara* is to cut or set a boundary. The intelligent person will understand [what I am alluding to]." His cryptic concluding remark, which can be found in numerous instances in his commentaries, suggests that his understanding of the text deviates in a significant manner from the traditional rabbinic perspective, and goes to the heart of the controversy over the meaning and intent of the opening verse of Scripture. The traditional view is that the Bible teaches the belief in creation from nothing, a concept in Jewish theology that many consider essential. Even though Rashi argues that the first verse cannot be construed as stating this, he does not even implicitly argue against the concept itself. Ibn Ezra, however, by translating *bara* as cutting or setting a boundary, appears to be suggesting that creation was from something that could be delimited, some eternal substance endowed with form, a highly contentious proposition in Judaic thought and one which he was unprepared to express openly and explicitly. It has been observed by some that Ibn Ezra has here adopted the neo-Platonic argument, which asserts that the world came into being by emanation from God, a view held by many Kabbalists, and that what the first verse of Genesis teaches is that the creation consisted of God giving final form to that which had previously emanated from Him.

RADAK

David Kimhi (c. 1160–c. 1235), popularly known by the acronym Radak, was another major commentator from Narbonne in Provence, who apparently only wrote commentaries on Genesis, the books of the Prophets, and Psalms. Kimhi was both an exegete and achieved enduring fame as a Hebrew philologist and grammarian. In his commentary on the first verse of Genesis he took a position that completely rejected the arguments of his illustrious predecessors, arguing that *In the beginning* is the correct understanding of the Hebrew, and that the term *reshit* is not in a construct form and must be understood as an absolute, as evidenced by its use in this way by Isaiah: *Magid me'reshit aharit*, translated as *Declaring the end from the beginning* (Isa. 46:10), in which *beginning* is clearly not used in a construct sense. The meaning of the opening verse of the Bible, therefore, is that at the beginning God created the heaven and the earth, and afterward those things that came from them. However, he argues, the second word in the text, *bara*, meaning *created*, can refer to either that which has matter and form, such as the earth, or that which is completely ephemeral, such as the heavens. Thus, when it says that *in the beginning God created . . . the earth*, the term *created* must be understood in the sense of *yetzirah* or "formation," a term later applied only to the creation of things that are characterized by matter and form. But, most importantly, because *bereshit* means *in the [absolute] beginning* and not *in the beginning of [the process]*, the phrase *in the beginning God created . . . the earth* clearly means bringing the earth from a state of nonexistence into one of existence.[6] In other words, the world was created *ex nihilo*.

RAMBAN

Moses ben Nahman or Nahmanides (1194–1270), popularly known by the acronym Ramban, and in his native Catalan as Bonastruc da Porta, was born and spent most of his life in Gerona in Catalonia, ultimately emigrating to the Land of Israel in 1265. In addition to being one of the most influential biblical exegetes of the medieval period, he was also a profound talmudist, philosopher, kabbalist, poet, and physician. Nahmanides's commentary on the *TaNakh* is both an elucidation of the text, a critique of the major commentators who preceded him, especially Rashi and Ibn Ezra, as well as an exposition of his own theology. In a rather long commentary on the first verse of Genesis, he essentially adopts the same position as Kimhi, his much older contemporary. He rejects the views of both Rashi and Ibn Ezra with regard to treating *bereshit* as a construct form, and argues as did Kimhi earlier that the term must be understood as an absolute, using the same prooftext from Isaiah as support for his opinion.

Nahmanides concludes that the biblical use of the term clearly indicates the idea of *creation ex nihilo*, a notion that he elaborates on as follows: "Now listen to the interpretation of this text according to its plain meaning, in a correct and clear manner. The Holy One, blessed be He, created all creations from absolute nihility, and we have no other word in the holy tongue [Hebrew] other than *bara* [translated as create] to express the idea of bringing forth what has existence from nothingness. Indeed, there is nothing *made under the sun* [Eccles. 8:9] or above it that initially comes into being from not-being." By contrast with Kimhi, he argues that the term *bara* always means creation from nothing, but what was created was a primal substance referred to by the Greeks as "hylic matter," that had the intrinsic potential to permit other things to emerge from it. Once this hylic substance was created, nothing further was created from nothing; "God 'formed' and 'made' things—He brought all things into being from it and endowed them with forms and perfected them."[7]

RALBAG

Levi ben Gershom or Gersonides (1288–1344), commonly known by the acronym Ralbag, was probably born at Bagnols-sur-Cèze in Languedoc and spent most of his life at Orange, except for a brief stay at Avignon. Aside from this, very little is known about him other than that he was an accomplished mathematician, astronomer, philosopher, and biblical commentator, and composed works of note in each of these fields. In his massive commentary on the *Torah* he took the approach that everything presented therein, including the narrative portions of the biblical texts, was intended to teach an ethical, philosophical, or religious lesson, and his work is full of examples of these teachings. Thus, with regard to the story of Noah and the Deluge, he asserted that there were ten teachings inherent in the narrative, the fifth of which concerned the biblical text, which relates that *Noah went in, and his sons, and his wife, and his son's wives with him, into the ark* (Gen. 7:7), which implicitly suggests that the men went together and the women separately. Gersonides wrote that the lesson taught by this is "that it is improper for a person to indulge in pleasures at the same time that his neighbors are suffering, because this is a cause of squabbles and dissention among people that undermines the political order. And the Torah pointed this out to us when it mentioned that Noah and his sons and their wives were separated so that when they conceived, they did so after the Deluge and not while they were in the ark."[8]

As it turns out, this reading of the text had already been suggested by Rashi centuries earlier, who made the point somewhat more explicitly: "The men were separate and the women were separate because intercourse was forbidden since the world was engulfed by sorrow."[9] The principle, however, was already set forth in the Talmud, although not derived from the biblical text concerning Noah. "When the community is in trouble let not a man say, 'I will go to my house and I will eat and drink and all will be well with me' . . . But rather a man should share in the distress of the community."[10] None of this, however, detracts from Gersonides's original approach to interpreting the biblical texts, which tends to enhance the significance of the narrative portions as providing notable examples of proper or improper conduct, in effect transforming the relevant texts into a handbook of applied ethics.

Gersonides condemned allegorical interpretations of the texts and sought rational explanations of everything contained therein according to principles of logic. The most controversial aspect of his commentaries involved his attempts to rationalize the *halakhah*, which made his work anathema to some conservative scholars and rabbinic authorities. It is noteworthy that with regard to the question of the meaning of the term *bereshit*, he took the same position as Rashi and Ibn Ezra, asserting that the first verse intends to say that "At the beginning of creation, when God created the heavens and the earth and everything connected to this."[11]

ABRAVANEL

Moving from the medieval period, necessarily omitting many other significant commentaries, to that of the Renaissance, we encounter the towering figure of Isaac Abravanel (1437–1508), who was not only a philosopher and biblical exegete but also a statesman of note. Born and educated in Lisbon, he not only mastered the literature of Judaism but also had a solid grounding in the classics and the works of the foremost Christian theologians. Following in his father's footsteps he was deeply engaged in commerce and state finance throughout his life, serving as treasurer to King Alfonso V of Portugal. Following the latter's death in 1481, the country was destabilized for a time and Abravanel became suspected of conspiracy against João II and was forced to flee the country in 1483, and was sentenced to death *in abstentia* two years later. He relocated to Castile, where he soon entered the service of the royal house, but was forced to leave Spain in 1492 and went to Naples, where he was appointed a royal financial agent of Ferrante I and then Alfonso II. After the French sacked Naples in 1494, he relocated with the royal family to Messina and, after the death of Alfonso, went to Corfu, eventually settling in Venice in 1503, where he undertook diplomatic missions for the Venetian government. In the midst of his continuously hectic professional life he managed to compose a large number of commentaries on biblical books and other subjects of Judaic interest.

In his approach to the Torah he rejected allegorical and philosophical as well as kabbalistic interpretations of the texts. He nonetheless maintained that the Torah contained hidden subtexts in addition to the straightforward meanings of the texts, leading him to quote extensively from midrashic sources. However, he did not hesitate to criticize such sources when their interpretations deviated too far from the literal meaning of the text. The influence of earlier commentators, most notably Gersonides, is apparent throughout his commentaries. He does not comment on the text, verse by verse, but rather divides it into chapters or sections according to subject matter, beginning each discussion by pointing out what he perceives as issues implicit in the text as a means of initiating discussion of its content. That which is especially distinctive about his commentary is his frequent comparisons between biblical society and its issues and that of the European societies of his day, a preoccupation with Christian biblical exegesis and refutation of Christological interpretations, and his comprehensive introductions to the books of the prophets. His commentaries on the Torah are voluminous, sometimes repetitive, but at the same time comprehensive, and for the most part quite interesting and illuminating.

Abravanel's political experience is clearly reflected in some of his commentary, most especially with regard to the text in which Moses instructs the nation: *When thou art come into the land . . . and shalt say: 'I will set a king over me, like all the nations that are round about me'; thou shalt in any wise set him king over thee, whom the Lord thy God shall choose* (Deut. 17:14–15). The question as to whether, according to this text, a monarchy was mandated or optional had been a matter of contention since early biblical days. Abravanel's antimonarchist arguments reflect his perception of the relative beneficence of the republican forms of government he found in some Italian states. Coming to Italy in the wake of the expulsion of the Jews from Spain, he discovered in Venice a state that was free from the excesses of the monarchies that he had served as statesman and financier in Portugal and Spain. In his lengthy commentary on the biblical text he wrote:

> It is fitting that we should understand if the king is a necessary thing and self-obligatory upon a people, or whether it is possible to manage without one. The philosophers have already considered . . . that monarchy will realize three things: first—harmony and political participation; second—continuity and political change; third—the power of ultimate decision. We will see that in truth their views regarding the obligation to have a king as well as the necessity for one are fallacious, because they do not preclude there being among the people numerous leaders to organize and agree upon a common course, and that through them there should be leadership as well as justice, and this applies to the first consideration. And why should their leadership not be on an annual basis or for three years . . . or for less, and when their turn arrives, different judges and officers will take their places and examine the transgressions of their predecessors, and those who are condemned for their acts will pay compensation for their misdeeds, and this will apply to the second consideration. And should not the power of decision be delimited and structured in accordance with the laws and legal precepts which state that in the case of a minority and a majority, the law is as seen by the majority? For it is more likely that an individual will transgress the law . . . than that many people within a single entity will commit evil . . . and by their tenure being temporary, they will fear because they will be called to account in a short while. But why do we have to bring rational argument to this issue? Experience provides greater evidence. Look and see those lands that are ruled by kings. We have seen several lands that are governed by temporary judges and rulers, selected from among themselves . . . and still today, the rulership of Venice, mistress of nations and chief among states, and the government of Florence, an example to all other lands and governments, both small and large, have no king among them, and they are led by leaders who are selected for an allocated time . . . All this demonstrates that the presence of a king in a nation is not necessary.[12]

With regard to the question of the meaning of the term *bereshit*, Abravanel begins his commentary by asking, "if the text intends to relate the order of creation . . . how does it state that at first God created the heaven and the earth? After all, they encompass all material existence, both above and below, and if all this was created at the outset, what was it that was created afterward?" He then goes on to point out that earlier commentators, specifically Rashi, Ibn Ezra, and Gersonides, effectively resolved this problem by arguing that the text does not intend to set forth the order of creation. They therefore asserted that the word *bereshit* must be understood as being in a construct form, meaning not "in the beginning God created the heaven and the earth," but "in the beginning of God's creation of the heaven and the earth."

But Abravanel insists, "this interpretation has no validity at all for me," and takes about a hundred lines to discuss the problems it presents.

Abravanel's own partial solution to the problem is that Rashi, Ibn Ezra, and Gersonides are correct in their assessment that *bereshit* is in a construct form, meaning "in the beginning of," but were mistaken in their assumption that it meant to say "in the beginning of God's creation of the heaven and the earth." He suggests that the text does set forth the order of creation and in order to do so implicitly indicates the presence of a word that it does not articulate, namely, "time." That is, the text should be understood as saying, "In the beginning *of time* God created the heaven and the earth." He explains that the word "time" is not employed in the text because the text speaks of material creation and that the introduction of the notion of the creation of time is one that is difficult to grasp, suggesting that there are times when constructive ambiguity is appropriate.[13]

SFORNO

Obadiah Sforno (c. 1470–c. 1550) was born in Cesena, Italy, and studied philosophy, mathematics, philology, and medicine in Rome. He was both a practicing physician and a renowned biblical commentator who established a house of study in Bologna over which he presided during the latter part of his life. In this regard, it is of interest to note that during his time in Rome, at the recommendation of Cardinal Grimani, Sforno instructed the famous Christian humanist Johannes Reuchlin in the Hebrew language from 1498 to 1500.

Sforno's commentary on the Torah has since been considered a valuable source of insight into the biblical texts and continues to be published in editions of the Rabbinic Bible along with those of Rashi, Ibn Ezra, and Nahmanides. His commentaries on the texts are typically brief and to the point—he rarely cites *midrash aggadah* and avoids the mystical and kabbalistic interpretations that had become so popular among his contemporaries. At times, his insights are both incisive and surprising. Thus, with regard to the story of the failed attempt by the wife of his benefactor Potiphar to seduce Joseph, and her subsequent claim that the latter had attempted to assault her, the text relates: *And it came to pass, when his master heard the words of his wife, which she spoke unto him, saying: 'After this manner did thy servant to me'; that his wrath was kindled* (Gen. 39:19). Sforno comments that *his wrath was kindled* not against Joseph, who he did not believe would have done such a thing, but against his wife, but that he was compelled to preserve her honor and therefore had Joseph imprisoned to demonstrate his trust in her.[14] However, as soon as the opportunity came to get him released so that he could interpret the dreams that so troubled the Pharaoh, he did so with alacrity, since this did not affect the honor of his wife.

In a sense, Sforno was truly a man of the Renaissance, imbued with the humanism of the era, which is reflected in some of his commentaries. Thus, with regard to the text, *Now therefore, if ye will hearken unto My voice indeed, and keep My covenant, then ye shall be Mine own treasure from among all peoples* (Ex. 19:5), Sforno comments on the last clause of the citation, "even though all of humanity is more dear to me than all other lowly creatures . . . as the sages said 'beloved is man who was created in the image,' in any case you will be more treasured than all."[15] In other words the difference between Israel and the nations is only with regard to observance of the covenant.

With regard to the question of the meaning of the opening word of Scripture, *bereshit*, Sforno rejects the views of Rashi and Ibn Ezra, and defines the term as, "At the beginning of time, and this is the first undivided instant for there was no time before it."

EPHRAIM OF LUNTSHITS

Ephraim of Luntshits (1550–1619), a rabbi and renowned preacher, originated from Leczyca (popularly known as Luntshits among Jews) in Poland, and lived and preached in many places including Lublin, Lemberg, Jaroslaw, and Prague, where he served as president of the rabbinical court and head of its seminary from 1604 to 1618. His commentary on the Torah, *Kli Yakar* (Precious Instrument), one of the earliest to have a distinctive title, is rather different in style and content than those previously discussed. As a preacher, his approach to reading the biblical text was primarily homiletic, but is nonetheless of continuing great interest, a consideration that led to the frequent reprinting of his commentary in many editions of the Rabbinic Bible to this very day.

With regard to the question of the meaning of *bereshit*, Ephraim of Luntshits essentially ignores the philological issue and is more concerned with why the text starts out with it rather than with the name of God, which is only mentioned two words later. His response is to invoke a *midrash* that argues that the word *reshit* refers to Torah and to Israel, as in the biblical statement *The Lord made me as the beginning [reshit] of His way* (Prov. 8:22), which was said of Wisdom, which the sages equated to Torah, and *Israel is the Lord's hallowed portion, His first-fruits [reshit] of the increase* (Jer. 2:3). Understanding the *be* of *be'reshit* to mean "for" rather that "in" the text may therefore be read as saying "For the sake of Torah and Israel, God created the heaven and the earth." In other words, Ephraim argues, the use of *reshit* is intended to assert "that both (Torah and Israel) serve as an introduction to the acknowledgement of the existence of God," which both proclaim. The only other alternative to such knowledge, he argues, can be achieved through philosophical research that is beyond the ability of the average person. Nonetheless, he concludes the discussion by remarking that, according to its plain meaning, "it was necessary to begin the Torah with *bereshit* in order to establish the belief in creation from nothing (*creation ex nihilo*), because that is the foundation of the entire Torah; for if one postulated the eternity of matter, there would be no place for the Torah, which is predicated on a foundation of free will."[16] Although he is not explicit about it, this last comment implicitly suggests that he is in accord with the view that *bereshit* must be understood literally as, "in the beginning of time."

IBN ATTAR

Hayyim ibn Attar (1696–1743), rabbi and kabbalist, was born in Salé, Morocco, but later settled in Meknes where he taught and ran the family business in partnership with his father-in-law until about 1739 when he sought to emigrate to the Land of Israel, detouring through Italy, and eventually reaching Jerusalem two years later, where he established an academy. His best-known work is his commentary on the Torah, *Or haHayyim* (Light of Life), a play on his name, which became immensely popular in Germany and Poland, especially among the Hasidic communities, in many of which it was read along with the weekly portion of the Torah. As a result of the popularity of his work, it has been republished many times and is to be found in many editions of the Rabbinic Bible to this day. In his work, Attar introduces a good number of kabbalistic readings of the text, and frequently cites *midrash aggadah* as prooftexts for his interpretations.

With regard to the question of the meaning of *bereshit* and its implications, Attar begins his lengthy discussion by pointing out, presumably referring to Rashi, that it is said that the form of the word is construct; however, he observes, the term to which it is connected is missing, which by implication rejects the argument that it means "in the beginning of," as Rashi would have it. He then goes on to explain that the first verse of Genesis is intended to convey the idea that the entire universe was created in its entirety by the divine word at the very beginning, and that what took place on the following days of creation was the transformation of that which was created into the forms subsequently described.[17]

MALBIM

Meir Loeb ben Jehiel Michael (1809–1879), rabbi and preacher universally known by the acronym Malbim, is one of the most popular commentators on the *TaNaKH* of modern times. Born in Volhynia in the Ukraine, he ultimately moved to Bucharest where he became the chief rabbi of Rumania in 1858. His uncompromising stand against the Reform movement led to communal disputes and false accusations against him that forced him to leave Rumania in 1864, and to wander about Eastern Europe for the remainder of his life. Despite the vicissitudes of his precarious existence, Malbim managed to produce commentaries with the avowed purpose of demonstrating that the Oral Torah is of divine origin and that its essential teachings are to be found in the plain and implicit meanings of the text, which must be interpreted in accordance with accurate linguistic rules.

His commentary *HaTorah vehaMitzvah* ("The Teaching and the Commandment") is based on the guiding principles that there are no words or phrases in the Bible that are there for stylistic reasons alone; that as a result, every word in the text is essential to convey the true meaning of the text in accordance with the established rules of grammar; and that every biblical statement conveys a sublime thought and every metaphor is a repository of divine wisdom. He was convinced that the ancient sages had a firm grasp of all the principles of grammar and logic that enabled them to comprehend the significance of everything contained in the Torah. He compiled a compendium of these rules and principles in a small work, *Ayelet haShahar*, which he placed as a preface to his commentary on the *Sifra*, the classical collection of *midrash halakhah* on the book of Leviticus, in emulation of the similar placement of the thirteen hermeneutic rules of R. Ishmael in antiquity. The work consists of 613 paragraphs, which include 248 dealing with linguistic rules and 365 that explain verbs and synonyms, obviously paralleling the traditional 613 precepts of Judaism, divided into 248 positive and 365 negative commandments.

The first of the rules of grammar, according to Malbim, is that the sages agreed with the view of the medieval philologists that every root in Hebrew consists of no more than three letters, and that those that seem to do so are either composites or are adopted from other languages. The first of the rules regarding the meaning of verbs and synonyms (# 249) is that which points out that the term *adam* (man) is a noun, whereas the term *ish* (man) is an adjectival form describing the noun; as a noun, *adam* has no gender, as evidenced by the fact that there is no feminine form of the word, whereas *ish* is masculine, the feminine form of which is *ishah*. This consequently leads to the second rule (# 250), which is that *adam*, or any other noun which has no feminine derivative, must be understood in a generic sense.[18] This becomes clear when we consider the biblical text *And God created man [adam]* . . . *male and female created He them* (Gen. 1:27), and then the verse *And the man [adam] said . . . she shall be called Woman [ishah] because she was taken out of Man [ish]* (Gen. 2:23).

With regard to the question of the meaning of *bereshit*, according to Malbim, the Rashi-Ibn Ezra understanding of the biblical verse is grammatically problematic because the word *reshit* is always used in an absolute sense (which is itself a highly contentious proposition). That is, he says, if one wanted to describe the beginning of a process or sequence one would have to employ a different term than *bereshit* such as *berishonah*, the Hebrew *rishon* being an ordinal number—"first." Therefore, Malbim argues, the biblical use of *bereshit* at the outset of the creation narrative clearly suggests that the statement is intended to imply that the creation of heaven and earth were completed at the very outset of the process and not at its conclusion.[19]

HIRSCH

Samson Raphael Hirsch (1808–1888), rabbi and writer, was born in Hamburg, became lead rabbi of the principality of Oldenburg in 1830, moved to Emden in 1841 and in 1846 became leading rabbi of Moravia until 1851, when he became rabbi of the Orthodox congregation in Frankfort on the Main, where he remained until his death 37 years later. Hirsch was the foremost spokesman for Orthodoxy in Germany, a prolific writer, and indefatigable opponent of the Reform movement.

Hirsch is the one of the few commentators mentioned in this chapter whose work was not written in Hebrew; to meet the challenges faced by his community he translated the Torah into German and wrote his massive commentary in that language as well. Nonetheless, he wrote:

> We must also read the Torah in *Hebrew*—that is to say, in accordance with the spirit of that language. It describes but little, but through the rich significance of its verbal roots it paints in a word a picture of the thing. It only joins for us predicate to subject, and sentence to sentence; but it presupposes the listening soul so watchful and attentive that the deeper sense and profounder meaning, which lie not upon but below the surface, may be supplied by the independent action of the mind. It is, as it were, a semi-symbolic writing. With wakeful eye and ear, and with soul roused to activity, we must read; nothing is told us of such superficial import that we need only, as it were, accept it with half roused dreaminess; we must strive ourselves to create again the speaker's thoughts, to think them over, or the sense will escape us.[20]

In his approach to the biblical texts he thus focused on what they said to the heart and intellect, rejecting methods of interpretation that attempted to construe the meaning of the texts through the prism of history and historical context. His avowed aims in writing his commentary were to explain the text "out of itself," to determine the true meaning of a text by considering all of its nuances and implicit meanings, to ascertain the meaning of the words of the text by reference to how the word is employed elsewhere in the traditional literature, to understand the text through the prism of the traditions regarding the transmission of the texts and the worldview that is based on it, and finally to demonstrate that the ideas expressed in the Torah have eternal validity and are not merely a reflection of a particular moment in history.

In pursuing this approach in his work Hirsch sometimes makes lavish use of the method of "speculative etymology," interpreting the texts by exploring the meaning of Hebrew word roots by the interrelationship of sounds with their cognates, as illustrated below, an approach that on occasion may appear somewhat far-fetched. With regard to the question of the meaning of *bereshit*, Hirsch wrote:

> The phonetic relation of *rosh* [meaning "head," which is the root of *reshit*] to *raash* and *rahash* of which the one designates a physical movement and the other an internal one, teaches that we are to consider *rosh* as the seat of movement, as that organ from which all external and internal movement has its origin. Hence, *reshit* means the beginning of a movement, a beginning in time, never in space . . . [It] means: in the beginning of all coming into existence, it was God Who created, or taking it in connection with the two objects that follow: At the very beginning God created the heaven and the earth. In any case *bereshit* expresses the fact that nothing preceded God's creation, that heaven and earth came into existence solely by the creation of God. This affirms creation out of nothing *yesh mi'ayin* [*creation ex nihilo*], a fact that forms the foundation-stone of the understanding which God's Torah wishes to build up in us. The contrary belief, that matter always existed, and only ascribes to the Creator a formative function . . . is not only a metaphysical lie which has robbed the theories of mankind as to the origin of the world of the truth i.e. of agreement with actuality, but is the much farther-reaching pernicious denial of all freedom of will in God and Man, which undermines all morality.[21]

The commentators and their works discussed in this chapter represent what is widely considered to be the classical literature of biblical interpretation. It should be noted, however, that the list of significant commentaries written over the past seven hundred years could be greatly extended, especially if the discussion is expanded to consider the very large number of works devoted to metarational interpretations of the biblical writings. This has not been undertaken here because such works, generally speaking, merit separate treatment in a broader discussion of Jewish mysticism and kabbalah and its extensive literature.

Chapter 8

The Contemporary State of the Literature

It will be noted that the preceding chapter on biblical commentaries concluded with a discussion of an important nineteenth-century commentator, notwithstanding that a large number of Judaic commentaries on the various books of the *TaNaKH* were produced in the twentieth century and continue to be published at the outset of the present century. However, it would be difficult to identify any of these as having the same stature and influence as those discussed earlier. This is not to suggest that they are not valuable contributions to the interpretive literature, or that some future commentary will become the representative classic of the age, only that for reasons of space, they cannot be considered here. What is the case with biblical commentaries is also that with regard to the other forms of literature discussed in the other chapters of this book.

In the introduction to this book, it was pointed out that the state of Judaic thought and rabbinic literature at the outset of the twenty-first century is unquestionably more variegated than at any previous period in the long history of Judaism, and this is reflected in the outpouring of an unprecedented number of books and articles dealing with Judaism. Moreover, with the advent of the Internet, the volume of such material is becoming staggering, although it should be noted that a great deal of this electronic literature does not pass through any form of peer or even editorial review, making it necessary for the reader to be especially diligent in assessing its true merit. A number of explanations have been offered to account for this virtual flood of literary production, perhaps the primary one being that it is precipitated by a perceived need for accommodating Judaic thought to intellectual vistas that are uniquely modern in that they are not restricted to a small intellectual elite but are open to every intelligent person prepared to invest even a modicum of energy in exploring them.

Until quite recently this was primarily an evolving situation in the so-called Western world, where the democratization of higher education exposed ever greater numbers of Jews to nontraditional modes of thought, most notably with regard to the various fields of science and also in the realms of the humanities and social sciences. The popularization of secular knowledge and the education of many contemporary rabbis as professionals in diverse fields such as medicine, law, psychology, literature, and the natural and social sciences, has resulted in the proliferation of both scholarly and popular publications, many of which purport to interpret traditional Judaic teachings in the light of these disciplines. Space constraints in this book do not permit a review and analysis of the large number of such works; however, it is important to recognize that more than a few of these that seek to exploit the current popular interest in topics such as mysticism and kabbalah are quite superficial and hardly merit consideration as serious works of Judaic thought.

One of the consequences of this explosion in learning and knowledge over the course of the last hundred and fifty years or so has been an increasing inability on the part of many who have absorbed and been influenced by a secular education to reconcile their perceptions and emerging worldviews with many of the traditional teachings reflected in the various forms of rabbinic literature. This has resulted in the emergence over the past century of a genre of Jewish literature that has not been discussed in this book, primarily because it does not fit well in any of the categories of classical Judaic thought and rabbinic literature with which this book is concerned. This genre consists in the main of books about Judaism as each individual author conceives it. As suggested, this is for the most part a modern development although its roots can be found in the classical and medieval Jewish philosophical literature, which requires separate treatment. What primarily distinguishes most modern works *about* Judaism from the traditional works *of* Judaism is that the former consider Judaism as a religion, a minority one at that, which needs to be explained to those unfamiliar with it, Jew and Gentile alike. By contrast, the latter works for the most part consider Judaism as a civilization that encompasses the entire gamut of social, political, economic, moral, and religious life, a civilization in which they live or aspire to live, and wish to elaborate on for the benefit of those with similar orientations. The former genre tends to be apologetic in character, explaining why Judaism is compatible with democracy, liberalism, or conservatism, depending on the intended audience, whereas the latter is generally speaking quite uninhibited and self-assured, and often not particularly concerned about how Judaism is perceived by the surrounding society. The former is essentially literature written by Jews intended for a broad audience, the latter is basically literature written by Jews for Jews.

The general problem of acculturation to a non-Judaic environment and its impact on Judaic thought and literature has been further exacerbated by the flowering of what was known in the nineteenth century as the Science of Judaism and today as the academic study of Judaism, both reflecting approaches to the study of Judaic thought and literature using disciplinary tools and analytic protocols adapted from their application in several fields of secular studies. While there certainly is some validity and utility in these approaches, which have not always been employed judiciously, all too often the works produced by contemporary scholars of Judaism, which may be found suffused with academic jargon and circumlocutions, appear to be designed more to appeal to academic colleagues than to educate interested nonspecialist readers.

By contrast, there is also a growing body of Judaic literature emerging from the various movements or trends in modern and contemporary Judaism, the primary purpose of which is to educate the present generation with regard to the various aspects of their Judaic heritage, from religious matters to ethics and social relations. Much of contemporary and relatively recent rabbinic writing is concerned with *halakhah* and religious observance, either in support of or in deviation from the literature discussed in the third, fourth, and sixth chapters of this book. It is in regard to these broad subjects that the literature of the various contemporary movements or trends in Judaism is most distinctive, reflecting widely differing theological and historical perspectives, a full treatment of which is beyond the scope of the present work. Suffice it to note at this point that the antipodes of the spectrum of contemporary Judaic thought and rabbinic literature, particularly in the United States, are to be found in the Orthodox and Reconstructionist movements, the latter a distinctively American phenomenon, with the larger Conservative and Reform movements occupying the broad middle ground. The situation is somewhat different in Israel where Orthodoxy dominates the religious scene in the primarily secular Jewish society, the Conservative and Reform movements currently serving as a religious point of reference for a relatively small number of adherents in the country.

The ideological differences between the movements or trends in Judaism are reflected in their literatures in a variety of ways, including their approaches to understanding the meaning and implications of the biblical texts that provide the underpinning for all of Judaic thought. This is reflected in the fate of the fairly literal Jewish

Publication Society (JPS) 1917 translation of the Bible, which was broadly considered the "authorized" version by the Jewish community for a half century, notwithstanding its archaic modes of expression. The literality of translations is especially critical for those who must rely on them when considering their use in the midrashic literature, discussed in the second and fifth chapters of this book, which is intimately and inextricably linked to the nuances of the Hebrew texts of the biblical writings. This literalist, old JPS version has now effectively been made obsolete by a variety of new translations, ranging from the close to literal to what sometimes appears to be a paraphrase rather than a translation, produced by the various contemporary movements in Judaism or by those whose outlooks tend to converge with those of the several movements. As a result, there are today at least six different "Jewish" translations in circulation, including the widely used 1962 new JPS translation produced by a committee of noted scholars. There is some irony in the fact that the JPS has recently produced a series of voluminous commentaries on its own new JPS translation of the Torah, in which the commentators repeatedly challenge the accuracy and validity of the translation, often rejecting it out of hand and offering alternatives considered to be more in keeping with the intent of the biblical author.

Hebrew readers have a distinct advantage in this regard in that there is only one "authorized" Hebrew text, the Masoretic. Thus, in Hebrew scholarly studies, the biblical text is presented without translation and its understanding by the writer is relegated to his commentary, where he indicates or hopefully explains how he interprets the text. Moreover, the so-called Rabbinic Bible, the *Mikraot Gedolot* ("Great Scriptures"), may have as many as ten different commentaries, and notes on the commentaries accompany the text, thus providing a range of possible interpretations of the text without prejudicing one's consideration of the text by a translation that actually reflects a particular interpretation. A forthcoming, closely literal English translation of the *Mikraot Gedolot* on the Pentateuch will prove a boon to anyone interested in trying to understand how the biblical texts can be read in a variety of ways.

In addition to the growing number of classical biblical commentaries now appearing in English, new translations and commentaries on the *Mishnah*, the Babylonian and Jerusalem Talmuds, and various works of Midrash, are also becoming available, opening up what has long been a virtually inaccessible body of Judaic literature to the English reader. Indeed, this may be reckoned as perhaps the most significant contemporary development and achievement in the field of Judaic thought and rabbinic literature.

Notes

CHAPTER 1

1. *Babylonian Talmud: Sanhedrin* 21b (henceforth cited as *B.T.*).
2. *Jerusalem Talmud: Sotah* 5:6 (henceforth cited as *J.T.*).
3. *B.T. Megillah* 15a.
4. *B.T. Avodah Zarah* 25a.
5. *B.T. Sotah* 36b.
6. Ibid., 48b.
7. *B.T. Shabbat* 13b; *B.T. Hagigah* 13a.
8. David Noel Freedman, *The Nine Commandments*, pp. 122–124.
9. Josephus, *Against Apion* 1:39.
10. *B.T. Baba Batra* 14b.
11. Ibid.
12. Joseph Caro, *Shulhan Aruch: Yoreh Deah* 283:5.
13. *B.T. Baba Batra* 14b.
14. *Mishnah Yadaim* 3:5.
15. *B.T. Shabbat* 14a.
16. *Tosefta Yadaim* 2:13.
17. *B.T. Megillah* 27a.
18. For an extensive discussion of the various aspects and history of the Masorah, see the book-length article "Masorah" among the supplemental entries in Volume 16 of the Encyclopaedia Judaica.
19. Joseph H. Hertz, *The Pentateuch and Haftorahs*, on Gen. 3:1.
20. *B.T. Baba Batra* 14b–15a.
21. Both views are cited by Adin Steinsaltz, *Talmud Bavli: Baba Batra*, vol. 1, p. 61.
22. Saadia Gaon, *Perush Rabbenu Saadiah Gaon al haTorah* on Deut. 27:3.

23. Abraham ibn Ezra, *Perushei haTorah* on Deut. 27:3.
24. Spinoza, *A Theologico-Political Treatise*, ch. 8–10.

CHAPTER 2

1. *Sifra* "Behukotai," Perek 8:13
2. *B.T. Gittin* 60b.
3. *Mishnah Avot* 1:1
4. Hayyim (Hugo) Mantel, *Anshei Knesset ha-Gedolah*, pp. 63–80.
5. *B.T. Yevamot* 76b.
6. *B.T. Baba Metzia* 59b.
7. Ibid.
8. Melamed, Ezra Zion. *Mavo leSifrut haTalmud*, pp. 13–16.
9. *Mekilta de-Rabbi Ishmael*, vol. 2, pp. 260–261.
10. Ibid., vol. 3, pp. 67–68.
11. *B.T. Baba Kamma* 83b–84a.
12. *Mekilta de-Rabbi Ishmael*, vol. 3, p. 68.
13. *Sifre al Sefer Bamidbar*, Piska 134, p. 178. See also *B.T. Baba Batra* 109a.
14. Ibid., Piska 58, pp. 55–56.
15. *Sifra*, "Kedoshim," Parshata 2:13.
16. *B.T. Baba Metzia* 62a.
17. *Sifra*, "Behar," Parshata 5:3.
18. *Sifre* on Deuteronomy, Piska 273, p. 268.
19. Ibid., Piska 280, p. 272.

CHAPTER 3

1. Josephus, *Antiquities of the Jews* 13:10:6.
2. Herman L. Strack, *Introduction to the Talmud and Midrash*, p.12.
3. *Mishnah Eduyot* 8:4. For discussion of these rulings, see *B.T. Avodah Zarah* 37a–b.
4. For a list of the major scholars on both sides of the argument, see Strack, *Introduction to the Talmud and Midrash*, pp. 18–19.
5. *Sifre* on Deuteronomy, Piska 273, p. 268.
6. *Mishnah Sanhedrin* 11:1.
7. *Mishnah Peah* 1:2.
8. Ibid., 1:4.
9. Ibid., 1:5.
10. *Mekilta de-Rabbi Ishmael*, vol. 2, p. 253.
11. Ibid., vol. 3, p. 197.
12. *Mishnah Shabbat* 7:2.
13. *Sifre* on Deuteronomy, Piska 194–197.
14. *Mishnah Sotah* 8:2.
15. Ibid., 8:5.
16. Ibid., 8:7.

17. *Mishnah Eduyot* 1:4.

18. Ibid., 1:5.

19. Ibid., 1:6.

20. *Mishnah Hullin* 5:1.

21. *Mishnah Niddah* 5:6.

22. *Mishnah Pesahim* 10:2.

23. *Tosefta Pesahim* 10:2–3.

24. *B.T. Pesahim* 114a.

25. *Mishnah Kiddushin* 1:1.

26. *Tosefta Kiddushin* 1:1–3.

27. *B.T. Kiddushin* 9a–10b.

28. *B.T. Shabbat* 31a.

29. H. Freedman, *B.T. Shabbat* 31a (Soncino edition), n. 8, p. 141.

30. Louis Finkelstein, "Introductory Study to *Pirke Avot*," pp. 14–15.

31. Judah Goldin, "Avot," *Encyclopaedia Judaica*, vol. 3, p. 983.

32. Simha ben Samuel of Vitry, *Mahzor Vitry*, p. 461.

33. *B.T. Berakhot* 16b.

34. *Tosefta Tebul Yom* 1:10.

35. *Mishnah Eduyyot* 1:4.

36. David Z. Hoffmann, *HaMishnah HaRishonah*, p. 28.

37. Samson Raphael Hirsch, *Chapters of the Fathers*, ad loc.

38. Herbert Danby, *The Mishnah*, p. 332.

39. Jacob Emden, *Siddur Beit Yaacov*, ad loc.

40. For an in-depth study of *Avot*, see my *The Moral Maxims of the Sages of Israel*.

41. *Mishnah Avot* 2:1.

42. *B.T. Tamid* 28a.

CHAPTER 4

1. *B.T. Sanhedrin* 17b; *J.T. Shabbat* 5:4.

2. The term *Gemara* is derived from the verb *gamar*, meaning to complete, that is, to complete the Oral Torah.However, in the Babylonian Talmud, the term *gemara* (which is not used at all in the Jerusalem Talmud), for reasons that remain a mystery, is employed to refer to "received teaching," that is, what was received from earlier generations, as opposed to rationalizations offered by scholars to explain those teachings.

3. Adin Steinsaltz, *The Essential Talmud*, p. 4.

4. Ibid., p. 6.

5. Christine Elizabeth Hayes, *Between the Babylonian and Palestinian Talmuds*, p. 35.

6. Jacob Neusner, *Invitation to the Talmud*, p. 267.

7. Yosef Reinman, in Ammiel Hirsch and Yosef Reinman, *One People, Two Worlds*, p. 208.

8. *Mishnah Baba Metzia* 1:1.

9. *B.T. Baba Metzia* 2a.

10. *B.T. Baba Kamma* 70a–70b.

11. *Mishnah Baba Kamma* 7:2.

12. This account is repeated in *B.T. Baba Batra* 56b.

13. *Mishnah Niddah* 6:11.

14. *Mishnah Kiddushin* 1:1.

15. *B.T. Kiddushin* 2a–b.

16. *Mishnah Kiddushin* 2:1.

17. *B.T. Berakhot* 52a.

18. *Tosefta Pesahim* 10:2–3.

19. *J.T. Berakhot* 8:1.

CHAPTER 5

1. Isidore Epstein, "Foreword," *Midrash Rabbah* (Soncino Edition), vol. 1, p. xvi.

2. Louis Finkelstein, "The Oldest Midrash: Pre-Rabbinic Ideals and Teachings in the Passover Haggadah," *Harvard Theological Review*, vol. 31, 1938, p. 293.

3. The translation and discussion of the Haggadah is from my *A Passover Seder Companion and Analytic Introduction to the Haggadah*, pp. 74–91.

4. *Sifre Deuteronomy*, Piska 301.

5. *B.T. Yoma* 74b. The translation of the euphemism is from the Soncino edition of the *Babylonian Talmud*.

6. *B.T. Sukkah* 45b.

7. See references in Finkelstein, "The Oldest Midrash," p. 297, n. 10.

8. *Midrash Rabbah*: Genesis 1:15 (1:21 in some editions).

9. Norman Bentwich, *Hellenism*, pp. 255–256.

10. *Midrash Rabbah: Numbers*, 1:7 (1:6 in some editions).

11. *Midrash Rabbah: Lamentations*, Poems, 2, p. 2.

12. Ibid., 1:1.

13. *Midrash Tanhuma* (Rosen edition) 2; *Midrash Tanhuma-Yelammedenu*, p. 16.

14. *Midrash Mishlei*, ch. 17; *The Midrash on Proverbs*, p. 85.

15. For a more comprehensive discussion of this issue, see Martin Sicker, *Judaism, Nationalism, and the Land of Israel*, ch. 3.

16. *Mishnah Avot* 4:1.

17. *Tanna debe Eliyahu*, ch. 1; *Tanna debe Eliyahu* (Braude and Kapstein translation), p. 3.

18. *Pesikta deRab Kahana*, Piska 12; *Pesikta de-Rab Kahana*, pp. 226–227.

19. The bracketed passage does not appear in the text of the Hebrew edition of *Pesikta Rabbati* used in the preparation of this section, but does appear there as a footnote.

20. *Pesikta Rabbati*, ch. 16, end; *Pesikta Rabbati* (Braude translation), vol. 1, pp. 358–359.

21. *Pirke Rabbi Eliezer*, ch. 15; *Pirke de Rabbi Eliezer* (Friedlander translation), pp. 102–103.

CHAPTER 6

1. Maimonides, *Mishneh Torah: Hilkhot Matenot Aniyim* 10: 7–14; *The Book of Agriculture*, pp. 91–92.
2. Maimonides, *Mishneh Torah: Sefer haMadda*, Introduction, pp. 14–15.
3. Jacob ben Asher, *Arba'ah Turim: Orah Hayyim*, Introduction.
4. *B.T. Makkot* 23b.
5. Maimonides, *The Commandments*, Negative Commandment #32.
6. *Sefer haHinukh* #1.
7. *Teshuvot haGeonim: Shaarei Teshuvah* #7.
8. *American Reform Responsa*, p. 193.
9. Isaac Klein, *Responsa and Halakhic Studies*, p. 123.
10. Cited in Irving J. Rosenbaum, *The Holocaust and Halakhah*, pp. 146–147.

CHAPTER 7

1. *Mishnah Shabbat* 6:4
2. *B.T. Shabbat* 63a.
3. Rashi, *Perushei Rashi* on Gen. 1:1.
4. Rashbam, *Perush haTorah*, preface to the section beginning with Ex. 21:1, p. 113.
5. Abraham ibn Ezra, *Ibn Ezra's Commentary on the Pentateuch*, p. 1.
6. David Kimhi, *Perush Radak al haTorah* on Gen. 1:1.
7. Nahmanides, *Perushei haTorah* on Gen 1:1.
8. Levi ben Gershom, *Perushei haTorah*, vol. 1, p. 91.
9. Rashi, *Perushei Rashi* on Gen. 7:7.
10. *B.T. Taanit* 11a.
11. Gersonides, *Perushei haTorah*, vol. 1, p. 22.
12. Isaac Abravanel, *Perush haTorah*, "Devarim," pp. 26a–b.
13. Ibid., "Bereshit," pp. 1a, 3b–4a.
14. Obadiah Sforno, *Biur al haTorah* on Gen. 39:19.
15. Ibid., on Ex. 19:5.
16. Ephraim of Luntshits, *Perush Kli Yakar haShalem*, pp. 1–3.
17. Hayyim ibn Attar, *Or haHayyim* on Gen. 1:1.
18. Malbim, *HaTorah vehaMitzvah*, vol. 1, pp. 455, 474.
19. Ibid., pp. 2–3.
20. Samson Raphael Hirsch, *The Nineteen Letters of Ben Uziel*, pp. 14–15.
21. Hirsch, *The Pentateuch* on Gen. 1:1.

References

CLASSICAL RABBINIC WORKS

The Babylonian Talmud. 18 vols. London: Soncino Press, 1978.

Mekhilta deRabbi Yishmael. With Notes by H.S. Horovitz and I.A. Rabin. Jerusalem: Wahrmann Books, 1970.

Mekilta deRabbi Ishmael. 3 vols. Edited by Jacob Z. Lauterbach. Philadelphia: Jewish Publication Society, 1949.

Midrash Mishlei. Edited by Solomon Buber. Vilna: Romm Brothers, 1893; Facsimile: Israel, 1965.

The Midrash on Proverbs. Translated and Annotated by Burton L. Visotzky. New Haven: Yale University Press, 1992.

Midrash Tanhuma. 2 Vols. Commentary by Abraham M. Rosen. Warsaw, 1878; Reprinted New York: Ateret, 1969.

Midrash Tanhuma. 2 Vols. Edited with Introduction by Solomon Buber. Vilna; facsimile edition: Jerusalem: Ortsel, 1964.

Midrash Tanhuma-Yelammedenu: An English Translation of Genesis and Exodus. Translated by Samuel A. Berman. Hoboken, NJ: Ktav Publishing House, 1996.

The Mishnah. Edited by Herbert Danby. London: Oxford University Press, 1967.

The Mishnah: A New Translation. Edited by Jacob Neusner. New Haven: Yale University Press, 1988.

Pesikta deRab Kahana. Edited by Solomon Buber. Mekitze Nirdamim, 1868.

Pesikta de-Rab Kahana: R. Kahana's Compilation of Discourses for Sabbaths and Festal Days. Translated by William G. Braude and Israel J. Kapstein. Philadelphia, PA: Jewish Publication Society, 1975.

Pesikta Rabbati. 2 vols. Translated by William G. Braude. New Haven: Yale University Press, 1968.

Pesikta Rabbati deRab Kahana. Warsaw, 1913; Reprinted with additional materials, Jerusalem-Bnei Brak, 1969.

Pirke de Rabbi Eliezer. Translated and Annotated by Gerald Friedlander. New York: Sepher-Hermon, 1981.

Pirkei Rabbi Eliezer. With Commentary of David Luria. Warsaw: Bamberg, 1852: Reprinted, New York: Om Publishing, 1946.

Shishah Sidrei Mishnah. 3 vols. Jerusalem: Eshkol, 1955.

Shishah Sidrei Mishnah. 13 vols. Jerusalem: Meorot, 1976.

Sifra devei Rav im Perush Rabbenu Hillel. Jerusalem, 1961.

Sifre. Commentary by Naphtali Zvi Berlin. 3 vols. Jerusalem: n.p., 1977.

Sifre: Midrash Halakhah leMidbar veDevarim. Commentary by David Pardo. 4 vols. Jerusalem: Lev Sameah, 1990.

Sifre: A Tannaitic Commentary on the Book of Deuteronomy. Translated with Notes by Reuven Hammer. New Haven, CT: Yale University Press, 1986.

Sifre al Sefer Bamidbar veSifre Zuta. Edited by Hayyim S. Horovitz. Jerusalem: Shalem Books, 1992.

Sifre al Sefer Devarim. Edited by Louis Finkelstein. Berlin: Judischer Kulturbund in Deutschland, 1939; Republished New York: Jewish Theological Seminary, 1969.

Talmud Bavli. Edited with Commentary by Adin Steinsaltz. 32 Volumes. Jerusalem: Israel Institute for Talmudic Publications, 1974-.

Talmud Bavli veYerushalmi. 20 vols. New York: Otzar Hasefarim, 1963.

Talmud Yerushalmi. 3 vols. Zhitomer: 1866; Facsimile Edition, Jerusalem: Torah MiTziyon, 1968.

Tanna debe Eliyahu: The Lore of the School of Elijah. Translated by William G. Braude and Israel J. Kapstein. Philadelphia, PA: Jewish Publication Society, 1981.

Tanna debe Eliyahu: Rabba veZuta. Jerusalem: Loewe, 1906; Reprinted in New York, 1990.

Torat Kohanim im Perush Derekh haKodesh. 2 vols. Hosiatin, 1908; reprinted, Israel, 1968.

Torat Kohanim im Perush Hadash beLashon Katzar veTzah. Jerusalem: Sachs, n.d.

Tosefta. Edited by Moshe S. Zuckermandel. New Edition. Jerusalem: Wahrman, 1970.

MISCELLANEOUS WORKS

Abravanel, Isaac (1437–1508). *Perush haTorah.* Warsaw: Levenssohn, 1862; facsimile edition: Jerusalem: Torah veDaat, n.d.

Albeck, Hanokh. *Mavo leMishnah.* Jerusalem/Tel Aviv: Bialik Institute/Dvir, 1974.

American Reform Responsa: Collected Responsa of the Central Conference of American Rabbis 1889–1983. New York: Central Conference of American Rabbis, 1983.

Attar, Hayyim ben Moses ibn (1696–1743). *Light of Life: A Compendium of the Writings of Rabbi Chaim ben Attar.* Translated by Chaim Feuer. North Hollywood, CA: Newcastle Publishing, 1986. (BS1225)

————. *Or haHayyim al haTorah*. 2 Vols. Jerusalem, 1999.

Bentwich, Norman. *Hellenism*. Philadelphia: Jewish Publication Society, 1919.

Ephraim Solomon of Luntshits (1550–1619). *Perush Kli Yakar haShalem*. 2 vols. Jerusalem: Horev, 1999.

Emden, Jacob. *Siddur Beit Yaacov*. Lemberg: n.p., 1904.

Finkelstein, Louis. "Introductory Study to *Pirke Avot*," *Journal of Biblical Literature*, vol. 57, 1938.

————. "The Oldest Midrash: Pre-Rabbinic Ideals and Teachings in the Passover Haggadah." *Harvard Theological Review*, Vol. 31, 1938.

Freedman, David Noel. *The Nine Commandments: Uncovering a Hidden Pattern of Crime and Punishment in the Hebrew Bible*. New York: Doubleday, 2000.

Gersonides (Levi ben Gershom [Ralbag], 1288–1344). *Perushei haTorah leRabbenu Levi ben Gershom*. 5 Vols. Edited by Yaacov Leib Levi. Jerusalem: Mossad Harav Kook, 1992–2000.

Goldin, Judah. "Avot." In *Encyclopaedia Judaica*, Vol. 3.

Hayes, Christine Elizabeth. *Between the Babylonian and Palestinian Talmuds*. New York: Oxford University Press, 1997.

Hirsch, Ammiel and Yosef Reinman. *One People, Two Worlds*. New York: Schocken Books, 2002.

Hirsch, Samson Raphael (1808–1888). *Chapters of the Fathers*. Translated into English by Gertrude Hirschler. New York: Philipp Feldheim, 1967.

————. *The Nineteen Letters of Ben Uziel*. Translated by Bernard Drachman. New York: Bloch Publishing, 1942.

————. *The Pentateuch*. 6 vols. Translated by Isaac Levy. New York: Judaica Press, 1971.

Hoffmann, David Z (1843–1921). *HaMishnah HaRishonah*. Translated from German by Samuel Gruenberg. Berlin, 1914; Reprinted: Jerusalem: n.p., 1970.

Ibn Ezra, Abraham (1089–1164). *Ibn Ezra's Commentary on the Pentateuch: Genesis*. Translated and Annotated by H. Norman Strickman and Arthur M. Silver. New York: Menorah Publishing, 1988.

————. *Perushei haTorah leRabbenu Avraham ibn Ezra*. 3 vols. Jerusalem: Mossad Harav Kook, 1976.

Jacob ben Asher (c. 1270–1340). *Arba'ah Turim*. 7 vols. New York: M.P. Press, 1959–60.

Josephus. *Josephus: Complete Works*. Translated by William Whiston. Grand Rapids: Kregel, 1977.

Kimhi, David (Radak, c. 1160–c. 1235). *Perush Radak al haTorah: Bereshit*. Pressburg: 1842; Facsimile: Jerusalem, 1968.

Klein, Isaac. *Responsa and Halakhic Studies*. New York: Ktav Publishing House, 1975.

Maimonides (1135–1204). *The Book of Agriculture*. Translated by Isaac Klein. New Haven and London: Yale University Press, 1979.

————. *The Commandments*. Translated by Charles B. Chavel. London and New York: Soncino Press, 1967.

————. *Mishneh Torah*. 16 vols. Jerusalem: Mossad Harav Kook, 1966.

————. *Sefer haMitzvot*. Commentary by Yosef Kafih. Jerusalem: Mossad Harav Kook, 1966.

Malbim, Meir L (1809–1879). *HaTorah vehaMitzvah*. 2 vols. Jerusalem: Pardes, 1956.

Mantel, Hayyim (Hugo). *Anshei Knesset ha-Gedolah*. Tel Aviv: Dvir, 1983.

Melamed, Ezra Zion. *Mavo leSifrut haTalmud*. Jerusalem: Kiryat Sefer, 1954.

Nahmanides (1194–1270). *Perushei haTorah*. 2 vols. Edited by Charles B. Chavel. Jerusalem: Mossad Harav Kook, 1959.

———. *The Torah: With Ramban's Commentary: Genesis*. 2 Vols. Translated, Annotated and Elucidated by Yaakov Blinder. New York: Mesorah Publications, 2004–2005.

Neusner, Jacob. *Invitation to the Talmud*. Revised and Expanded Edition. San Francisco: Harper & Row, 1984.

Notes on the New Translation of the Torah. Edited by Harry M. Orlinsky. Philadelphia: Jewish Publication Society, 1970.

Plaut, W. Gunther. *The Torah: A Modern Commentary*. New York: Union of American Hebrew Congegations, 1981.

Rashbam (Samuel ben Meir, c. 1080–1085 to c. 1174). *Perush haTorah*. New York: Om Publishing, 1949.

Rashi (Solomon ben Isaac, 1040–1105). *Perushei Rashi al haTorah*. Edited by Charles B. Chavel. Jerusalem: Mossad Harav Kook, 1983. (BS1225)

———. *The Torah: With Rashi's Commentary Translated, Annotated, and Elucidated by Yisrael Isser Zvi Herczeg*. 5 vols. New York: Mesorah, 2000.

Rosenbaum, Irving J. *The Holocaust and Halakhah*. New York: Ktav Publishing House, 1976.

Scherman, Nosson. *The Chumash* (Stone edition). New York: Mesorah, 1993.

Sefer haHinukh. Edited by Charles B. Chevel. Jerusalem: Mossad Harav Kook, 1966.

Sforno, Obadiah (c. 1470–c. 1550). *Biur al haTorah*. Edited by Zev Gottlieb. Jerusalem: Mossad Harav Kook, 1980.

Sicker, Martin. *Judaism, Nationalism, and the Land of Israel*. Boulder: Westview Press, 1992.

———. *The Moral Maxims of the Sages of Israel: Pirke Avot*. Lincoln: iUniverse, 2004.

———. *A Passover Seder Companion and Analytic Introduction to the Haggadah*. Lincoln: iUniverse, 2004.

Simha ben Samuel of Vitry. *Mahzor Vitry*. Edited by Simeon Hurwitz. Berlin, 1889. Reprinted, Jerusalem: Alef, 1963.

Steinsaltz, Adin. *The Essential Talmud*. Translated by Chaya Galai. London: Weidefeld and Nicolson, 1976.

Strack, Hermann L. *Introduction to the Talmud and Midrash*. Cleveland and Philadelphia: World Publishing and Jewish Publication Society, 1959.

Teshuvot haGeonim: Shaarei Teshuvah. Edited by Zev Wolf Leiter. New York: Feldheim, 1946.

Index

About the Author

MARTIN SICKER is author of over 30 books on Jewish and Middle East history, geopolitics, political theory, and Biblical studies. He is a private consultant, writer, and lecturer. His books include *The Rise and Fall of the Ancient Israelite States, Political Culture of Judaism, The Islamic World in Ascendency, The Middle East in the Twentieth Century*, and many others.